Rich Democracies, Poor People

RICH DEMOCRACIES, POOR PEOPLE

How Politics Explain Poverty

David Brady

OXFORD

UNIVERSITY PRESS

2009

OXFORD

UNIVERSITY PRESS

cae

Oxford University Press, Inc., publishes works that further
Oxford University's objective of excellence
in research, scholarship, and education.

Oxford   New York
Auckland   Cape Town   Dar es Salaam   Hong Kong   Karachi
Kuala Lumpur   Madrid   Melbourne   Mexico City   Nairobi
New Delhi   Shanghai   Taipei   Toronto

With offices in
Argentina   Austria   Brazil   Chile   Czech Republic   France   Greece
Guatemala   Hungary   Italy   Japan   Poland   Portugal   Singapore
South Korea   Switzerland   Thailand   Turkey   Ukraine   Vietnam

Published by Oxford University Press, Inc.
198 Madison Avenue, New York, New York 10016

www.oup.com

Library of Congress Cataloging-in-Publication Data

Brady, David.
Rich democracies, poor people : how politics explain poverty / David Brady.
p. cm.
Includes bibliographical references and index.
ISBN 978-0-19-538587-8; 978-0-19-538591-5 (pbk.)
1. Poverty.   2. Poverty—Government policy.   3. Welfare state.   I. Title.
HC79.P6B653 2009
339.4′6—dc22   2009000980

9 8 7 6 5 4 3 2 1
Printed in the United States of America
on acid-free paper

Acknowledgments

Like social equality, this book really is the product of a collective effort. The experience of writing it was much richer because of the family, friends, and colleagues who helped me along the way. I owe a great deal to all those who have offered suggestions and support.

As with most professors, I've learned far more from my students than they could ever learn from me. I'm very grateful to the Duke students who read this book as part of my classes Politics and Markets in the Global Economy in the spring of 2008 and Comparative Social Stratification in the fall of 2007. Moreover, I thank current and former students Yunus Kaya, Nate Martin, Sara Pilzer, Megan Reynolds, and Ben Sosnaud for offering the most detailed, critical, and constructive suggestions on the manuscript. Working through the ideas in this book was only possible because of the tough-minded criticisms and intellectual energy of my students.

Friends and colleagues have given a great deal of their time to me and this book. I only hope I can return the favor. Andrew Fullerton, Denise Kall, and Jennifer Moren Cross have collaborated with me on projects related to this book, and these partnerships have certainly made this book a lot better. Also, I received specific suggestions and careful readings by Jason Beckfield, Judith Blau, Katie Bolzendahl, Mitch Duneier, Mike Ezell, Katy Fallon, Herbert Gans, Arseniy Gutnik, Alex Hicks, Thomas Hirschl, M.E. Hughes, Matt Hunt, Kevin Leicht, Nan Lin, Jeff Manza, Jane McLeod, Stephanie Moller, Phil Morgan, Angie O'Rand, Emilio Parrado, Andrew Payton, David Reimer, Jason Schnitker, Martin Seeleib-Kaiser, Ken Spenner,

Ed Tiryakian, and John Wilson. Over the years, I have presented portions of this work to several scholarly audiences. Among others, I thank the attendees at the Duke Sociology Department colloquium, the University of North Carolina political and cultural sociology workshop, the political economy workshop at Indiana University, and the MIT-Harvard economic sociology seminar.

This project began as a dissertation at Indiana University, where I was very lucky to have a host of terrific teachers and fellow students. I thank my first-class dissertation committee of Art Alderson, Dave Reingold, and Rob Robinson for constructive and rigorous guidance. Mike Wallace chaired that committee and was an extraordinary mentor. Mike always set high expectations, demanded rigor, took meticulous care, and spent remarkable amounts of time in my development as a scholar. I hope the final product is something he can be proud of. Few scholars are as lucky as I have been in having a booster like Clem Brooks. Clem has had an unwavering, limitless, and never-ending enthusiasm for my work. I would have never written this book had Clem not insisted it was worth doing. His passion and energy for scholarship and his enthusiasm and encouragement for students are my model.

At Duke, Lisa Young, Claudette Parker, Gary Thompson, Rob Marks, Bob Jackson, Theresa Shouse, Jessica Ellington, and Jesse Riggan have made my job a lot easier and more fun. David Jesuit, Teresa Munzi, Emilia Niskanen, and all the members of the Luxembourg Income Study went above and beyond the call of duty to help me conduct the analyses.

In the fall of 2007, an amazing stroke of good luck occurred when I met James Cook, my editor at Oxford University Press. James has believed in this book from day one, offered smart editing and even better judgment, and has done everything possible to encourage me to write the book I wanted to write.

My family has been a great source of support in this book and everything I do. I thank my Mom, Pat Brady, for always encouraging me and for having so much confidence in what I could accomplish. My wife, Sandra Jaramillo-Busquets, has made an enormous difference on a daily and long-term basis. She has always been willing to hear my thoughts and has cheerfully tolerated my obsessions with this book, baseball, and other things. There is no way I could have finished this book without her love, kindness, and encouragement.

Just as I was beginning this project, my father, Frank Brady, passed away unexpectedly. I could never have become the scholar or person I am without him. I can trace my lifelong interest in traveling and other countries and cultures to him. He taught me everything I know about the values of equality and a love of learning. For that and so much more, I will forever be grateful. Just as I was finishing this project, my son, Dylan Brady, was born. He has provided unlimited joy in our lives and taught me to keep everything in perspective. I hope I can pass on to him at least a fraction of what my father taught me. To my father and son, I dedicate this book.

Contents

Rich Democracies, Poor People

1

Beyond Individualism

By the accident of birth, people face incredibly different odds of experiencing poverty. We are born into families that predict much of our socioeconomic attainment in life. Yet, even more consequentially, we are born into countries that carry with them a probability of poverty for their citizens. Poverty has existed as long as there have been markets, but what is striking about the contemporary world is how much poverty varies across countries. Those born into egalitarian countries are much more likely to be economically secure in their youth, sickness, and old age. In other countries, a much larger share of the population will be poor at some point in their life. For the most part, we do not get to choose the probability of poverty we face. Instead, our societies contextually shape the odds that an individual in a given country will be poor. Obviously this is true if one compares affluent democracies of Western Europe, like Sweden, to struggling Sub-Saharan African countries, like Sudan. But this is also true if one compares Sweden to the United States.

Even among these rich democracies, cross-national and historical variation in poverty is profound. In the postindustrial era, there have been dramatic differences between the affluent Western democracies and between the 1970s, 1980s, and 1990s. The United States maintains nearly twice as much poverty as its neighbor Canada. Even more striking, the United States has three times as much poverty as some West European countries. Nearly 20% of Americans are poor, and almost a fourth of U.S. children and elderly are poor. Though the United States might be the richest country in the history of the world, roughly 50 million Americans are relatively deprived. And despite commentary to the contrary, these high levels of U.S. poverty have been stable for decades. In 1974, 16.8% of the United States was poor. In 2000, 18% was poor. There is nothing necessary or natural about these extremely high levels of U.S. poverty. There are many varieties of capitalism that perform efficiently without these levels of relative deprivation. Compared to all other affluent Western democracies, the United States is iconically unequal.

Yet, this is not only a story of American exceptionalism. There is substantial cross-national and historical variation among other affluent Western democracies, as well. In 1987, only 6.7% of Austria was poor, but by 1995 nearly 11% was poor. Denmark's poverty declined from more than 10% in 1987 to 5.2% in 1995. Poverty in the Netherlands doubled from less than 4% in 1983 to more than 8% in 1994. The United Kingdom, previously far more egalitarian than now, has seen poverty rise from 5.5% in 1969 to around 9% in the 1970s and 1980s, all the way to 14.5% in the 1990s. Canada used to have high poverty, but its poverty has declined precipitously in recent decades. Ireland, Spain, and Australia have about twice as much poverty as the Scandinavian countries. The United Kingdom has much more poverty than the Netherlands, and Switzerland has more poverty than Germany.

Figure 1.1 maps the 18 affluent Western democracies for which data exist in the Luxembourg Income Study (LIS)—the leading international data source on poverty. Each country is shaded according to its average level of poverty from 1969 to 2002. The shading represents the percentage of the entire population that is poor. The Scandinavian countries, the "low countries" of Belgium, Luxembourg, and the Netherlands, and Germany have maintained average poverty levels of less than 7% of the population. Indeed, Belgium, Finland, Luxembourg, the Netherlands, and Norway even had years when less than 5% of the population was poor. Not far behind are Austria, France, and Switzerland, with an average of less than 10% poverty. At the other end of the spectrum is the United States, alone among the affluent Western democracies with average poverty levels greater than 17%. In between are Australia, Canada, Ireland, Italy, Spain, and the United Kingdom, with more than 10% poor but with less poverty than the United States. By focusing only on affluent Western democracies, one cannot fall back on the tautology that rich countries have less poverty and poor countries have more. All of these countries are "rich" compared to the vast majority of countries and people in the world. But even within these affluent democracies, there is enormous cross-national and historical variation in the amount of poverty.

This variation in poverty is important not only because egalitarian societies might be more just. This variation is also significant because countries with high poverty experience more crime and suicide, greater health problems, weaker economic productivity, and undermined development and well-being among children.[1] Indeed, it is reasonable to suggest that the

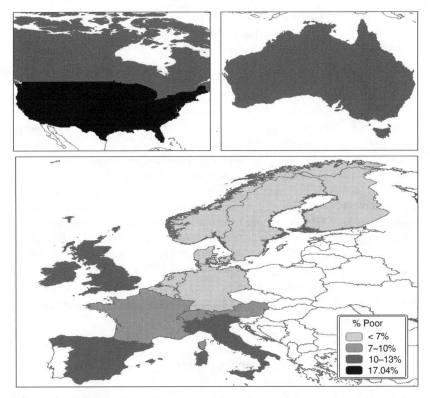

Figure 1.1.   Average Poverty in 18 Affluent Western Democracies, 1969–2002

United States would not have its astronomical rates of imprisonment—now highest in the world at more than 1% of the population—if poverty was not so high. Plausibly, if poverty was lower in the United States, fewer of our cities would contain ghettos. If poverty was lower, millions more children would have a real chance at the American dream. Conversely, if Europe had poverty levels like the United States, it is not hard to imagine how deeply and irrevocably different life in those countries would be. With this variation in poverty, we are examining some of the most crucial differences between countries that exist in the modern world.

What explains this tremendous variation in poverty across the affluent Western democracies? This question represents a serious challenge to any theory of poverty. Theories of poverty should be able to explain why some affluent Western democracies maintain substantial poverty and others are more egalitarian and accomplish low levels of poverty. Yet, the conventional approach in poverty studies is to analyze only the United States and to compare the characteristics of poor people (perhaps in poor neighborhoods) to nonpoor people. It is not an exaggeration to say that the vast majority of poverty studies explain why one group of people within a country are more likely to be poor, or why some individuals are poor while others are not. Thus, conventional poverty research stops short of confronting the enormous cross-national differences.

In contrast, I contend that these cross-national and historical differences in poverty are principally driven by politics. This book makes the simple claim that the distribution of resources in states and markets is inherently political. I explicitly seek to challenge the mainstream view that poverty is an inescapable, if perhaps unfortunate, outcome of an individual's failings or a society's labor markets and demography. Instead, I argue that societies make collective choices about how to divide their resources. These choices are acted upon in the organizations and states that govern the societies, and then become institutionalized through the welfare state. Where poverty is low, equality has been institutionalized. Where poverty is widespread, as most visibly demonstrated by the United States, there has been a failure to institutionalize equality. Thus, this book answers Herbert Gans's request that "The principal subject of poverty research ought to be the forces, processes, agents, institutions that 'decide' that a proportion of the population will end up poor."[2] In sum, *institutionalized power relations theory* is my answer to this question of the differences in poverty across affluent Western democracies.

Institutionalized Power Relations Theory

There are four key components to institutionalized power relations theory: (a) welfare generosity, (b) Leftist collective political actors, (c) latent coalitions for egalitarianism, and (d) institutionalized politics. Poverty is lower and equality is more likely to be established where welfare states are generous, Leftist collective political actors are in power, latent coalitions for egalitarianism exert influence, and all of this is institutionalized in the formal political arena.

At this point, it is useful to acknowledge that this book clearly stands on the shoulders of giants. The giant in studies of the politics of the welfare state and equality is power resources theory. Power resources theory provides a compelling narrative of how the working class can mobilize to overcome the power of business in order to expand the welfare state.[3] In particular, power resources theory appreciates that business maintains greater political power in capitalist democracies. Only when the working class is allied with the middle class can their power resources be sufficiently mobilized in the polity to push for redistribution. My institutionalized power relations theory is partly inspired by power resources theory. Much like power resources theory, this book disputes the naive pluralist view that politics is a game among equals. Consistent with power resources theory, I fully appreciate the realistic premise that political power is unequally distributed in a capitalist democracy. Power resources theory correctly emphasizes that opponents to social equality rest in a position of default dominance in the electoral arena. Nevertheless, there are salient differences between institutionalized power relations theory and power resources theory. This book aims to take the criticisms of power resources theory seriously and offer new directions for theories of the politics of social equality.

Welfare State Generosity

The central element of this theory is the generosity of a country's welfare state. The welfare state is defined as the complex of social policies and programs that distribute economic resources disproportionately to a nation's vulnerable populations. Every nation has vulnerable people, but welfare states differ in the extent to which they protect the vulnerable against economic insecurity. Broadly, welfare states include progressive taxes, cash and near-cash assistance, publicly funded services such as health care, public programs that guarantee economic security, and government activities to ensure social inclusion and economic capability. The welfare state relieves citizens from being forced to exclusively depend on the private market for economic resources. Moreover, welfare states define whether citizens are entitled to the "social right" of economic security. Welfare generosity is the proximate and primary influence on a nation's level of poverty. Countries with more generous welfare programs and more extensive welfare services have far lower poverty.

The influence of welfare states on poverty can be spelled out in terms of the three crucial roles welfare states play. First, welfare states manage risk. Welfare states are public insurance programs that protect people who have experienced a loss or are stuck in a vulnerable position. For example, welfare states plan for the chance that a worker will lose a job, become a mother, face disability, or simply grow old. To protect against such risks, welfare states facilitate saving and provide social insurance through publicly mandated and publicly subsidized programs.

Second, welfare states organize the distribution of economic resources. Through governing the rules of exchange, or regulating currencies and business, or providing public goods like education and health care, or by facilitating transportation and communication, or even simply by creating jobs, the welfare state shapes how much income each household receives. Normally, this mechanism is understood as *redistribution*. However, this framing obscures the welfare state's impact. For doing so leads to the neglect of how welfare states, or states more generally, govern the accumulation of profits and income for the affluent as well as the poor. The imagery of redistribution artificially insinuates that there is a two-step process, where markets naturally distribute income and states only subsequently intervene to redistribute. But no such two-step process exists. States do not simply follow what markets have initiated; states constitute markets.[4] As the Nobel Laureate Douglass

North once wrote, "The polity and the economy are inextricably inter-linked in any understanding of the performance of an economy."[5] Rather than framing welfare states as narrowly about redistribution, this study postulates welfare states as organizing distribution.

Third, welfare states institutionalize equality. Welfare states are both a cause and an effect of a society's ideologies about equality.[6] These ideologies define how societies normalize collective expectations about whether vari-ous economic distributions are considered appropriate and acceptable. By creating the social conditions to govern markets, states enact a wide variety of a society's formal and informal rules.[7] Thus, the welfare state is the culmination of a society's beliefs for how economic resources ought to be distributed. At the same time, welfare states shape a society's norms and values and create constituencies of beneficiaries (the groups of citizens who subscribe to and benefit from welfare programs). These norms and constitu-encies feed back into the political process as key bases of support for welfare states. Thus, welfare states reflect politics, but they also have what scholars call "feedback effects" into subsequent politics. In turn, public support for welfare programs is partly a product of the welfare programs themselves. Of course, scholars have often written about how a confluence of ideology and interest shape the welfare state. Welfare states, ideology, and interest are so bound up in each other that it is not necessary to sort out which came first. What is important is understanding how social equality results from the reciprocal relationships among welfare states, ideologies, and interests. Through these relationships, countries socialize the responsibility of pre-venting citizens from being poor. By saying welfare states "institutionalize equality," this is meant to emphasize that welfare states are caused by and cause collective expectations that widespread poverty is not politically and socially acceptable.

Leftist Collective Political Actors

Institutionalized power relations also reflect the indirect effect of Leftist collective political actors, or "Leftist politics" for short. Leftist politics in-clude the organizations and institutions committed to a more equal distribu-tion of a society's resources. Among the more prominent Leftist political actors are labor unions and Leftist parties (i.e., Social Democrat, Labor, Socialist/Communist, and Green parties). Leftist politics, however, also in-cludes the percentage of women in the legislature, the percentage of the electorate that votes, and even the rules of the electoral arena. Where Leftist politics have historically been strong, the welfare state is more generous and less poverty results.

This book advocates for the view that political action occurs at a collec-tive, group, and macro level. While individual political behavior may matter for other outcomes, it is collective political behavior and the power relations among collective political actors that matters to poverty.[8] Only collective actors have the resources to leverage power over other actors in the national electoral arena. Being a participant in the national politics of the welfare state is extremely costly. Collective political actors need to maintain a constant presence in national capitals, be able to monitor fine-grained information about policy, communicate to dispersed constituents and supporters, and be able to threaten to or actually challenge the power of officeholders and elites.[9] Moreover, collective political actors need to be embedded in networks of other collective actors and to use this embeddedness for influence. In the politics of poverty, the key players are almost never individuals because individuals almost never have these sorts of resources. Institutionalized power relations theory emphasizes the centrality of collective, not individual, political actors for the welfare state and poverty.

Institutionalized power relations theory considers Leftist collective political actors to be a "fundamental cause" of poverty. In an influential article on the social influences on health, Bruce Link and Jo Phelan explain that the fundamental causes, such as class, of disease should get more attention than proximate risk factors.[10] They explain that even if interventions reduce risk factors, the fundamental cause will find a new risk factor to trigger inequalities in disease. This book utilizes the idea of fundamental causality to explain how Leftist politics influences poverty. By fundamental cause, the notion is that Leftist politics embodies the power relations that determine the generosity of the welfare state and affects poverty through multiple mechanisms, including some beyond the welfare state. Consequently, Leftist politics may maintain an association with poverty even given changes in the welfare state and/or net of the welfare state. In chapter 5, I elaborate this point to explain that there are two plausible causal pathways between Leftist politics, the welfare state, and poverty: channeled and combined. These pathways involve the direct and indirect effects of politics on poverty, and both incorporate the welfare state as a central factor. Because I argue that poverty is ultimately a political problem, the fundamental cause of poverty is politics. As an illustration, consider Leftist parties and labor unions.

Much of the impact of Leftist parties probably channels through the generosity of the welfare state. As many studies show, Leftist parties are a key political force that triggers welfare state expansion. Welfare states are more generous where Leftist parties have historically controlled the government. Some of the power of Leftist parties occurs through the threat to elected officials, and some occurs by replacing those officials with ones that are sympathetic to economic egalitarianism. Tightly linked to Leftist parties are labor unions. Unions regulate the labor market, ensure greater pay and benefits for workers, and restrict the compensation of executives and owners. Unions represent the organized power of workers. However, unions also represent the poor who might aspire to be workers and the workers who seek to avoid falling into poverty. In addition, unions facilitate coordinated labor market arrangements (often called "corporatism"), which encourage equitable compensation and stabilize countries during boom-and-bust cycles. This contributes to protecting workers with long-range planning, formal cooperation, and power sharing between workers and managers. In this sense, unions might combine with the welfare state to pressure for an egalitarian distribution of business profits. Finally, these two reinforce each other. Unions contribute to the electoral success of Leftist parties, and Leftist parties enable the organizing of unions.

Latent Coalitions for Egalitarianism

This book proposes that, at least regarding poverty, Leftist politics is the manifestation of what can be called latent coalitions for egalitarianism. These latent coalitions are the diffuse, unanticipated, and often accidental groups of diverse citizens who come together to support generous welfare states and social equality. These latent coalitions are ideologically committed to normative expectations about alleviating poverty and establishing social equality. Because many of the members of these latent coalitions are not personally faced with the possibility of poverty, most of the mobilization of these actors is driven by ideology. For example, many scholars have shown that professionals tend to vote for Leftist parties even though it might not strictly be in their economic interest.[11] I call these coalitions "latent" because what brings them together in support of egalitarianism and welfare states is not always anticipated or intended.[12] These latent coalitions are often accidental partners in support of welfare generosity and the poor.

Playing a central role in these latent coalitions are the constituencies of beneficiaries who receive government assistance, public pensions, and welfare services. This point incorporates the aforementioned feedback effects of welfare states on Leftist politics. Although the elderly, for example, may seemingly have little in common with single mothers, the elderly are often a key reason Leftist collective political actors push for more generous social policies that end up alleviating poverty among single mothers. Thus, these latent coalitions can be understood as the diffuse and diverse publics that back and vote for Leftist collective political actors. Often, these latent coalitions become visible in the public support for a generous welfare state or social equality. For example, when a mix of public opinion and advocacy groups opposed President George W. Bush's attempts to privatize Social Security, this reflected the latent coalitions for egalitarianism in the United States. By emphasizing ideology and constituencies of beneficiaries as the microfoundations of Leftist politics, this book moves away from power resources theory's exclusive focus on the material interests and rational choices of the working class.

Institutionalized Politics

As another departure from power resources theory, this book aims to place greater emphasis on how the politics of poverty is institutionalized.[13]

Institutionalized power relations theory explicitly prioritizes the role of formal organizations of Leftist political actors participating in the formal political arena. This theory is called *institutionalized* power relations instead of simply power relations in order to highlight that politics matters most for poverty when it occurs in the formal political system. The Left, probably more than the Right, has a romantic and nostalgic fondness for disorderly, defiant, grassroots, and militant resistance—what Frances Fox Piven and Richard Cloward call "dissensus politics."[14] Strikes play a central role in power resources theory because of the ability to disrupt business profits, and much of labor's power supposedly came from the threat to strike. Of course, it is fair to concede that such anti-institutional politics in civil society may play a marginal role in the background. Maybe strikes, riots, and student protests help cultivate an environment where Leftist formal organizations are more likely to thrive.

However, this book proposes that the effects of dissensus politics on poverty are far less consequential than the effects of formal organizations in the formal political arena. While dissensus politics is often romanticized among Leftists, I contend that the bureaucratic formal organizations of parties and unions are simply more important. Formal organizations solve the coordination problems of groups, multiply the power of otherwise disconnected individuals, have the necessary resources to make a difference, and carry greater legitimacy in the national political arena where welfare policy gets decided.[15] As Max Weber famously wrote in his essay "Politics as a Vocation," "Politics is a strong and slow boring of hard boards."[16] Regarding poverty especially, it is the formal organizations in the formal political arena that end up doing this slow and hard work.

Because I argue that the welfare state is the primary influence on poverty, it follows that politics are most germane when they involve the welfare state. There is an old line about the aging bank robber Willie Sutton who, when asked why he robbed banks, replied "Because that's where the money is." Regarding poverty, formal politics revolving around the state are more important because the state is where the money is. No nongovernmental or charitable organization can come close to the economic resources that the state controls because of its power to tax. No other entity has the resources the state can marshal on behalf of poor people, and protests disconnected from the state are unlikely to make any difference to the poor. This book suggests that Leftist romanticization with dissensus politics may even lead to an underappreciation of the more consequential political negotiations in formal political arenas.

In addition, Leftist politics is institutionalized because the politics of poverty is path dependent. By path dependent, I mean that the politics of poverty is locked into a routine that was established in the past. One of the limitations of power resources theory is that it represents the struggle over welfare states as an iterative game of interest-driven action. Instead, I represent politics as the confluence of interest and ideology in slowly evolving and routinized negotiations.[17] Leftist political actors not only make the decision to mobilize for welfare generosity by calculating how many of their members will gain or lose with a new policy. Rather, Leftist actors instinctively and reflexively establish egalitarianism through slow, often small, but cumulative historical increments. Instead of viewing each election as an opportunity to reduce poverty and inequality, I contend that welfare generosity is locked in place and only very slowly can evolve toward or away from egalitarianism. Thus, the politics of poverty is habitualized. Earlier settlements over the welfare state reinforce the ongoing politics of poverty.

To help make sense of how institutionalized power relations theory explains poverty, the failed Clinton health care reform serves as a useful example.[18] In 1994, President Clinton unveiled a moderate reform that mixed private- and public-sector health insurance and only modestly increased taxes. This was not a substantial move toward socialized medicine, as it left the responsibility of health insurance mainly to employers. Although many factors drove its defeat, one can interpret this policy-making episode with the key elements of institutionalized power relations theory: welfare state generosity, Leftist collective political actors, latent coalitions for egalitarianism, and institutionalization.

Had the Clinton plan become law, this book suggests that poverty would have declined (see chapter 4). With an even more generous government-run "single-payer" plan like we see in several Western European countries, the United States could have become a substantially more egalitarian society. Health care reform would have provided better social insurance against the risk of getting sick or losing one's job. The higher taxes to pay for the reform would have distributed economic resources downward toward the vulnerable. Also, socializing the medical system more fully could have institutionalized the collective responsibility of health for all citizens. The privatized health care system that remains after the failed reform is emblematic of the meagerness of the U.S. welfare state.

The failed health care reform also illustrates the weakness of Leftist collective political actors. Former Senate Majority Leader Tom Daschle and colleagues explained that although a minority of congressmen tried to push for a plan closer to socialized medicine, they never got much support. A single-payer bill sponsored by Representative Jim McDermott and Senator Paul Wellstone had 90 cosponsors in Congress and the support of many unions and advocacy groups but was never seriously considered. Prior to Clinton's election in 1992 and after the 1994 congressional elections, there was stiff opposition from President George H.W. Bush and from the Republican Congress. Moreover, prior to and even after Clinton's election in 1992, conservative Democrats effectively resisted greater government involvement in health care. Particularly important was Texan Lloyd Bentsen, who was chair of the Senate Finance Committee and subsequently Clinton's Secretary of the Treasury. Also consequential were the many conservative Democrats who favored a private-sector solution. Clinton himself, as governor of

Arkansas, had campaigned as a "New Democrat" opposed to "big govern-ment" policies, and as president once famously proclaimed, "The era of big government is over."[19]

The latent coalitions for egalitarianism were outmaneuvered, outhustled, and outspent by the opponents. Two of the most potent actors were the National Federation of Independent Business (NFIB) and the Health Insur-ance Association of America (HIAA). In noting that opponents outspent supporters by a margin of more than 6 to 1, Daschle and colleagues recall, "Unions and some other liberal groups rewarded the president's proponents in Congress with substantial support, but their overall lobbying effort was anemic compared to the exertions of the other side."[20] The latent coalitions for egalitarianism that did exist were not able to mobilize nearly as effective-ly partly because of divisions amongst themselves. This manifested in public opposition to Clinton's plan. As the sociologist and former Clinton advisor Paul Starr explained, "The problem was not so much that the opponents had more resources, but that the supporters could not mobilize theirs. While the antagonists had great clarity of purpose, the groups backing reform suffered from multiple and complex fractures and were unable to unite."[21]

The institutionalized nature of this episode is reflected in the deep ideo-logical opposition to and almost knee-jerk reaction against "socialized med-icine." It says a lot about American ideology that there was so much susceptibility to advertising campaigns deriding Clinton's plan. It also turned out to be tremendously difficult to reform health care because of the path-dependent politics driven by insurance companies and stakeholders interested in maintaining the current system.[22] The HIAA had gained a great deal from the private health insurance system, and the NFIB had a great to deal to lose if employers had to pay more taxes or were required to insure their employees. Finally, the institutionalized nature of this episode is clear, as protests, strikes, and civil disobedience had absolutely no discer-nable effect.

Ultimately, the Clinton plan lacked the political support necessary to push through substantial reform against the resistance of business and those opposed to welfare generosity. The Clinton plan never even got out of committee or resulted in an actual vote in Congress. As Daschle and colleagues write, "The great health-care debate of the early 1990s expired with barely a whimper."[23] The continuing lack of a generous welfare state including health care explains much of why the United States has such high poverty.

In sum, institutionalized power relations theory is a strongly political explanation of the levels of poverty in society. These arguments are summa-rized in figure 1.2, which outlines the relationships between the key concepts. Ideologies and interests manifest in latent coalitions for egalitari-anism. These latent coalitions influence Leftist collective political actors and welfare generosity, which itself is partly driven by Leftist politics. Leftist politics and welfare generosity shape poverty. Finally, the levels of poverty

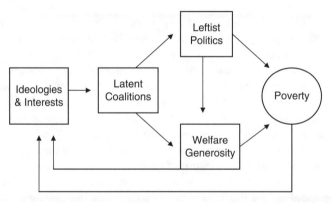

Figure 1.2.   Conceptual Model for Institutionalized Power Relations Theory

and welfare generosity feed back into ideologies and interests. Variations in the power of latent coalitions for egalitarianism, the Leftist politics that are the manifestation of these coalitions, and what they are able to enact via the welfare state shape the amount of poverty in society.

The Individualist Perspective

This book's strongly political argument stands in sharp contrast to prevailing social science explanations of poverty. Instead of devoting much attention to collective politics and states, the study of poverty is driven implicitly and explicitly by individualism. Even though it is more of a taken-for-granted perspective than a theory, individualism might even be said to dominate the scholarship of poverty.[24] Individualism encompasses methodological individualism—the presumption that all causal explanations be specified in terms of individual behavior.[25] Linked to methodological individualism, poverty scholars normally analyze individual-level data. The widespread practice is to compare the characteristics and behaviors of poor individuals against nonpoor individuals.[26] As Mark Rank explains in *One Nation, Underprivileged*, the social sciences tend to present poverty as an "individual failing" and individual attributes as the cause, resulting in models of individual characteristics predicting individual behavior.[27]

On balance, individualist research has made real contributions by clarifying which types of individuals are more at risk of being poor.[28] For illustration, it is helpful to consider three common individualist explanations for why people are poor. Perhaps the consensus approach in the social sciences, individualism is often used to identify the demographic and labor market characteristics of the poor. Many focus on identifying vulnerable family or job positions. Individuals in single-mother families, individuals that are old, young, or women, and individuals who experience parenthood early in life are more likely to be poor. Individuals who are unemployed or marginally employed are more likely to be poor. In tandem, those with less human capital—education, experience, and skills—are more prone to poverty. Most findings have been established in studies of specific countries with large survey data sets. Probably the best example is the status attainment research tradition in sociology. At least since Peter Blau and Otis Duncan's classic *The American Occupational Structure*, sociologists have sought to identify how parents' socioeconomic status and education predict children's likelihood of attaining a socioeconomic status removed from poverty.[29] As exemplified by Christopher Jencks and colleagues' classic *Who Gets Ahead?*, many have identified the demographic and labor market predictors of who falls behind.[30]

Beyond demographic and labor market traits, individualism manifests in behavioral or cultural accounts of poverty. Those vulnerable family and job positions have been typically viewed as the result of individual choice or behavior. For example, there is an undercurrent of voluntarism in the individualist study of the poor's single parenthood and unemployment. Adults that fail to get married or to secure education and maintain a stable job have exhibited counterproductive or self-destructive behavior. In that vein, the noted poverty scholar Isabel Sawhill recently offered a "behavioral" theory of poverty stressing the characteristics of poor households and poor individuals. Sawhill emphasizes three behaviors: "Those who graduate from high school, wait until marriage to have children, limit the size of their families, and work full-time will not be poor."[31] Often, problematic individual behavior is linked to choice.[32] Because much social science presumes that individuals make choices following incentives and constraints, individualist accounts of poverty basically imply that the poor have simply made bad choices. Other times, this problematic behavior is connected to a pathological culture. Much of what readers of the poverty literature know as the "culture of poverty" is simply a theory of how the poor supposedly make so many bad choices and engage in so many problematic behaviors.

Taken to its end point, individualism often arrives at biological explanations. Sooner or later, poverty scholars start to ask *why* the poor make so many bad choices, and almost inevitably, this leads to a search for the innate limitations of poor people.[33] If the demographic and labor market characteristics of the poor really do reflect bad choices and problematic behaviors, maybe the poor have "hard-wired" traits that constrain their socioeconomic achievement. Maybe the poor do not just succumb to a deviant or pathological culture, but are essentially unable to make better choices and engage in more productive behavior. The most visible manifestation of this radical individualism is, of course, Richard Hernstein and Charles Murray's *The Bell Curve*.[34] Among other arguments, Hernstein and Murray allege that the poor have lower IQs and less intelligence. As those authors argue, "Among people who are both smart and well-educated, the risk of poverty approaches zero....In sum: Low intelligence means a comparatively high risk of poverty."[35] Of course, many have shown that Hernstein and Murray's book is based on flawed measures, inappropriate manipulation of the data, and dubious statistical analyses.[36] Nevertheless, poverty scholars should not lose sight of the fact that *The Bell Curve* was one of the best-selling social science books in recent decades. Thus, there is a real individualist tradition that contends that the poor make bad choices and engage in problematic behavior because they are biologically inferior.

The popularity of individualism can be explained by the confluence of ideology and science. Many have shown that Americans are extremely individualistic in their beliefs about poverty, especially compared to other countries.[37] When accounting for poverty, it is normal to talk of how that individual made bad choices, engaged in self-destructive behavior, or had the bad luck of possessing some disadvantageous characteristic (e.g., old age or being born into a single-parent family). Purportedly, individuals may have been born with insufficient natural intelligence or lack a work ethic or long-term mentality. To the extent that the dominant ideologies of the United States influence the way the world thinks about poverty, individualism's prominence can be linked to this distinctively American faith in individualism. As long as the United States subscribes to a deeply individualistic ideology, the focus on individual traits will probably continue to be reinforced in the study of poverty.

Beyond ideology, individualism represents the dominance of methodological individualism in the social sciences. Methodological individualism is anchored in the most prominent social science: economics. For many social scientists, individualism is beyond question—it is an assumed truth about the world. Unlike abstract phenomena like "society," the behavior of individuals is one of the few phenomena that social scientists can actually observe. For others, individualism presents the best, among many imperfect, ways of thinking. With individualism, a scholar can shorten the time between cause and effect, and isolate the immediate mechanisms. Finally, many are justifiably appreciative of the substantial contributions that individualism has made. A lot has been learned from individualist social science of poverty, and one should not dismiss those advances in understanding poverty.

All that said, the social sciences fall into a trap if they have no other explanations beside individualism. In order for the study of poverty to advance, this book contends that we must acknowledge the limitations of and move beyond individualism. When faced with the question of the enormous cross-national and historical variation in poverty displayed by the affluent democracies, individualism is simply inadequate. By extension, social science's inability to answer this crucial question of cross-national and historical variation is partly due to our overreliance on exclusively individualist perspectives on poverty.

The Problems of Individualism

There are at least three major reasons why an individualist perspective turns out to be inadequate for explaining the cross-national and historical variation in poverty in affluent Western democracies. First, not all causes of poverty can be reduced to the micro level. Some causes simply exist, and are best understood and studied, at the macro level.[38] The social sciences of inequality have convincingly demonstrated the reality of the effects of macro-level units like culture, neighborhoods, political parties, and labor unions. Adhering exclusively to a strict individualist explanation forces one to either deny that these macro-level units and their effects exist or attempt to reduce them to individual-level phenomena. Denying the reality of the effects of macro-level units is clearly problematic, because rigorous evidence has demonstrated that culture, neighborhoods, parties, and unions do actually matter. The empirical results in this book provide further support for the reality of such macro effects. These macro effects demonstrate that not all causes of poverty are the characteristics or properties of individuals.[39] In addition, reducing macro-level causes to micro-level mechanisms is not always sufficient. By trying to reduce everything to a micro-level mechanism, social scientists end up neglecting that there are multiple causal processes in many cause—effect relationships. In turn, reductionism often obscures as much as it illuminates. To fully understand the effects of macro-level units, social scientists must appreciate that some causes are best studied as collective in nature.

Trying to reduce all causes to the micro level also results in the methodological problem of cross-level inference. This problem occurs when a social scientist analyzes data at one level of analysis and then attempts to generalize a causal explanation at another level of analysis. Probably reflecting the bias for methodological individualism, the problem of cross-level inference is usually raised to critique ecological inference (commonly called the ecological fallacy). The ecological inference problem occurs when one tries to explain individual-level causal processes based on aggregate, group-level, ecological data analyses. Ironically, social scientists often trigger this same problem in reverse by extrapolating macro-level relationships from individual-level patterns. If seeking to explain macro-level relationships, a social scientist should examine macro-level patterns.[40] Presuming that societal patterns can be explained by their individual parts is what Amos Hawley calls a reductionist fallacy.[41] Hence, I take the classical sociological position that societies, groups, and, in turn, macro-level patterns are more than the sum of their individual parts. Countries, like any group, have emergent properties, and one cannot rely exclusively on the analysis of individuals in order to understand them. As C. Wright Mills famously wrote in his classic *The Sociological Imagination*:

> When, in a city of 100,000, only one man is unemployed, that is his personal trouble, and for its relief we properly look to the character of

the man, his skills, and his immediate opportunities. But when in a nation of 50 million employees, 15 million men are unemployed, that is an issue, and we may not hope to find its solution within the range of opportunities open to any one individual. The very structure of opportunities has collapsed. Both the correct statement of the problem and the range of possible solutions require us to consider the economic and political institutions of the society, and not merely the personal situation and character of a scatter of individuals.[42]

This book applies the same logic to poverty that Mills applied to unemployment. The rule is that the means of analysis should be consistent with the phenomena in question. If we seek to explain why countries differ in terms of poverty, then we should analyze countries.

Second, individualistic perspectives end up neglecting two crucial dimensions of social life: relations and context.[43] If one can explain poverty simply with demographic and labor market characteristics, choices and behaviors, or biological traits, there is no need to investigate relations among people. However, this book objects to this essentialist concentration on individual attributes. As Gans writes, "Trying to determine how family or neighborhood influence poverty ignores how much both are themselves caught in and responding to the poverty that agents and forces in the larger society impose."[44] People exist in a social world where they are connected to other people and participate in the collective construction of how we experience, navigate, and influence each other. Following Charles Tilly's influential *Durable Inequality*, I contend that relations are a more valuable direction for the social science of inequality than are individual traits. As Tilly remarks, "Instead of reducing social behavior to individual decision-making, social scientists urgently need to study the relational constraints within which all individual action takes place."[45]

Moreover, the individualist focus on characteristics neglects why a characteristic is linked to poverty in a social context. Almost no individual characteristic has an unbreakable bond with poverty universally across all affluent Western democracies. Even single-mother families are not disproportionately poor in some affluent democracies.[46] Moreover, the extent to which a characteristic is associated with poverty varies dramatically across countries. Societies make collective choices about *which* insecure labor market and family situations will not be protected. If certain characteristics associate with poverty only in some contexts, it tells you at least as much about that context as it does about poverty. If a particular characteristic is associated with poverty, this suggests that in that national context, citizenship has not been defined so as to ameliorate the economic insecurity associated with that characteristic. Whether and how much an individual characteristic is linked to poverty are questions of politics. In order to make progress in understanding cross-national and historical variation in poverty, social scientists must interrogate why and how national contexts shelter only some groups from poverty.

Third, the empirical performance of individualist explanations is unsatisfactory. If one extends the individualist enterprise as discussed above, one is forced to defend some rather dubious arguments. For example, following Hernstein and Murray, would it be reasonable to argue that the United States has more poverty than Sweden simply because we have a greater share of dumb people? Indeed, the inability of biology to explain really big differences between countries or across history was one of the most important critiques of Hernstein and Murray's controversial book. Even if we can provide persuasive evidence of the individual characteristics associated with poverty, this can contribute little to explaining why some countries have more poverty than others.[47] Relatedly, the macro-level elaborations of individualist explanations have also been insufficient. Even if one builds macro-level models from our best individualistic accounts, those macro-level models can be shown to leave too much unexplained. In chapters 6 and 7, I evaluate two macro-level explanations that elaborate and extend leading individualist accounts: liberal economics and structural theory. As I show, these two theories provide an incomplete understanding of poverty in affluent Western democracies. This weak empirical performance may even be the most critical limitation of individualism. If an analysis of individuals cannot yield an effective model for predicting macro-level patterns of poverty, an individualistic perspective is not sufficient as a scientific theory of poverty. After all, explaining and predicting phenomena are the fundamental purpose of scientific inquiry. Further, if scientific explanations cannot predict macro-level phenomena, they are severely limited for public policy. Policies are implemented and expected to have effects at the macro level, not simply on an individual level.

Given these limitations, the study of poverty needs a theory that contrasts explicitly with individualism. Instead of explaining why the poor are different from the nonpoor, we need a theory that explains why poverty varies cross-nationally and historically. This book proposes institutionalized power relations theory as a step in that direction. As the following chapters demonstrate, welfare state generosity and Leftist politics more effectively explain poverty than prevailing individualist explanations or explanations extended from individualism to the macro level.

Returning to the notion of fundamental causality, we need to invert the prioritization of individualism with narrowing the distance between cause and effect. Instead of trying to assign the proximate characteristic associated with poverty, this book seeks to push the explanation backward toward the fundamental causes of poverty. Rather than isolating the risks of poverty, the aim is to explain the origins of the political context that makes poverty more likely. Rather than asking "who gets ahead?" or who falls behind, this book asks why some societies have so many that fall behind while other societies have so few.[48]

Empirical Analyses

This book articulates institutionalized power relations theory and compares it against alternative explanations of poverty. Because I argue that a macro-level approach is appropriate when one's question and theory are at the macro level, the data analyses are conducted at the macro level. My analyses are based on cross-national and historical comparisons of 18 affluent Western democracies: Australia, Austria, Belgium, Canada, Denmark, Finland, France, Germany, Ireland, Italy, Luxembourg, the Netherlands, Norway, Spain, Sweden, Switzerland, the United Kingdom, and the United States. The period of analysis is from 1969 to 2002, what some might consider an era of postindustrialism.[49] All of the data are at the country level, and the sample contains several time points for each of the 18 countries. The unit of analysis is the "country-year," which is each time point for a particular country. Just like the orienting question of the book, the empirical analyses examine why poverty varies across countries and over time.

It is beyond the bounds of this study to examine less developed countries, and, unfortunately, data are not available for Japan and a few affluent democracies, like New Zealand, Greece, Portugal, and Iceland. Similarly, it is not possible to analyze every year for the 18 countries. Thus, I sample the total number of country-years during this period based on data availability. My analyses typically include 104 country-years or slightly more than five observations per country on average.

Rather than detailing the minute methodological details in the text, most of that information is presented in the appendix. Suffice to say that the analyses utilize random effects models. Although random effects models have some limitations, I explain in the appendix that they are a defensible strategy for theoretical and methodological reasons (albeit among imperfect alternatives).[50] It is worth pointing out that although I present several tables, the statistical results are displayed graphically whenever possible. Whenever I do so in the text, however, I present the detailed results in tables in the appendix. Although these chapters build on my previous research, all of the empirical results in this book are new and are a product of new analyses. In my prior articles, I detailed all of my methodological choices and modeling strategies. To make this book more accessible to readers, I refer the specialized reader to those articles for anything not detailed in the appendix.[51]

Outline of Chapters

Beyond developing institutionalized power relations, this book offers a comprehensive study of poverty in affluent Western democracies. Before proceeding to the analyses, however, it is essential to scrutinize the measurement of poverty. The only defensible approach is to justify the measurement of one's dependent variable conceptually before moving on to test theories of that dependent variable. When social scientists select their measures of poverty based on convenience, the study of poverty is compromised. Worse, when social scientists cherry-pick a poverty measure that biases the results in favor of their favored theory, one cannot trust the conclusions. To correctly understand the causes of poverty, one must first justify one's measure of poverty. Thus, I devote two chapters to the measurement of poverty. The aim is to advocate for the most sophisticated state-of-the-art measures and to more fully incorporate those measures into empirical analyses.

Chapter 2 reviews advances in the conceptualization of poverty. Most of the U.S. social science of poverty relies on the flawed official U.S. measure, which is lacking in both reliability and validity. In chapter 2 I argue that the official measure should be abandoned. Instead, I advocate for a set of theoretical and methodological criteria for poverty measurement. After establishing how to measure poverty, Chapter 3 empirically explores the patterns in poverty with alternative measures. With data from the LIS, I examine what these measures mean for cross-national and historical comparisons. In addition to the entire population, patterns in child, elderly, adult female, and adult male poverty are considered.

Chapter 4 analyzes the welfare state, establishing the first of two parts of the institutionalized power relations theory. I explain the mechanisms by which the welfare state influences poverty and then consider which dimensions of the welfare state might influence poverty, whether there are different effects across different types of welfare states, and whether the welfare state's effects have changed over time. The results demonstrate that the welfare state has a robust and powerful negative influence on poverty. Moreover, this influence is remarkably stable across welfare state regimes and over time.

As the second part of institutionalized power relations theory, chapter 5 examines the impact of Leftist collective political actors. This chapter outlines the contributions and limitations of power resources theory and articulates how institutionalized power relations theory moves beyond that theory. I then test six measures of Leftist politics, and all six are shown to significantly reduce poverty. Their effects are mostly channeled through the welfare state, and only one measure partly combines with the welfare state. Leftist politics fundamentally causes poverty, but the welfare state remains the proximate and direct influence.

Chapters 6 and 7 evaluate the two alternative theories of poverty. Chapter 6 examines liberal economics, the leading explanation in economics, and chapter 7 examines structural theory, the leading explanation in sociology. One can also consider these two theories to be the macro-level extensions of the prevailing individualist approaches to poverty. Chapter 6 demonstrates that liberal economics provides a weak model of poverty. Many of its claims are wholly unsupported, and only economic growth has a robust effect in the expected direction. More importantly, I show that institutionalized power relations theory is a far more effective explanation. Chapter 7 shows that manufacturing employment, female labor force participation, the elderly population, and children in single-mother families all play a role in explaining poverty. Thus, structural theory is a respectable rival explanation to institutionalized power relations theory. Nevertheless, I argue that an exclusive commitment to structural theory—as tends to exist in U.S. sociology—leads to an incomplete understanding of poverty.

In the concluding chapter 8, institutionalized power relations theory is presented as the most useful explanation of poverty across affluent Western democracies. In the process of reviewing the scholarship of poverty, this chapter advocates for a theoretical reorientation. Even though some view the United States as simply too unique in terms of race and ethnic diversity, chapter 8 also demonstrates that the idiosyncrasies of United States do not undermine institutionalized power relations theory. Finally, I articulate a few policy implications of this study.

Like so many students in the 1990s, my original inspiration for studying poverty came from trying to come to grips with the concentrated inner-city poverty profiled in works like William Julius Wilson's *The Truly Disadvantaged*.[52] In the wake of the crack epidemic, decaying and hypersegregated neighborhoods, rows of shuttered factories, and the federal government's wholesale abandonment of a generation of poor children, the puzzles of endemic poverty in such a rich country were inescapable. It was the stark ethnographies that opened my eyes to the depths of America's social problems, whether it was Mitchell Duneier's documentation of the working poor, Elijah Anderson's accounts of Old Heads in blighted West Philadelphia, Sudhir Venkatesh's tales of the towers of the Robert Taylor Holmes projects on the south side of Chicago, or Katherine Newman's and Kathryn Edin and Laura Lein's windows into the trials and tribulations of single-mother poor families just trying to make it.[53]

Yet, as I studied poverty, the most enigmatic question became why these social problems are so much more common in the United States. No other affluent democracy has so normalized poverty for so much of its population. Sure, Barcelona has the precarious immigrant enclave of El Raval, and Paris has troubled suburbs where riots break out and youth unemployment is widespread. Yet, it is only in the United States where such deep divides between rich and poor appear to be so intractable and so, for lack of a better word, ordinary. This book seeks to maintain my generation of students' deep concern for the truly disadvantaged. At the same time, this book seeks to ask what makes poverty so entrenched in some affluent democracies while it is a solvable problem in others.

2

Rethinking the Measurement of Poverty

At the end of every summer, American citizens engage in a rather insincere ritual. Usually in the last week of August, the Census Bureau releases the "official" rates of poverty for the previous year. Poverty might be 12.6% this year, whereas it was only 12.3% last year. Pundits, professors, politicians, the press, and even the president rehearse their annual empty remarks on why poverty is higher or lower than last year, and attribute this failure or success to things that really have nothing to do with poverty's true causes. We talk about the trends in official poverty in the United States and use these statistics to frame public debate and policies regarding poverty. These official poverty statistics shape how Americans think about poverty and construct and constrain the national discussion. The statistics take on a life of their own and, by doing so, make the entire episode remarkably dishonest.

The dishonesty is not really the fault of the hardworking government statisticians distributing the figures. One such statistician, Mollie Orshansky, constructed the formula for the official measure in 1963. She developed this poverty line purely for research, never intended it for policy, and quickly renounced it once it became the "official" measure. The Census Bureau, aware of its problems, presents alternative estimates, publishes criticisms of it, and does not really resist calls to revise the official measure.

The dishonesty of official poverty statistics is only partially the responsibility of politicians. Though guilty of an unwillingness to revise the official measure, it would be unusual for politicians to intentionally misrepresent poverty statistics. In contrast to how commonly politicians willfully caricature budget or tax details, for example, political debate on poverty statistics seems quaintly sincere.

Unfortunately, a great deal of the responsibility falls on social scientists. The official measure lacks any justification as a social science measure. And yet we continue to use it. By doing so, we contribute to how it frames our understanding of poverty. Every year, we spend a great deal of time and energy reporting, debating, and scrutinizing an official statistic that is not a valid and reliable measure of poverty. By participating in the commentary, and especially by using the official measure in our research, social scientists give unwarranted credibility and legitimacy to a flawed measure. This acceptance and use of the official measure is the underlying reason the ritual is so insincere. This chapter proposes that social scientists should move beyond the official measure and, in the process, rethink the measurement of poverty.

During this time that social scientists have continued to use the deeply flawed official measure, scholars have actually made tremendous progress in improving poverty measurement.[1] These poverty measurement experts have devised innovative and useful alternative measures of poverty. For example, Amartya Sen received a Nobel Prize in Economics in 1998 for work that included his "Ordinal Approach" to measuring poverty. Though some of these new techniques are impractical, there have been many significant theoretical and methodological advances.

In the studies surrounding these advances, one thing has become tremendously clear: how one measures poverty truly does matter. The measurement of poverty determines how many people are counted as poor and how deeply in poverty they are considered to be.[2] Indeed, one gets different results for the level, composition, and trends in U.S. poverty depending on the measure chosen. Simply answering the question of whether U.S. poverty has increased in the last several decades basically depends on which poverty measure is used.[3] Thus, there are very real consequences to poverty measurement. Unfortunately, however, these important advances in measurement remain incompletely realized in the social science of poverty. This book advocates for these advances and, in the process, demonstrates that poverty measurement is an essential concern of any study of poverty. By utilizing state-of-the-art measures of poverty, this book offers a more accurate account of patterns in and causes of poverty. Therefore, one contribution of the book is to ground debates about the causes of poverty in more sophisticated and justifiable measures of poverty.

This chapter begins by reviewing the shortcomings of the official U.S. measure. Then, I discuss the major theoretical and methodological advances in poverty measurement and advocate for five criteria: (1) measure comparative historical variation effectively, (2) be relative rather than absolute, (3) conceptualize poverty as social exclusion and capability deprivation, (4) incorporate taxes and transfers, and (5) integrate the depth of poverty. Overall, the aim is to facilitate the integration of theoretical and methodological advances into the empirical measurement of poverty. What is more, this integration is the basis for how poverty is measured in the analyses in the remainder of the book.

Shortcomings of the Official U.S. Measure

The vast majority of U.S. research on poverty is based on the official U.S. measure.[4] Occasionally, scholars modestly alter the measure or supplement it with other indicators. However, most survey data sets supply researchers with variables identifying respondents as below or above the official level. Typically, analysts just use these simple "dummy" (coded 0/1 or "binary") variables. Others analyze and present historical trends in official poverty and debate whether poverty has increased since the official measure was adopted in the early 1960s. This widespread use of the official measure stands in stark contrast to what social scientists know and have written about the limitations of the official measure.

In the past few decades, a consensus has emerged that is deeply critical of the official measure. Indeed, almost all serious poverty scholars acknowledge the measure is flawed.[5] William Julius Wilson argues that the official measure "does not capture the real dimensions of hardship and deprivation, it also does not reflect the changing depth or severity of poverty," and that its income thresholds are "arbitrary."[6] In 1988, the U.S. Congress passed the Family Support Act, which called for a scientific review of the measure. In 1995, the National Research Council (NRC) Panel on Poverty and Family Assistance published the results of this review. The NRC panel, which included many of America's most influential poverty researchers, concluded that the official measure is so problematic that it should be abandoned. In addition, the NRC panel noted that these problems had gotten worse over the previous three decades and that, as a result, we cannot trust comparisons of poverty across groups or over time.[7] Since the NRC panel's report, many have reiterated the official measure's limitations. Indeed, those that examine the official measure closely almost uniformly end up seeking to move beyond it.

The history of how the measure was constructed begins to illustrate its problems.[8] Mollie Orshansky, a statistician in the Social Security Administration, constructed the measure in 1963. She used family consumption data from 1955 and what she called a "crude" calculus of family budgets.[9] Orshansky used the U.S. Department of Agriculture's (USDA) "low-cost food budget" and multiplied the dollar amount by 3. Even though it was never very firm, she postulated that food amounted to one-third of a family's expenses. She developed the line purely as a tool for research, and never intended it for setting policy. Contrary to her intentions, President Johnson's Office of Economic Opportunity went ahead and adopted it as the official measure. Yet, they only did so after substituting the USDA's "economy food plan," which was about 25% below the low-cost food budget. Orshansky clearly preferred the low-cost food budget, and pointed out that the economy food plan would only provide families with sufficient money in emergencies or on a temporary basis.[10] The food budgets have never been revised since the 1955 data, and the measure was only adjusted for inflation. Partly because the adjustments over time were quite rough and partly because inflation involves many items besides food, the original link between food budgets and income no longer even exists.[11] Even though scholars often defend the threshold for being based on food budgets, this has not been accurate since the 1960s.

Historians such as Alice O'Connor and Michael Katz have even provided evidence that the threshold was intentionally set low in order to make the elimination of poverty an easier political goal as part of Johnson's "War on Poverty."[12] The official threshold was at least partly a political maneuver to classify millions of people as "not poor" who reasonably should have been considered poor. By defining these millions as not poor, the Johnson administration could more easily claim to have won the war. Soon after the measure became official, Orshansky wrote articles criticizing it and explaining that her work had been misused.[13] As Orshansky explained in 1969, "The best you can say for the measure is that at a time when it seemed useful, it was there."[14] At the very least, the dubious origins and amount of time since the measure's inception suggest the need for revision. The NRC panel went one step further and argued that the official measure should not be retained.

In addition to identifying its questionable origins, one can judge the official measure in terms of the two main ways that social scientists assess measurement: reliability and validity. By both standards, the official measure is deeply problematic.

Reliability

The official measure is the same across the entire United States and for all population groups and has been basically the same since its adoption in the mid-1960s. Thus, it may seem odd to fault its reliability. However, because it is constantly applied across time, regions, and demographic groups, the measure has become clumsily incompatible with the changing realities of family life in the United States.[15] Significant demographic, economic, and policy changes have been ignored. The official measure was constructed during a time when the "typical" family included two parents: a male breadwinner and a mother at home with the children. Now that many of the U.S. poor are single-parent or dual-earning couples, the official measure is inadequate for appreciating the increased labor force participation of mothers and the related escalating need and expenses for child care. The original family size adjustments are now antiquated and do not capture the realities of contemporary U.S. families. Also, the economic insecurity of the growing elderly population—and their growing average ages—is not captured well by the official measure. Partly this is because the official measure does not budget for chronic health conditions or health care necessities like medication.

Relatedly, the share of family budgets devoted to different goods and services has changed dramatically.[16] Food no longer amounts to one-third of a typical family's expenses, and more accurately is about one-sixth. Because it should set the line at food multiplied times six instead of food multiplied times three, the official measure severely underestimates a household's economic needs. Moreover, the inflationary adjustments to the official measure are based on the cost of a basket of goods for the entire U.S. population (or all urban consumers). Because the poor are such a unique population, these price increases probably do not capture the distinct price increases they face. As a result of these and other problems, the U.S. measure has depreciated from its value in 1963 and underestimates what a family really needs to avoid poverty. Because of rising consumption and living standards, the NRC concluded that updating the poverty threshold solely with inflation has become inadequate. In short, the U.S. measure lacks reliability due in large part to the weak adjustments to the measure since its inception.

Validity

Because the official measure systematically underestimates poverty, it lacks validity as well. Many essential but burdensome family expenses, for example, health insurance, were not included in the household budgets underlying the official measure. So the official measure understates how much money a household needs to make ends meet. A household is defined as poor or not poor based on its income before taxation, yet taxes (especially payroll and sales taxes) deeply affect the disposable income of the poor. Also, "transfers" like in-kind public assistance and near-cash benefits are entirely ignored when defining a household's income. Neglecting taxes and transfers results in an inaccurate estimate of the real economic resources a household has at its disposal.[17] The earned income tax credit, housing subsidies, and food stamps have clearly raised the economic resources of such households, but payroll taxes have increased since the official measure was created. Considering all taxes and transfers together, the official measure probably underestimates U.S. poverty.[18]

These validity problems have fluctuated over time and place and, in turn, further compound reliability problems.[19] Some taxes vary across the United States, and other taxes have increased since the measure's inception. Also, policy initiatives have not been incorporated into the measure. When the Children's Health Insurance Plan and the Food Stamp program were implemented and when Medicare was expanded, the official measure was never revised. Finally, these validity problems prevent a reliable comparison across population groups. For example, Social Security pensions, a major resource for the elderly, count as income for the official measure, but major resources for young families like food stamps, housing subsidies, and child care vouchers, do not. In the past 15 years, the Earned Income Tax Credit (EITC) has grown into the largest assistance program for families with children—even larger than Temporary Assistance for Needy Families (TANF, previously called Aid to Families with Dependent Children [AFDC]).[20] Unfortunately, since the official measure is based on pretax income, the EITC is ignored.

As a result, the U.S. measure lacks both validity and reliability and warrants revision. We should be cautious in reading any social science that solely relies on this problematic official U.S. measure. We should question any conclusions drawn from the official measure. While the government lacks the political will to implement a better measure, social scientists have no justification for continuing to rely on this fundamentally flawed measure.

Measuring Comparative Historical Variation

A poverty measure must be appropriate within and across different national and historical contexts. Such a measure must allow for valid and reliable comparisons across different countries and over recent time periods. At the same time, a poverty measure should be meaningful within each of those comparative historical contexts. As the international poverty scholar Timothy Smeeding and colleagues explain, "A poverty standard cannot be established independently of the economic and social context within which needs arise and are defined."[21]

Unfortunately, the official U.S. measure is woefully inadequate for conducting comparative historical analyses. The official measure's thresholds are even more problematic if applied in other affluent democracies. One cannot simply adjust the official measure for the exchange rates or purchasing power parities of other countries because the official measure is invalid and unreliable in the United States to begin with. Even if the official measure made sense in the United States, it is unlikely that the thresholds would reasonably differentiate the poor from nonpoor in other countries. For example, even if the official threshold of roughly $20,000 for a family of four was appropriate in the United States, it would make little sense in Germany or Canada. Those countries have publicly provided health insurance and health care, so the meaning of and need for disposable income is fundamentally different. Thus, converting the official measure to other countries' currencies will not produce a meaningful threshold in those countries. Instead, social scientists need poverty measures that are grounded in each specific comparative historical context.

Many have shown that the biggest variations in poverty are cross-national.[22] There are bigger comparative differences between affluent Western democracies than there are over time within such countries. Hence, explaining these significant cross-country differences is an essential task for theories of poverty. At the same time, several challenges emerge when comparing poverty across nations because different measures of poverty produce small but noticeable differences in the ranking of nations.[23] Therefore, scholars need to be careful when drawing cross-national comparisons. One should probably replicate cross-national comparisons with different measures to ensure that any differences are robust. Also, analysts have to be careful that measures appreciate cultural differences in the definition of what constitutes a family or household. Hence, a number of methodological issues must be addressed in order to conduct cross-national analyses.

Though cross-national differences are probably larger, historical variations are important to the study of poverty as well. As mentioned above, simply answering whether U.S. poverty has increased or decreased over time remains controversial.[24] Though some research finds that poverty levels have remained relatively stable within affluent Western democracies, significant historical variation has occurred. Several countries, like the United Kingdom and Ireland, have experienced a substantial increase in poverty since the 1970s. Others, like Canada, have seen poverty fall precipitously in the past few decades. To understand poverty, scholars must scrutinize and explain both cross-national differences and historical changes.

To enhance our understanding of comparative historical variation, two issues need to be carefully addressed. First, given the diverse meanings and nature of poverty across societies, scholars need to broaden the definition of poverty. To assess what are essentially culturally specific and historically contextualized phenomena, scholars need a comprehensive definition of poverty. Second, given the difficulty in comparing poverty across countries and time, to make general inferences about causes scholars need measures that grasp the same phenomena in each society. While seemingly contradictory, the next two sections explain how we can embrace both concerns simultaneously.

Conceptualizing Poverty as Social Exclusion and Capability Deprivation

In order to construct valid and reliable measures of poverty, it is essential to first theoretically define ("conceptualize") what poverty means. Together, the linked notions of social exclusion and capability deprivation provide the most useful conceptualization of poverty.

Social Exclusion

European scholars have advanced the idea of social exclusion as way of thinking about poverty and disadvantage.[25] In a masterful review, Hilary Silver explains that social exclusion has many meanings in different contexts and for different purposes.[26] Nevertheless, she contends that a central element of social exclusion is the antithesis of Emile Durkheim's concept of solidarity. Social exclusion therefore means marginalization, irrelevance, and isolation from a community. Other theorists characterize social exclusion to entail "the multi-dimensional character of disadvantage and exclusion in modern market economies,"[27] multiple deprivation or "cumulative misery,"[28] those "who suffer from an accumulation of disadvantage which cannot be reached by macro-policies,"[29] and those difficult to reach with social policy.[30] In sum, social exclusion means incomplete, unequal, or disadvantaged access to the status, benefits, and experiences of typical citizens in society.[31]

Social exclusion unites many of the definitions of poverty implicitly conveyed by scholars of poverty. The notion of social exclusion echoes Michael Harrington's concern that "the poor are losing their links with the greater world."[32] In addition, social exclusion is consistent with William Julius Wilson's concept of social dislocation, which he describes as limited differential opportunities for economic resources, political privileges, organizational influence, and cultural experiences.[33] Similarly, in his classic *The Affluent Society*, John Galbraith defines poverty as when people's income "falls radically behind that of the community." Galbraith emphasizes that poverty involves more than simply having enough to physically survive and is better understood as lacking what the "community regards as the minimum necessary for decency."[34]

Theories of social exclusion have also been deeply influenced by the political philosopher John Rawls's difference principle.[35] Rawls argued that a society can be judged according to how it treats the "least advantaged" or "least fortunate group in society." Rawls was concerned with these people "being drawn into the public world and seeing themselves as full members of it"[36] and that the least advantaged are included as equal members of society.[37] Anthony Atkinson explains that a Rawlsian definition of poverty applies this concept of the "least fortunate group" to the concept of social exclusion.[38]

Capability Deprivation

In addition to pioneering measures of poverty that I discuss below, Sen and Martha Nussbaum have developed the concept of capability deprivation.[39] Capability refers to the ability or capacity to function effectively in society— as Nussbaum describes, "what people are actually able to do and to be."[40] Capability also implies having the freedoms to participate fully and equally with the mainstream of society. The concept of capability also links to Rawls, who argued that basic liberties should be prioritized in a society.[41] A society that deprives people of basic liberties can be understood as depriving those people of capability. Sen has built his definition of poverty in terms of the poor's lack of substantive freedom of choice to achieve valuable "functionings" and the capability to acquire well-being. In turn, a functioning member of society must have basic freedoms (or capabilities) to participate in society.[42] As Lee Rainwater and Tim Smeeding explain, "Without a requisite level of goods and services, individuals cannot act and participate as full members of their society."[43]

Uniting the Two

In many ways, capability deprivation and social exclusion share common ground. A person who is socially excluded has a limited capability to effectively participate in society. Atkinson integrates the two concepts by explaining that poverty involves "people being prevented from participation in the normal activities of the society in which they live or being incapable of functioning."[44] Similar to social exclusion, capability deprivation involves people lacking the basic liberties to participate equally in society. Thus, the concepts of social exclusion and capability present an engaging direction for analysts of social inequality.

However, because poverty is primarily an economic status, whereas social exclusion and capability deprivation appear to be multifaceted and complex, some readers might see them as incompatible. It might seem inappropriate to treat social exclusion and capability deprivation as market phenomena, rather than as something cultural, institutional, or social.

Yet, the economic market is one of several main mechanisms triggering social exclusion and capability deprivation. In affluent Western democracies, a low level of economic resources is a principal source of social exclusion and capability deprivation. Brian Barry has argued that an interest in social exclusion requires an interest in economic inequality, and that "[a] government professing itself concerned with social exclusion but indifferent to inequality is, to put it charitably, suffering from a certain amount of confusion."[45] Bea Cantillion claims, "There is probably not a single characteristic that the 'socially excluded' have in common, except perhaps, not having a stable well-paying job."[46] Atkinson exemplifies social exclusion as lacking a telephone in the home: "A person unable to afford a telephone finds it difficult to participate in a society where the majority have telephones."[47] While owning a telephone or lacking a job is based mainly on a person's economic resources, these simple conditions lead to more elaborate social processes of dislocation and marginalization. Even while conceptualizing poverty with the broader and more nuanced notions of capability deprivation and social exclusion, it is still reasonable to define poverty in terms of a minimal level of economic resources.

Thus, escaping poverty is at least a necessary—if not wholly sufficient—qualification to avoiding capability deprivation and social exclusion. In order to participate in society and community life, it is essential to have an adequate income.[48] Social exclusion and capability deprivation entail marginalization from society's core institutions, and the market is one such core institution.

Relative versus Absolute Poverty Measures

For many years, a lively debate has occurred between those advocating relative versus absolute measures of poverty.[49] Relative and absolute measures involve different notions of deprivation, reflect different accounts of the nature and experience of poverty, and produce different estimates of how much poverty exists. Despite how long this debate has gone on, poverty scholars generally have come to a consensus. The poverty literature generally concludes that a relative measure is more justified in *affluent democracies*, whereas absolute measures of "basic needs" or "well-being" are most useful in *less developed countries*.[50] By reviewing the strengths and weaknesses of absolute and relative measures, I advocate a relative measure for the study of affluent democracies.

Absolute Measures

Absolute measures set a cross-nationally and historically constant threshold, and this threshold distinguishes poor from nonpoor across all contexts. Absolute measures assume that a certain level of material resources purchases an essential bundle of goods necessary for well-being. For example, except for inflationary adjustments, the U.S. measure is meant to be absolute over time, regions, and family types. The World Bank defines poverty absolutely as living on less than one dollar per day in Sub-Saharan Africa and less than two dollars per day in Eastern Europe. Thus, absolute measures tend be tied to the concept of well-being and indicators of basic needs such as caloric intake. Sen contends that when studying developing countries, absolute measures remain useful.[51] Nevertheless, absolute measures suffer from serious limitations when applied to developed countries.

Most international poverty analysts have become understandably skeptical that absolute measures are valid and reliable in affluent democracies. Such scholars realize that a fixed bundle of goods or absolute threshold of well-being cannot represent the complexity of poverty. Indeed, attempts to measure such absolute thresholds tend to be based on a series of dubious decisions. Thus, an absolute veneer is placed on top of a set of problematic indicators. Smeeding and his colleagues avoid an absolute measure because it "conveys an unwarranted objectivity."[52] Aldi Hagenaars contends that "the resulting estimates are not as absolute and objective as they are claimed to be."[53] Rainwater and Smeeding even go so far as to conclude "The more experience countries have with absolute poverty definitions, the more obvious becomes the absurdity of the rationale for them."[54]

Nevertheless, proponents of absolute measures counter that it is valuable to tap into concepts of well-being and basic needs. After all, if basic needs are unmet or well-being is low—in terms or physiological subsistence and physical health—poverty is clearly present. For example, families that suffer from homelessness or hunger must obviously be poor. Some scholars provide evidence of a historical decline in U.S. poverty based on measures of absolute consumption. While the argument is not new—economist Milton Friedman made the argument in the 1960s, and many made it before him—a number of economists contend that that U.S. poor presently are more affluent than the middle class in previous decades.[55] As popularized in. W. Michael Cox and Richard Alm's *Myths of Rich and Poor*, the U.S. poor consume like the middle class in previous generations, with access to refrigerators, televisions, cars, and indoor plumbing.[56] If one concentrates on basic needs or well-being, perhaps it is fair to say that poverty is not a serious problem in the contemporary United States.

On the surface, such absolute measures of consumption or well-being are intriguing. But as one digs deeper, one finds a number of shaky assumptions and questionable decisions.[57] The greatest concern is with how these measures conceptualize and measure poverty divorced from cultural and historical context. Absolute measures explicitly presume that being poor is the same thing in the United States in the 1950s or 1990s, the same thing in Spain as in Sweden, or even the same in Kenya as in Germany. Thus, in order to adopt an absolute measure, an analyst must assume that being poor is the same thing in all contexts.

Upon reflection, however, it is more reasonable to conclude that any definition of "need" is full of culturally and historically contextualized norms.[58] It is quite unlikely that if one interviewed social scientists in each of these time periods and cultural contexts, there would be much agreement about the basic needs of people or what constitutes poverty. Patricia Ruggles has shown that consumption patterns have changed so dramatically over the past 40–50 years that agreeing on the basic needs of American families is actually quite difficult.[59] Martin Ravallion notes that perceptions of "well-being" depend on what is the comparison group and argues, "There is an inherent subjectivity and social specificity to any notion of 'basic needs.' "[60] Hagenaars points out that nutritionists cannot agree about levels of calories needed for various ages, sexes, occupations, and living conditions.[61] Even U.S. policy makers have long conceded that as a society's standard of living rises, more expensive consumption is forced on the poor to remain integrated into society.[62] Peter Townsend concludes, "Any rigorous conceptualization of the social determination of need dissolves the idea of 'absolute' need."[63] Therefore, attempts to come up with a list of basic needs that differentiate poor from nonpoor across all cultural and historical contexts have failed to stand up to scrutiny.

Just like the concept of need, the concept of well-being has limitations as a way to define poverty. Sen has explained that one of the problems of absolute measures is that they conflate "poverty" and well-being. He persuasively distinguishes between these two by pointing out that some people have low well-being without being poor and some are poor without low well-being. Poverty is better thought of as question of economic resources, whereas well-being is an outcome that is often undermined by a shortage of economic resources. As Sen emphasizes, "Poverty is not a matter of low well-being, but of the inability to pursue well-being precisely because of the lack of economic means."[64]

Of course, most readers can probably agree that a desperate absolute level of deprivation does exist under which families are definitely poor. The problem is that it is nearly impossible to define a valid and reliable absolute standard above the most basic subsistence levels. Of course, people are poor if they are homeless or starving. But such a minimal standard sets the line so low that only a tiny share of the population would be "poor" in affluent democracies. Certainly, there is more to escaping poverty than simply avoiding starvation or meeting "basic needs." When one tries to discern any absolute poverty definition above such minimal levels, it becomes problematic to distinguish poor from nonpoor. For these reasons, most international poverty researchers have abandoned absolute measures for developed countries.

Relative Measures

Relative measures specify poverty thresholds for each society at each point in time based on the distribution of economic resources within that context. Relative measures do not try to capture absolute deprivation, but instead embrace relative deprivation.[65] As I explain below, the leading approach is to define relative poverty as those households with less than 50% of the median income. People below this culturally and historically specific threshold are considered too far down in the queue for the scarce resource of income to be fully integrated into society.[66] Hence, relative measures assess the difference in living conditions between the poor and the majority of society, or the difference between the poor and conventional customary standards for normal households. More specifically, relative measures have three major advantages.

First, relative measures are most compatible with the leading concepts of poverty as social exclusion and capability deprivation.[67] In 1984, when the European Commission constructed measures of poverty, the Council of Ministers explicitly linked its measures to social exclusion by defining poverty as "persons whose resources are so limited to exclude them from the minimum acceptable way of life in the Member State in which they live."[68] The European Union's statistical service, Eurostat, utilizes relative measures of poverty due to a theoretical interest in such concepts as social exclusion.[69] Returning to Rawls, he offered the example that the "least fortunate group" could be defined as those with less than half of the median income and wealth. Rawls even suggested that this could form a meaningful poverty standard.[70] Rawls certainly thought of his difference principle in terms of relative deprivation, writing that it implies a "social minimum [that] depends on the content of the public political culture."[71] This social minimum "is *not* given by the basic needs of human nature taken psychologically (or biologically) apart from any particular social world."[72] Throughout his writings, Rawls is concerned with equal citizenship and how it is threatened by inferiority and deference, inequalities, and social status.[73] Although Sen argued that there was value in absolute poverty measures when studying developing countries, he was clear that poverty should be measured relatively in developed countries. Indeed, Sen stressed that the relatively poor in rich countries are capability deprived, even though they are well off compared with most of the people in the world. Sen explained, "Relative deprivation in terms of *incomes* can yield *absolute* deprivation in terms of *capabilities*."[74] Based on these theoretical ideas, international poverty scholars have critiqued absolute measures on the grounds that they are disconnected from key concepts like social exclusion and capability deprivation. In sum, relative measures are superior because they better represent these leading conceptualizations of poverty.[75]

Second, relative measures have the virtue of being entirely grounded in national and historical context.[76] Relative measures recognize that poverty must be meaningful according to each particular society's cultural norms and customary, prevailing standards of necessities. It is worth noting that, while coming up with what became the official U.S. measure, Orshansky was actually concerned with "the *relative* well-being of both individuals and the society in which they live" and what families need for "keeping with American consumption patterns."[77] In the classic *The Other America*, Harrington stressed that poverty should be gauged according to the living standards and historical conditions of the mainstream of contemporary society. In a telling passage that is worth revisiting, Harrington wrote:

> Shall we say to them [the American poor] that they are better off than the Indian poor, the Italian poor, the Russian poor?...In the nineteenth century, conservatives in England used to argue against reform on the grounds that the British worker of the time had a longer life expectancy than a medieval nobleman....Indeed, if one wanted to play with figures, it would be possible to prove that there are no poor people in the United States, or at least only a few whose plight is as desperate as that of the masses in Hong Kong. There is starvation in American society, but it is not a pervasive social problem as it is in some the newly independent nations. There are still Americans who literally die in the streets, but their numbers are comparatively small....Those who suffer levels of life below those that are possible, even though they live better than the medieval knights or Asian peasants, are poor....The American poor are not poor in Hong Kong or in the sixteenth century; they are poor here and now, in the United States. They are dispossessed in terms of what the rest of the nation enjoys.... To have one bowl of rice in a society where all other people have half a bowl may well be a sign of achievement and intelligence; it may spur a person to act and to fulfill his human potential. To have five

bowls of rice in a society where the majority have a decent, balanced diet is a tragedy.[78]

Thus, a relative measure advantageously focuses on one in comparison with or in relation to other members of the society in which he or she is a member. A person is considered poor compared with or in relation to the typical or average person in his or her society. In this sense, relative measures frame poverty as a social and, hence, sociological condition.[79] As Townsend eloquently elaborates, "Man is not a Robinson Crusoe living on a desert island. He is a social animal entangled in a web of relationships at work and in family and community which exert complex and changing pressures to which he must respond, as much in his consumption of goods and services as in any other aspect of this behavior."[80] Because relative measures define deprivation in relation to other people within a social context, they are better suited to the previously mentioned need to be sensitive to the comparative historical context. Relatedly, it is valuable to point out that people actually think of their social context when asked to define poverty. For example, when asked in a survey how to define poverty, most people come up with a poverty threshold that is roughly equal to a common relative threshold: 50% of the median income.[81] Moreover, the average person's definition of "necessities" tends to rise with the social context as living standards rise.[82]

Third, relative measures enable social scientists to gain a better understanding of the consequences of poverty. One of the conclusions of the aforementioned NRC review was to propose a new official measure that was based upon the relative consumption of contemporary U.S. families. A number of studies have analyzed how this proposed relative measure would change our understanding of poverty. This work has shown that historical trends in U.S. poverty would have been significantly different, poverty rates would have been considerably higher, and there would actually be smaller differences in poverty between some demographic groups (e.g., children vs. the elderly). Most important, Carolyn Hill and Robert Michael demonstrate that the NRC measure has much greater predictive validity than does the official measure. The NRC alternative better predicts a number of children's outcomes that should be affected by poverty: school grades and suspensions, achievement test scores, expectations of completing college, and avoiding pregnancy.[83] Thus, when we consider how child poverty matters to public policy and aspects of children's well-being, scholars have found that relative deprivation is most important.[84] In a different but equally informative literature, Michael Marmot documents in *The Status Syndrome* that relative, not absolute poverty, is more consequential for health in affluent democracies.[85] Although absolute deprivation matters to a point, once countries are developed, relative deprivation becomes the more salient predictor of well-being.

In sum, relative measures have three principal advantages over absolute measures. First, relative measures are much more consistent with the concepts of social exclusion and capability deprivation. Second, relative

measures are grounded in cultural and historical context and thus emphasize the social relations among people. Third, relative measures are more
useful for understanding the consequences of poverty. After a great deal of
debate on the topic, most international poverty researchers now agree that a
relative measure of poverty is most useful for affluent democracies.

Taxes, Transfers, and the State

A great deal of research has tried to untangle how taxes and government
benefits, what are called "transfers," shape people's income. One of the most
persuasive critiques of the U.S. measure of poverty is that it is mostly based
on pretax income and inconsistently neglects cash transfers and in-kind
benefits. Of course, taxes and transfers significantly affect a household's
finances. In fact, the deteriorating value of transfers may have contributed
to the worsening of child poverty in recent decades in the United States.[86]
Further, taxes on U.S. poor families have risen since the 1960s, and in turn,
their actual financial standing may be weaker than that of families with
similar incomes in earlier decades. This neglect of taxes and transfers in
calculating income violates Sen's Transfer axiom: "Given other things, a
pure transfer of income from a person below the poverty line to anyone
who is richer must increase the poverty measure."[87] To accurately estimate
a household's economic resources and, in turn, accurately estimate poverty,
it is essential to incorporate taxes and transfers.

Calculating the exact impact of taxes and transfers on household income
and poverty levels is a formidable task. Though taxes and transfers typically
are financial, in-kind and near-cash benefits like housing assistance and food
stamps are important, too. Ignoring these benefits biases our estimates of the
distribution of economic resources between households and leads to a misleading picture about the relative standing of various types of households.[88]
The Luxembourg Income Study has been the leader in calculating the most
comprehensive definitions of household income by incorporating taxes and
transfers. Tim Smeeding and colleagues have assessed the value of taxes,
transfers, and a variety of near-cash benefits and translated those values into
the estimate of household income. It is important to keep in mind that
benefits accrue from both the private and the public sector. Although public
benefits probably have a bigger impact, private pensions, rental income, self-
employment earnings, and other private compensation matter as well. There
are national differences in the different kinds of benefits, and private and
public taxes and transfers should always be incorporated when calculating a
household's income.

One common strategy used to untangle the consequences of taxes and
transfers for household income has been to calculate the distribution of
economic resources *before* taxes and transfers (what is called "pre-fisc").

The conventional approach is to estimate a household's income while adding back the value of taxes paid and subtracting the value of transfers. This is supposed to simulate what income would look like before taxes and transfers. This simulated counterfactual might appear useful when analyzing individual employed adults. Because the majority of their income comes from labor market earnings, perhaps it is not unreasonable to estimate what a working adult's pre-fisc income might have been. Many analysts have extended this logic to calculate pre-fisc poverty rates or pre-fisc inequality levels for the entire population. Pre-fisc is supposed to represent the private sector or labor market earnings. By contrast, "post-fisc," which measures household income after subtracting taxes and adding transfers, is supposed to incorporate the state. Indeed, it has become conventional to estimate pre-fisc and post-fisc poverty or inequality and then take the rate of change between the two and call that "redistribution."[89] Despite its widespread use, there are serious micro-level and macro-level problems with this approach.

On a micro level, pre-fisc has no meaning for much of the nonemployed population. The elderly, for example, usually have little pre-fisc income because they often rely on public pensions. Even with working adults, an estimate of pre-fisc income does not truly gauge private economic resources. In every labor market, an adult has gained greatly from state investment. Human capital, an essential factor behind any labor market earnings, is shaped deeply by state involvement in all societies. Public primary and secondary education clearly affects private labor market earnings, and owners and managers profit from this public sector investment. But those with higher education have also benefited from government investment in universities—directly in the form of subsidized or free education and/or state-subsidized loans and grants, and indirectly via the enormous amount of money collected by universities from government grants and contracts. Also, vast numbers of working adults are employed in public-sector jobs or at private-sector employers who have government grants and contracts. Yet, pre-fisc would have us act as if these earnings were independent of the state. In reality, no household exists in, and there is no such thing as, a pretax and pretransfer world. Thus, it is disingenuous to simulate what income would be "before the state." Even a working adult's income cannot be separated from state involvement since the state permeates and shapes every individual's labor market opportunities.

On a macro level, it is unrealistic to reify these simulations of individual pre-fisc income into national-level estimates of poverty, inequality, and redistribution. One of the emerging conclusions of economic sociology is that states and markets inherently constitute each other.[90] States are always involved in the allocation of economic resources to workers, managers, and especially owners. States do not simply respond to what markets have initiated; states define and constitute markets. The state is heavily involved in the operation of markets by setting rules on how goods and services are bought and sold, by setting standards for labor and production, by defining who and what has property rights, by funding the infrastructure on which markets unfold, and by backing the currencies and credit that make exchange possible. The private sector *always* benefits from *some* state influence—even if just by protecting property rights. All of these state interventions are central for markets to even happen, and the distribution of income that results from a market cannot be said to be independent of the state. As Erik Wright articulately explains, "It is therefore misleading to talk about a clear distinction between pure 'distribution' of income and a process of politically shaped 'redistribution.' "[91] Since the state is *always* involved in the market, there really is no such thing as income *before* the state. One can also point out that the historical record shows that most markets did not exist prior to the state, because the process of market formation requires state formation.[92] Thus, it is artificial to define taxes and transfers as "re"-distribution, and it is not realistic to calculate what the income distribution would be "before" the state.

Confirming these theoretical arguments, Andreas Bergh has recently convincingly demonstrated that pre-fisc estimates are deeply problematic.[93] These estimates are biased by the fact that state taxes and transfers actually do affect how much people earn and whether people work, retire, or leave the labor force to care for family. Bergh demonstrates specifically how (1) welfare states redistribute both between individuals and over the life cycle, (2) pre-fisc incomes actually depend upon and are shaped by taxes and transfers, (3) pre-fisc estimates incorrectly describe the redistributive effect of social insurance that crowds out market insurance, and (4) welfare states influence the distribution of earnings through education. People consider their expected taxes and transfers when making decisions about labor market behavior, and this biases pre-fisc estimates. Imagine the typical wealthy person in the United States. This person undoubtedly has an accountant whose job is to identify ways to maximize income by avoiding taxes and collecting transfers. In turn, this person's supposedly pre-fisc income is actually strategically dependent on taxes and transfers. Precisely because people are influenced by the state when earning income, a person's pre-fisc income is not severable from taxes and transfers. Thus, we cannot accurately estimate the income distribution as if the state does not exist.

As a final illustration of the problems of pre-fisc estimates, consider the Earned Income Tax Credit (EITC) in the United States. Because the EITC is a tax refund, and pre-fisc is a simulation of one's income excluding all taxes paid and transfers received, studies treat the EITC in confusing, contradictory, and inconsistent ways. The EITC mostly refunds labor market earnings that were taxed. So, it is pre-fisc income, but it is also "post-fisc" because the state gives it back at the end of the year after receiving some paperwork. Also, there is a transfer component of the EITC because it gives more to the bottom of the earnings distribution. Certainly, the majority of EITC recipients are aware of it, and probably factor it into their labor market behavior. For example, the EITC creates an incentive to increase "pre-fisc" earnings, because the EITC

requires people to work to gain benefits. Pre-fisc income may be underesti-
mated because people are being taxed, and alternatively, redistribution might
be overestimated because they are mostly just getting those pre-fisc earnings
back. Very small in previous decades, the EITC has grown into the largest
family assistance program in the United States (much larger than TANF).
As a result, ignoring the EITC severely undermines reliable comparisons of
pre-fisc income or redistribution over time. Because the United States heavily
relies on the EITC to alleviate poverty whereas most other affluent democracies
rely more on transfers, international comparisons of pre-fisc income or redistribution are probably not trustworthy.

The poor, like everyone, live with the benefits and constraints of state
involvement. People live in a posttax and posttransfer world. In order to
effectively measure the economic resources of households, it is essential
to incorporate taxes and transfers as comprehensively as possible. As a
result, poverty scholars should focus on poverty after taxes and transfers.[94]

The Depth of Poverty

One of the pioneering innovations in poverty measurement was Sen's ordinal measure of poverty.[95] Indeed, Sen's contribution was so important that
Hagenaars referred to it as the "ordinalist revolution."[96] Sen's contribution
can best be explained by considering a series of measures that build on each
other. Table 2.1 displays the definitions and the advantages and disadvantages of each of these measures. All of these measures can be defined
relatively.

Poverty is measured commonly with the *headcount*, the percentage of the
population that is below a certain threshold of income. The headcount is a
binary measure of poverty, offering an either/or account of who is denied the
basic minimum rights of citizenship, social inclusion, or capability. The
headcount is usefully simple, providing an easy-to-interpret and common-
sense rate of poverty. It allows one to describe what percentage of people are
poor and how that rate has changed over time or differs across countries.
Thus, the headcount is a standard way to measure and think about poverty.
Nevertheless, the headcount has received some criticism.[97]

Sen calls the headcount "crude" because it ignores the income distribution among the poor and contains no information on the depth of poverty.
Using the headcount, we treat all poor below the threshold as equal regardless of how deeply in poverty different people are. Sen articulated this
criticism of the headcount as the "monotonicity axiom: given other things,
a reduction in income of a person below the line must increase the poverty
measure."[98] This axiom can be explained best by way of example. Societies A
and B, with equal rates of poverty with the headcount, would be considered
equivalent. However, while the poor in A may cluster close to the threshold,
the poor in B may cluster close to zero income. The headcount would be

Table 2.1. Alternative Poverty Measures Emerging From the Ordinalist Revolution

	Definition	Advantages	Disadvantages
Headcount	Percent population below 50% of median income	Simple, dichotomous measure of the percentage of the population who are poor	Ignores the depth of poverty among the poor
Income gap	Difference between population's median income and mean income of poor, standardized by the population's median income	Continuous variable of the average depth of poverty among the poor	Ignores the quantity of poor people
Intensity	Product of Headcount and Income Gap	Simple, parsimonious measure combining quantity and depth of poverty	Does not weight index with the distribution of income of the poor
Ordinal	Intensity × (1 + coefficient of variation)	Weights measure so the deeply poor have more impact than the barely poor	May add unimportant information or unneeded complexity

unable to detect this difference in depth. Further, if the income distributions in A and B were identical at one point in time, the headcount would be unable to detect if the poor in A suffered severe income loss and fell to zero income while the poor in B were unchanged. Relatedly, one salient critique of the official U.S. measure—which is a headcount measure—is that it underestimates the positive impact of welfare programs.[99] Welfare programs might make families less poor without necessarily lifting them above the poverty threshold. Changes in headcount poverty rates would also understate the effect of welfare when cutbacks lead to already-poor families becoming even poorer. In short, welfare could be quite effective at reducing poverty without having an effect on the headcount. Though it is still useful for describing the proportion of the population that is socially excluded or the rate of capability deprivation, the headcount is considered imperfect because it ignores the depth of poverty.

To address these concerns, one should estimate the depth of poverty among the poor. Usually, the depth is measured as the difference between the poor's average income and either the poverty threshold or the median of the entire income distribution. This average deprivation, the *income gap*, is then standardized by the median income or poverty threshold to render it comparable across populations. By considering the income gap, rather than simply the headcount, scholars more realistically capture the continuous quality of poverty. In reality, poverty is not a discrete condition that is immediately acquired or shed by crossing a particular line. Rather, poverty is an interval variable, because the desperately poor with no income are worse off than the poor just below the poverty threshold. Sometimes poverty researchers address this concern by calculating the "income to needs ratio" as a household's income divided by the poverty line.

Still, though, the income gap is imperfect as well. While the headcount tells us the percentage of the population that is poor, it is insensitive to the depth of poverty. While the income gap tells us the depth of poverty of this subpopulation, it is insensitive to how many are poor. One solution is to simply calculate the product of the headcount and the income gap. The prevailing name for this product is *poverty intensity*.[100] Both the headcount and income gap are valuable because neither by itself tells the whole story about poverty intensity.

In addition to addressing the limitations of the headcount, a poverty intensity measure has the advantage of being less sensitive to the business cycle. When the economy grows, the median income is likely to increase (though this is often not the case—e.g., recent U.S. history). If the poverty threshold is 50% of the median income, that threshold will often rise and the number of poor will automatically increase. At the same time, households with the same income will mechanically move from nonpoor to poor. This has been one of the more common criticisms of relative measures. Fortunately, poverty intensity is far less sensitive to movements in the median income and threshold since newly and barely poor households would have a very small poverty gap. Such households would reduce the income gap, so although the headcount would increase, intensity would increase only minutely.

At this stage, Sen made his key contribution. He imposed axiom R, that the poverty gap should be weighted to correspond to the rank order in the interpersonal welfare ordering of the poor.[101] Basically, Sen argued that intensity should be weighted such that the poorest of the poor had more influence on the index. In practice, intensity should have a weight attached for the income inequality among the poor. Doing so augments the intensity measure into what he called the *ordinal measure* of poverty. The ordinal measure simply takes the intensity measure and multiplies it by a factor of the inequality among the poor.[102] Additionally, the ordinal measure is easily decomposed into three parts—the headcount, the income gap, and inequality among the poor—and each can be analyzed separately to understand their specific influence.[103]

Sen's contribution provoked a lot of research. In addition to the headcount, scholars began to use more sophisticated measures, including the income gap, intensity, and ordinal measures. As table 2.1 displays, each measure has advantages and disadvantages. If one wants a rate of poverty and does not care about the depth of poverty, the headcount remains useful. By itself, the income gap is normally less useful since it is insensitive to how many people are poor. If an analyst seeks a parsimonious measure that incorporates both the quantity and depth of poverty, intensity is preferred. By contrast, if one decides that the deeply poor should disproportionately affect the index, the ordinal measure should be used.

Even while appreciating Sen's contribution, many have become skeptical of the ordinal measure. Unlike intensity, the ordinal measure reflects a rather strong judgment that the deeply poor are more important than those near the threshold. Not everyone agrees with this judgment. Additionally, studies have recently shown that most of the variation in the ordinal measure is captured by the poverty intensity measure.[104] There is little real-world difference in patterns of poverty if one uses the ordinal or intensity measure. Also, most of the time, we do not have sufficiently good data at the very bottom of the income distribution, which is key to estimating the inequality among the poor, so it becomes harder to trust estimates of ordinal poverty. Thus, the ordinal measure often adds unneeded and unimportant complexity and may actually obscure international comparisons.[105] Ultimately, if one seeks a sufficient yet parsimonious measure and prefers to avoid the complexity and assumptions of the ordinal measure, intensity may be preferable. Prompted by the empirical patterns in my and others' research, it is probably sufficient to evaluate the headcount and intensity, thus omitting the ordinal measure from this book. While it is essential to consider the depth of poverty and to examine intensity along with the headcount, the ordinal measure may be unnecessary.

Conclusion

This chapter aimed to advance theoretically and conceptually how the social sciences measure poverty. Unfortunately, much of U.S. social science, and especially U.S. sociology, still relies on the official measure despite its overwhelming methodological problems. These problems almost certainly limit social science's contribution to understanding the causes and effects of poverty. As an alternative, this chapter synthesizes a number of advances in the conceptualization and operationalization of poverty. The end result is a set of criteria for better measuring poverty. To summarize, this chapter has provided five criteria for the measurement of poverty, as summarized in table 2.2. Each of these criteria emerges from an existing theoretical literature that

Table 2.2. Criteria for Measures of Poverty

1. Measure comparative historical variation
2. Conceptualize poverty as social exclusion and capability deprivation
3. Be relative rather than absolute
4. Assess the impact of taxes, transfers, and state benefits
5. Integrate the depth of poverty

has established its relevance to poverty measurement. Driven by these criteria, poverty analysts should focus on the headcount and poverty intensity measures.

In chapter 3, I put these theoretical and methodological advances to work. In particular, I explore the empirical patterns in poverty across and within affluent democracies with these measures. Now that the conceptual foundations have been laid for how to measure poverty, we can assess different dimensions of poverty as they actually exist. By integrating these conceptual advances with empirical data, one can gain a better and more complete understanding of poverty in modern societies.

3

Mythical and Real Patterns in Poverty

How big are cross-national differences in poverty? Which countries have the most poverty and which have the least? Has poverty increased or declined in the United States over the past few decades? Is women's poverty higher than men's poverty, and if so, are they correlated? Is poverty low among the elderly but high among children? This chapter investigates these patterns in poverty since the late 1960s between and within the 18 affluent democracies. By carefully scrutinizing these patterns, we gain insight into the variation in poverty that the rest of the book seeks to explain. Also, this chapter provides the dependent variables for the remaining chapters in the book.

Though there are many taken-for-granted and commonly understood views about poverty, only some stand up to empirical scrutiny. For example, one of the most repeated claims about poverty is that the elderly have become much less likely to be poor, while child poverty has grown partly as a result of the decline of elderly poverty. The results in this chapter demonstrate that this account is most likely incorrect. This chapter seeks to challenge some of the myths about the patterns in poverty and to offer a more accurate reading.

Data

Countries and Years

In order to analyze the empirical patterns in poverty, I calculated the levels of poverty for several different years for each of 18 affluent Western democracies: Australia, Austria, Belgium, Canada, Denmark, Finland, France, Germany, Ireland, Italy, Luxembourg, the Netherlands, Norway, Spain, Sweden, Switzerland, the United Kingdom, and the United States. Thus, the analyses include 2 North American countries, 15 Western European countries, and Australia. For each country, I had access to surveys of the population that allowed me to calculate poverty in different given years. Each of these surveys becomes a case in the analyses—each case will be sometimes referred to as a "country-year." Generally, each country contributed a case in the 1970s, around 1980, the mid-1980s, 1990, the mid-1990s, and 2000. Canada, for example, has nine country-years: 1971, 1975, 1981, 1987, 1991, 1994, 1997, 1998, and 2000. However, the analyses do not have an equal number of cases for each country, and thus the sample is unbalanced. For instance, the sample includes four cases for Spain and eight for the United Kingdom. In total, the sample includes poverty statistics for 104 country-years across these 18 countries, for an average of 5.8 cases per country.

Household Income

The poverty estimates are derived from the Luxembourg Income Study (LIS). The LIS is the world's leader in data on household income and is based on cross-nationally and historically comparable individual-level data sets. The LIS provides nearly standardized data—what the LIS staff call "Lissified" data with similar variables across data sets, similar samples, and equalizing weights, which all allow for population estimates and international comparisons. Of course, the LIS data are not perfect.[1] However, the advantages outweigh the disadvantages, and the LIS has perhaps the greatest capacity to advance scholarship on poverty of any international data set.

Following the practices of other LIS analysts and the state of the art in inequality research, I build the poverty estimates from household income after taxes and transfers.[2] Thus, these measures of household income combine all sources of private income, add cash and near-cash benefits provided by the government, and subtract the taxes a household pays. In the United States, for example, these income estimates include all salaries, earnings, private pensions, and other income and add that dollar amount to transfers, including food stamps, housing allowances, and refundable tax credits like the Earned Income Tax Credit (EITC). Then, all taxes are subtracted to equal total net disposable income.

Because people reside in households and pool the resources and expenses of members of the household, it is more justified to assess whether a person is poor based on the household's total income. One can assume that if a household is poor, every member of that household is poor. Because households with more members naturally have more expenses, I standardize each household's income by an "equivalence scale." Following recent precedent, I divide household income by the square root of household members.[3]

The analyses focus on income, but not wealth or consumption. A number of social scientists have recently argued that wealth is a better measure of a household's economic resources, while some economists contend that consumption is most important. Certainly, there are advantages to wealth and consumption as measures of economic resources.[4] Nevertheless, there are also strong reasons to continue to analyze income. Methodologically, survey research probably has a greater aptitude for collecting data on income.[5] People have reasonably good records and memory regarding income. Fewer high-quality data exist on wealth, and people simply do not have good information on their consumption. If asked, most readers would be hard-pressed to tell a survey interviewer their net worth or the value of what they have consumed in a period of time. Even the market value of one's home, the most widespread asset in the United States, would be beyond most of us. But people can easily recall how much income they earned in the past or present year.

Moreover, low-income households—the population we are interested in when studying poverty—have very little wealth.[6] The recently available Luxembourg Wealth Study demonstrates this point. In the United States in 2001, poor people had a median net worth of only $400–650. Poor children resided in households with a median net worth of zero. In comparison, the median net worth for all people was $41,700–48,500.[7] Most low-income households have little savings or investments and do not own their homes. For studying wealthy or middle-class households or the inequality between all households, certainly wealth inequality will be greater and may be more salient. But, for calculating the economic resources of low-income households, income is probably the key measure. To define a household as poor, what is relevant is their income relative to other low-income households who also have little to no wealth and relative to the incomes in the middle of the income distribution.[8]

Measures of Poverty Overall and among Groups

In order to represent the patterns in poverty, I estimated poverty among the entire population as well as among several demographic groups. Following the conclusions of chapter 2, the presentation concentrates on the headcount and intensity measures. Again, the *headcount* is the percentage of the relevant population with less than 50% of the median income for the entire population. *Poverty intensity* multiplies that headcount times the average depth (income gap) in poverty among the poor. The income gap is measured as the difference between the mean income of the poor subsample and the median income of the entire population and then standardized by the median income of the entire population.

In the following sections, I first discuss the cross-national and historical patterns in poverty for the entire population. I then explore the patterns in poverty among adult and working-age women and men. Finally, I analyze patterns in poverty among the elderly and children. Ultimately, the evidence demonstrates that regardless of which demographic group one is examining, the patterns in poverty are, surprisingly, quite consistent.

Poverty in the Entire Population

Cross-National Variation

Table 3.1 displays the descriptive statistics for the poverty measures and their related components for the maximum number of observations for the entire population. Besides the mean and standard deviation, also listed are the coefficient of variation and the minimum and maximum.

In the average country-year across the sample, 9.4% of the population is poor (according to the headcount mean). The headcount ranges from a low of only 3.9% poor to a high of 18.1% poor. The average income gap is 0.643, and this variable ranges from 0.57 to 0.77. To illustrate what this income gap means substantively, we can apply this mean to the United States in 2000. The median household income in 2000 was almost $42,000. Roughly speaking, this translates into an average income gap of about $27,000, and the average poor household's income was about $15,000.[9]

The average poverty intensity is 6.09. Remember the intensity measure is the product of the headcount and the income gap, and the income gap is always less than 1. As a result, the intensity measure will always, by definition, be lower than the headcount. Just like the headcount, however, bigger values of poverty intensity translate into greater poverty. So, one can compare poverty intensity across countries but should not compare intensity against the headcount.

Table 3.1. Descriptive Statistics for Poverty Measures Based on Luxembourg Income Study Data, 1967–2002 (N = 104)

Statistic	Mean	Standard Deviation	Coefficient of Variation	Minimum	Maximum
Headcount	9.413	3.687	0.392	3.893	18.085
Income Gap	.643	.035	.055	.566	.767
Poverty Intensity	6.087	2.496	0.410	2.314	12.191

As the coefficient of variation displays, there is not as much variation in the income gap, because all countries are close to the mean income gap of 0.64. By contrast, there is far more variation in the headcount and even more in poverty intensity. Hence, what really differentiates countries is what percentage of the population falls below the poverty threshold. The intensity measure complicates this variation slightly more, but the bigger differences between countries are in the headcount.

To get a sense of the variation in poverty across affluent democracies, one can examine the levels of poverty across countries. Figure 3.1 displays the headcount and poverty intensity estimates for a recent LIS data set for each of the 18 affluent Western democracies. According to the headcount measure shown in figure 3.1A, the United States leads all countries, with a headcount greater than 17%. The next closest countries include Ireland and Spain, with nearly 15% in poverty. The Netherlands has the least poverty, at 4.9%, or less than one-third the amount of poverty in the United States. Luxembourg and the Scandinavian countries all feature low poverty, 6.6% or less.

According to the poverty intensity measure shown in figure 3.1B, there is a generally similar pattern of results, with a few notable exceptions. Again, the United States has the most poverty by a substantial margin. Ireland and Spain repeat as the next two highest, but Italy has a slightly higher poverty intensity than Australia (reversed from the headcount). The Netherlands, the Scandinavian countries, and Luxembourg also have the lowest poverty intensity. Because they have relatively large income gaps, Belgium and the United Kingdom are one notch higher with the intensity measure compared to the headcount. The cross-national rankings of intensity differ slightly from the rankings of headcount. As a result, it is worthwhile to explore the patterns with both measures.

Similar patterns can be shown with these two measures if one confines the estimates of poverty to working-age adults. While my preference is to examine the entire population, working-age poverty mirrors overall poverty. Indeed, the bivariate correlations, with both the headcount and intensity measures, between working-age and overall poverty are greater than .92.

Because data exist for multiple time points for each country, poverty also varies over time within each country. Table 3.2 shows the means, coefficients of variation, and number of cases for each of the 18 affluent democracies in the sample.

Several interesting conclusions emerge from table 3.2. First, many of the cross-country differences are fairly stable over time. Just as with most recent country-years in figure 3.1, the United States has the highest average headcount and intensity among these countries. The United States is also the only country with an average headcount that exceeds 13%, and it is substantially greater than all other countries at 17%. The United States is the only country with a more than 8.25 poverty intensity, and it far exceeds that number with an average intensity of 11.5. Thus, the United States stands out both in recent years (figure 3.1) and over the past several decades. Basically consistent with

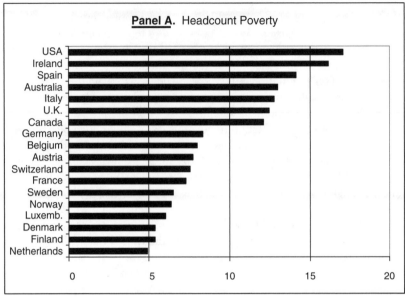

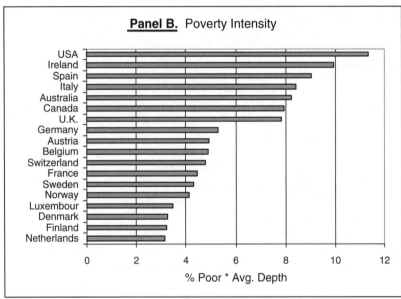

Figure 3.1.   Cross-National Patterns in Poverty in LIS Data: Headcount (A) and Intensity (B)

figure 3.1, Finland and Luxembourg have had the lowest average levels of poverty over time.

Second, there is substantial variation in how much countries changed over the past several decades. The coefficient of variation provides insight into the historical variation within countries in these measures of poverty.

Table 3.2.   Poverty Across 18 Affluent Western Democracies, 1969–2002 (Mean and Coefficient of Variation)

Country, Time Period	Headcount		Income Gap		Intensity		
	Mean	CV	Mean	CV	Mean	CV	N
Australia, 1985–2001	11.953	.058	.640	.007	7.644	.052	5
Austria, 1987–2000	8.342	.175	.647	.044	5.431	.220	5
Belgium, 1985–2000	6.462	.296	.618	.016	3.999	.301	6
Canada, 1971–2000	12.561	.129	.655	.020	8.249	.151	9
Denmark, 1987–2000	6.982	.329	.630	.043	4.426	.354	4
Finland, 1987–2000	5.154	.131	.612	.018	3.160	.142	4
France, 1979–2000	8.520	.185	.658	.068	5.656	.252	6
Germany, 1973–2000	6.829	.174	.635	.028	4.342	.183	8
Ireland, 1987–2000	12.872	.151	.605	.037	7.785	.159	5
Italy, 1986–2000	12.081	.154	.648	.038	7.867	.187	8
Luxembourg, 1985–2000	5.183	.191	.584	.020	3.026	.192	5
Netherlands, 1983–1999	5.576	.295	.699	.049	3.904	.306	5
Norway, 1979–2000	6.383	.141	.636	.031	4.049	.121	5
Spain, 1980–2000	12.526	.147	.648	.029	8.132	.161	4
Sweden, 1975–2000	6.508	.106	.671	.044	4.371	.126	6
Switzerland, 1982–2002	8.040	.107	.675	.092	5.464	.208	4
United Kingdom, 1969–1999	10.511	.280	.627	.045	6.605	.289	8
United States, 1974–2000	17.036	.055	.673	.010	11.467	.055	7

The greater the coefficient of variation, the more a country's poverty levels have fluctuated over time. While Belgium, Denmark, and the Netherlands tend to have low poverty levels and the United Kingdom tends to have higher poverty levels, these countries have experienced substantial fluctuation over time. In three of these cases, interestingly, poverty rose considerably over recent decades: the headcount increased from a low of 4.5 to a high of 8 in Belgium, from 3.9 to 8.1 in the Netherlands (before declining to 4.9), and from 5.5 to 14.6 in the United Kingdom (before declining to 12.5). In Denmark, however, the headcount declined from 10.14 to 5.38. By contrast, the United States and Australia at the high end and Sweden at the low end have been very consistent in their levels of poverty. For example, the headcount was 6.5 in Sweden in both the first and last time point. Thus, this sample of country-years exhibits large cross-national *and* historical variation.

Readers may note that these patterns are broadly consistent with past research about differences between countries in social equality.[10] At the same time, however, the patterns do not collapse simply into the basic typologies that have dominated welfare state and inequality research over the past few decades. Some claim variously that the fundamental cleavage is between Europe and everyone else, or between Anglo-Saxon countries and others.[11] Most influentially, the welfare state typology of conservative/Christian Democratic, socialist/Social Democratic, and liberal regimes has dominated this literature at least since Gøsta Esping-Andersen's pivotal work.[12] Yet, these sweeping typologies are at best a mediocre fit with the real patterns in poverty across affluent Western democracies. True, three of the six countries that have the highest poverty are outside Europe (Australia, Canada, and the United States), but three of the six are European (Ireland, Italy, and Spain). The *most* Anglo-Saxon country, the United Kingdom, has had less poverty than Italy and Spain. The liberal countries like the United States do exhibit the highest levels of poverty. But, among the countries with the highest poverty, one finds the Mediterranean conservative/Christian Democratic countries Spain and Italy. Three continental European countries—plausibly classified as conservative/Christian Democratic— Belgium, Luxembourg, and the Netherlands, have some of the lowest levels of poverty. While the socialist/Social Democrat Scandinavian countries do indeed land among the lowest levels of poverty, in the middle of the distribution is a hodgepodge of countries that do not fit any of the typologies. Thus, it is too simplistic, and potentially even deceptive, to describe cross-national patterns in poverty solely with the prevailing typologies. Chapter 4 demonstrates the limited appropriateness of these typologies for explaining the relationship between the welfare state and poverty as well.

Poverty in the United States

The United States has the most poverty with both the headcount and intensity measures, in terms of the latest data and over the past several decades. Given that the United States is such an extreme case, it is worthwhile to give it a closer look. In particular, the United States provides an informative case to explore historical trends in poverty. Figure 3.2 shows the trends in the headcount, intensity, and official measures for the United States from 1974 to 2000.[13] According to the official U.S. measure, poverty rose from 11.2% in 1974 to a peak of 14.5% in 1994 and then subsequently fell. From 1974 to 2000, official U.S. poverty barely changed at all—rising one-tenth of 1% from 11.2% to 11.3%. Because this measure has many limitations, it is worthwhile to compare the two superior alternatives: the relative headcount and intensity. Though all three measures track a rise to the middle of the period, U.S. poverty shows a very different trend with these alternatives. From 1974 to 2000, poverty increased 7.5% according to the headcount and 4.5% according to the intensity measure. With the official measure, one gets a false impression that poverty did not increase over the period. But, with these more defensible measures, poverty increased substantially. Moreover, while the official measure suggests declining poverty from 1997 to 2000, both alternatives show increasing poverty. In sum, different historical trends emerge across measures, and a false understanding emerges with the official measure.

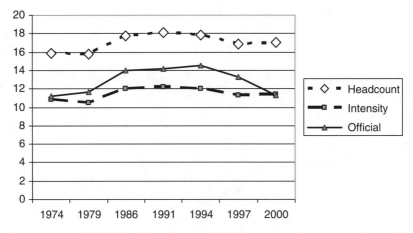

Figure 3.2.   Trends in U.S. Poverty with Alternative Measures, 1974–2000

As chapter 2 shows, the U.S. measure is flawed because it ignores taxes and transfers and its threshold is too low, so a comparison with the levels of these alternatives is illustrative. One can compare the quantity of households that would be misclassified as not poor by the official measure. As mentioned in chapter 2, previous studies have demonstrated sizable differences in poverty rates between the official U.S. measure and the National Research Council's alternative.[14] With the relative headcount and intensity measures, real differences materialize as well. As figure 3.2 indicates, 11.3% of the U.S. population was officially classified as poor in 2000. With the relative headcount, fully 17.05% of the population was poor. Therefore, the official measure inappropriately classified 5.75% of people as not poor. Given that the United States had about 282 million people in 2000, the official measure misclassified more than 16.2 million people as not poor. With the more defensible relative headcount measure, more than 48 million people would have been poor instead of the 31.6 million people that were "officially" poor.

A Comparison with Absolute Poverty

Chapter 2 presents a theoretical argument in favor of relative measures of poverty for affluent democracies and against absolute measures. Although there are clear theoretical advantages to relative measures of poverty, it might be informative to also consider the cross-national patterns in absolute poverty.[15] For this comparison, I use probably the most widely used absolute measure, one advocated by scholars like Lane Kenworthy.[16] I calculate the poverty line using the relative 50% of median income (divided by the square root of household members) for the United States in 2000 and then standardize this dollar amount across countries using purchasing power

Table 3.3. Comparison of PPP Absolute (U.S. Relative 2000) and Relative Headcount
Poverty in 18 Affluent Western Democracies

Country	Year	Headcount Absolute	Relative	Absolute Line in Equivalized Income	Percent Median Equivalized Income	Absolute Line for Family of Four
Australia	2001	**29.07**	13.01	16,685.08	69.98	33,370.16
Austria	2000	3.24	7.74	90,111.49	37.33	180,222.98
Belgium	2000	2.05	8.08	241,301.20	35.87	482,602.40
Canada	2000	**20.24**	12.37	15,540.62	61.94	31,081.24
Denmark	2000	**15.03**	5.39	105,230.50	62.02	210,461.00
Finland	2000	3.51	5.38	43,911.28	45.56	87,822.56
France	2000	5.01	7.31	44,814.81	45.28	89,629.62
Germany	2000	**22.29**	8.36	24,334.92	71.28	48,669.84
Ireland	2000	**30.66**	16.15	9517.12	73.86	19,034.24
Ireland	1996	**39.37**	12.31	7345.33	83.48	14,690.66
Ireland	1995	**42.65**	12.90	7217.58	88.79	14,435.16
Ireland	1994	**44.34**	11.88	6837.87	89.64	13,675.74
Ireland	1987	**60.95**	11.12	5633.66	118.94	11,267.32
Italy	2000	**43.62**	12.78	20,589,632.00	90.59	41,179,264.00
Luxembourg	2000	0.10	6.05	237,265.50	22.75	474,531.00
Netherlands	1999	**20.65**	4.91	26,021.50	71.25	52,043.00
Norway	2000	**11.29**	6.40	117,940.00	58.75	235,880.00
Spain	2000	9.77	14.16	807,449.60	43.80	1,614,899.20
Sweden	2000	**27.71**	6.61	119,686.90	78.12	239,373.80
Switzerland	2000	**11.65**	7.67	24,214.45	56.85	48,428.90
United Kingdom	1999	**31.65**	12.46	7,951.01	73.18	15,902.02
United States	2000	17.05	17.05	12,046.99	50.00	24,093.98

Boldface indicates absolute headcounts greater than relative headcounts.

parity (PPP) conversion rates.[17] So, this measure is really only "absolute" in
that it presumes a household needs the same amount of disposable income
across countries and time. Table 3.3 shows the absolute poverty rates, and
the details behind the measure, for each of the 18 countries. For comparison,
the relative poverty rates from figure 3.1 are displayed again. Many offer the
Irish case as an example of the problems of a relative measure, because
relative poverty rose in Ireland just as the economy was improving. In turn,
I also provide absolute poverty rates for Ireland for five time points, from
1987 to 2000.[18]

This comparison illustrates that absolute poverty is considerably higher
than relative poverty in 11 of the 18 countries, and at all five time points for

Ireland. The boldfaced entries indicate countries that have higher absolute than relative poverty. The United States would not have particularly high poverty with this measure. Also, Ireland would have experienced a substantial decline in absolute poverty. Thus, with this measure, one can fairly argue that Ireland's economic success has worked to reduce absolute poverty from 1987 to 2000. Because it is reasonable to argue that living and consumption standards have risen in Ireland since 1987, table 3.3 shows that a relative measure of poverty is not perfect.

Nevertheless, what table 3.3 really illustrates are the severe limitations of a supposedly absolute measure of poverty for international comparison. According to this absolute measure, many countries with moderate or low relative poverty would suddenly be defined as having extremely high poverty. Australia, Canada, Germany, Ireland, Italy, the Netherlands, Sweden, and the United Kingdom would all have poverty rates exceeding 20%— a level no country reaches with the relative poverty measure. Indeed, Ireland and the United Kingdom would exceed 30%, and Italy would have an astronomical 43.6% poor. Although Ireland would have experienced declining absolute poverty, almost 61% of Ireland would have been defined as poor in 1987. Clearly, these estimates lack face validity. There is no other evidence one could draw on that these countries have such extreme levels of poverty and deprivation. Given that we know these countries have much lower levels of inequality, these high rates of absolute poverty are quite dubious. Also, these extremely high rates speak to two fundamental problems with absolute measures of poverty.

First, in the United States, a household needs to purchase a wide variety of expensive items with its disposable income. Perhaps most crucial, most households have to use disposable income to purchase essential items like health insurance, health care, and child care. In other countries, the welfare state provides such public services, which enables members of a household to use their disposable income for other items. Thus, a typical household in other countries does not need to use nearly as much disposable income for such essential items. In turn, it is inappropriate to assume that the same disposable income is necessary to make ends meet across countries that do and do not have socialized medicine, publicly provided child care, and other welfare services.

Second, the three rightmost columns in table 3.3 display crucial information that is not usually revealed by proponents of these absolute measures. Most likely, if scholars were more aware of these details, there would be less support for absolute poverty measures. The fifth and seventh columns show how much money, in local currency, is necessary to be not poor per person and for a family of four. If we use this absolute measure of poverty, we are assuming a family of four needed almost 16,000 pounds in the United Kingdom in 2000 and more than 41 million lira in Italy in 1999. Moreover, we are assuming that an Irish household in 1987 would have needed more than 11,000 Irish pounds in real 2000 currency. This is a substantial amount of money for a typical British, Italian, or Irish household. It is very unlikely that people in those countries and time periods would have defined poverty with these very high thresholds. This point hits home when we examine the sixth column. The absolute measure of poverty assumes that, to be nonpoor, one would need more than 90% of the median equivalized income in Italy, more than 74% of median in the United Kingdom, and almost 119% of the median in Ireland in 1987. This demonstrates that this "absolute" measure of poverty is inappropriate for these countries and times. Problematically, this measure assumes that the dollar amount necessary to be not poor in the United States in 2000 is the same amount necessary to be not poor everywhere and always.[19]

As I argued chapter 2, the meaning of deprivation and what a household needs to make ends meet is culturally, historically, and nationally specific. Being poor depends on the standard of living and consumption of the typical households in a society (i.e., the median), not the typical household in a totally different cultural and historical context (i.e., the United States in 2000). Using Kenworthy's absolute measure of poverty, one can see the clear limitations of assuming that the same amount of disposable income is needed in every country to be nonpoor. These results raise significant questions about validity and reliability that have yet to be addressed by proponents of absolute poverty measures.

Poverty among Women and Men

Following Diane Pearce's coining of the term "feminization of poverty," several scholars have estimated the rates of poverty among women and men and shown that women are disproportionately represented among the poor.[20] Purportedly, women are less likely to be poor in a few countries (e.g., Sweden), but women are far more likely to be poor in the United States.[21] How much poverty is feminized supposedly varies cross-nationally and over time as well.

One of the uncertainties that lurks under the surface of this literature has been the apparent divergence between women's, men's, and overall poverty. Indeed, this uncertainty has lingered in debates about social equality for more than a century. In Donald Sassoon's seminal history of the West European Left, *One Hundred Years of Socialism*, a recurring theme is the tension between traditional commitments to economic egalitarianism and emerging expectations for gender equality.[22] Partly, these concerns are due to the perception that women's poverty, and in turn the feminization of poverty, is a unique social problem, with distinct or particularly complicated causes. Partly, these concerns are a product of the uncertainty over the compatibility between economic and gender egalitarianism. Despite great interest in this question, we actually know relatively little about whether countries with high overall poverty are also likely to have high women's or men's poverty. Moreover, it is unclear how much the feminization of poverty is associated with the levels of overall poverty. Even though there has been a paucity of research on these precise questions, one can discern two perspectives in the literature.

Some scholars seem to assert that the extent of societal gender inequality is a function of the extent of overall economic inequality. In an influential paper, Francine Blau and Lawrence Kahn showed that countries with greater returns to skill and greater earnings inequality tend to have greater gender pay differences.[23] Compounding the greater dispersion in wages and the fact that women are positioned less favorably in the labor market, the high wage inequality in the United States is considered the primary cause of its relatively high gender pay gap. Karen Christopher and colleagues offer a similar view as an account for low rates of women's poverty in social democracies.[24] In a study of affluent democracies in the mid-1980s, Robert Wright finds that countries with higher overall poverty tend to also have a greater representation of females among the poor.[25] If indeed there is a broad consistency between economic inequality and gender inequality, one should expect that overall, women's, men's, and feminized poverty cohere.

Other scholars are less confident that economic egalitarianism will ensure gender equality and point to resilient gender inequalities in societies that are relatively economically equal.[26] As Leslie McCall contends, gender inequality is simply not reducible to overall economic inequality.[27] Many of the social democratic and Christian democratic welfare states that accomplished low overall poverty and economic equality also maintained traditional breadwinner gender roles and low female labor force participation. Ann Orloff has explained that many egalitarian West European welfare states do not provide autonomy for women—the capacity to form economically sustainable independent households—and as a result leave women economically vulnerable.[28] The implication is that women's and feminized poverty are distinct from the economic standing of men.[29] Plausibly, in a country where poverty is very low for adult men and children but is higher for adult women, that country could maintain low overall poverty even with a significant feminization of poverty.

But, what evidence is there on this contentious question? To enhance our understanding, I analyze poverty among all adult women and men 18 or more years of age. An alternative would be to focus on working age adults (e.g., 18–65 years old), because some readers might suspect this is where poverty is most feminized. But, substituting the working-age adults for all adults does not change any of the conclusions, because women's and men's working-age and adult poverty are very highly associated. Further, elderly women are actually more likely to be poor than are elderly men, and there are more elderly women than elderly men. So, concentrating on working-age adults ends up underestimating the extent to which poverty is feminized.[30]

Figure 3.3 displays the association between overall and women's headcount poverty. The three-letter symbols mark each data point for each

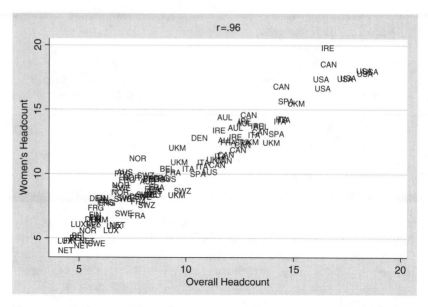

Figure 3.3.   The Association between Overall and Women's Headcount
Poverty ($r = 0.96$)

country. The U.S. is represented by "USA," Canada is represented by
"CAN," Germany is "FRG," and so forth (these symbols are used throughout
the rest of the book).[31] The correlation is overwhelmingly positive ($r = .96$),
demonstrating that there is a very strong correspondence between countries'
women's and overall poverty. All of the countries that have high women's
poverty have high overall poverty, and all of the countries with low
overall poverty have low women's poverty. No country departs from this
powerful pattern of symmetry.

Figure 3.4 displays the same association for the intensity measure. Again,
women's poverty is very highly associated with overall poverty. By social
science standards, these correlations are extremely high. The implication of
these findings is clear: there is no trade-off between having low overall
poverty and having low poverty for women. Women are much less likely to
be poor in countries that have low overall poverty.[32] Hence, when one
analyzes poverty in the overall population, one effectively gauges poverty
among women.

Perhaps, however, the better comparison would be between women's and
men's poverty. It could be that women's and men's poverty are not strongly
associated. Figures 3.5 and 3.6 display the association between adult wom-
en's and men's headcount and intensity poverty. Somewhat surprisingly, the
same pattern holds. There is a very strong association—albeit not quite as
strong as the association with overall poverty—between women's and men's
poverty. The headcounts correlate at 0.87, and the intensity measures

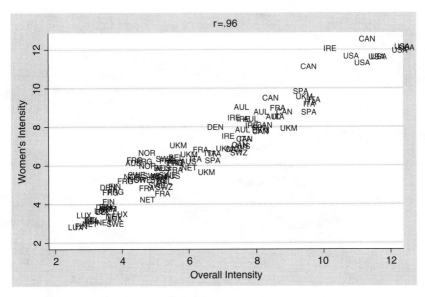

Figure 3.4. The Association between Overall and Women's Poverty Intensity (*r* = 0.96)

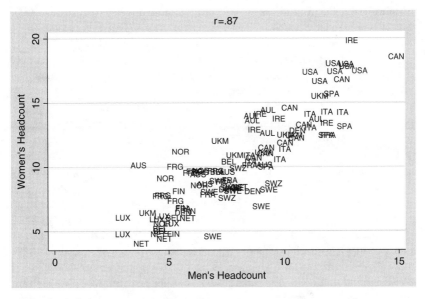

Figure 3.5. The Association between Women's and Men's Headcount Poverty (*r* = 0.87)

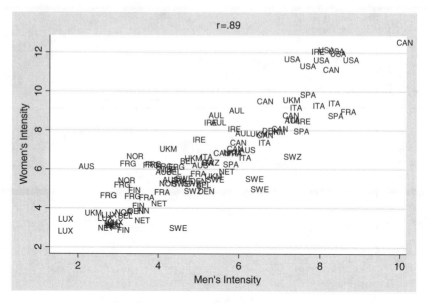

Figure 3.6.   The Association between Women's and Men's Poverty
Intensity (r = 0.89)

correlate at 0.88.[33] Countries that have low poverty for men are very likely to
have low poverty for women. Countries where women face a great deal of
economic insecurity and are more vulnerable to poverty also feature high
men's poverty. Obviously, this is partly due to the simple fact that many
women and men spend a number of years married, resulting in identical
rates of poverty. Because women's, men's, and overall poverty are so strongly
associated, we can be confident that measures of overall poverty track the
patterns in both women's and men's poverty.

Despite this telling correspondence between overall, women's, and men's
poverty, the issue can be complicated still. Though women and men face
similar probabilities of poverty across countries, the feminization of poverty
might be a separate matter. In this book, the focus is on the levels of poverty
across societies, but it could be that women are still disproportionately
represented among the poor. Thus, the feminization of poverty could diverge
from women's, men's, and overall poverty.

Table 3.4 displays the feminization of poverty, calculated simply as the
ratio of women's to men's headcount or intensity. Indeed, the mean shows
that poverty is quite feminized. Adult women are, on average, about 38%
more likely to be poor than are men, and women's poverty intensity averages
36% higher than men's. As I have shown in other research with Denise Kall,
the feminization of poverty is nearly universal across and within affluent
Western democracies.[34] Especially once the elderly are included in the

Table 3.4.   Patterns in the Feminization of Poverty in 18 Affluent Western
Democracies, 1969–2002 (N = 104)

	Feminization of Headcount	Feminization of Intensity
Mean	1.384	1.360
Standard Deviation	0.327	0.328
Correlations with:		
Overall Poverty	−.049	−.027
Women's Poverty	.133	.148
Men's Poverty	−.323	−.304

estimates of women's and men's poverty, almost all country-years exhibit
feminized poverty. Although the trends in women's and men's poverty do
certainly cohere, as explained above, there is a strikingly persistent difference between the levels of women's and men's poverty. Thus, the feminization of poverty is a crucial social problem that warrants study in its
own right.

What is also revealed by table 3.4, however, is that the feminization of
poverty is a social problem somewhat distinct from overall, women's, and
men's poverty. The correlations between the feminization of the headcount
and intensity measures and these three levels of poverty are very weak.
Especially compared to the overwhelming association between overall,
women's, and men's poverty, this feminization is simply not associated
with these other three measures. As shown above, the level of overall poverty
very effectively predicts the level of women's poverty. Thus, economic
egalitarianism and women's economic security seem quite compatible. However, economic and gender egalitarianism are not associated if one is interested in the feminization of poverty.

One helpful way to think about this is to compare Norway and Italy.
Norway has a low headcount poverty for adult women, as less than 9% of
women were poor in recent years. However, poverty is quite feminized in
Norway, as women are about 50% more likely to be poor than men. By
contrast, women are only about 20% more likely to be poor in Italy, but
women's headcount poverty is much higher—about 13% of women were
poor in recent years. It is important that poverty is quite feminized in Norway, but it is also important that Italy has a high rate of poverty for women.
Thus, the level of poverty (for women, men, or overall) is simply a different
topic than the feminization of poverty. Although the feminization of poverty
certainly demands scholarly attention, it represents a different problem—
indeed, a different research question. As my research with Denise Kall
shows, somewhat different processes drive the feminization of poverty as
well. This book is concerned with the level of poverty in society. So, hence-
forth, I concentrate on overall, women's, and men's poverty. The feminization of poverty is an equally salient but different concern.

Poverty among Children and the Elderly

One of the seemingly established "facts" about poverty is that child and elderly poverty are divergent. In the United States, child poverty has reportedly increased in recent decades, and elderly poverty has declined. As a result, children are supposedly much more likely to be poor than the elderly. Across the affluent Western democracies as well, the conventional wisdom among social scientists and commentators has been that children are more economically vulnerable than the elderly.

This conventional wisdom originates partly in Samuel Preston's influential 1984 presidential address to the Population Association of America.[35] Preston contended that child poverty, and child well-being in general, had dramatically worsened relative to the elderly. Poverty had become "juvenilized," resulting in the marginalization of poor children from the rest of society. Following Preston's lead, a great deal of scholarship decries generational inequities between children and the elderly and reiterates the conventional wisdom.[36] For example, Rebecca Blank writes, "The elderly are one of the biggest success stories for public policy; expansion in government benefits to the elderly has resulted in very low poverty rates."[37] Benjamin Page and James Simmons explain, "Poverty in the United States is now heavily concentrated among children, who have not been helped by government as much as the elderly have."[38] Thus, the conventional wisdom has been that child poverty diverges from elderly poverty and overall poverty, and that children are much worse off than the elderly.

Remarkably, these claims rest exclusively on evidence from the official U.S. measure of poverty. Because that measure has so many problems, a reconsideration of these conclusions is warranted. As pointed out in chapter 2, the official U.S. measure was intentionally designed such that a large portion of the elderly would not be defined as "officially" poor. Also, key economic resources for families with children, such as food stamps and the EITC, are excluded when calculating official poverty, yet the elderly's pretax Social Security pensions are included. Indeed, the Johnson administration appears to have drawn the line to ensure that many elderly would be just above it.

Before examining the associations between child, elderly, and overall poverty, it is important to acknowledge that children are more likely to be poor than are working-age adults. As revealed in table 3.5, the average child headcount poverty rate (10.3%) is significantly greater than the average overall headcount poverty rate (9.6%).[39] Thus, children are more vulnerable than the overall population. What is surprising, however, is the average elderly headcount poverty rate (14.7%).[40] The average elderly poverty rate is significantly greater than the average overall poverty rate. More strikingly, the average elderly poverty rate is also significantly greater than the average child poverty. Of course, one should be cautious to avoid arguing

Table 3.5.   Patterns in Child, Elderly, and Overall Headcount Poverty in 18 Affluent Western Democracies, 1969–2002

	Mean	Standard Deviation	N	Significance Level of Test That Overall Poverty Is *Less*	Significance Level of Test That Elderly Poverty Is *Greater*
Child Headcount	10.273	6.048	104	$p < .005$	$p < .001$
Elderly Headcount	14.493	7.610	103	$p < .001$	
Overall Headcount	9.413	3.687	104		$p < .001$

that elderly poverty is *worse* than child poverty, because a measure based on wealth might show different patterns than these measures based on income. Nevertheless, this finding directly challenges the claim that children are much worse off than the elderly. A much more accurate reading of the patterns across affluent Western democracies is that *both* children and the elderly are worse off than the overall population. Just as has been shown in the poverty literature as far back as Seebohm Rowntree's classic study more than 100 years ago, poverty is more likely to strike those at both the beginning and end of the life cycle.[41] There has not been a decline in elderly poverty that triggered higher child poverty—both children and the elderly are more likely to be poor.

The next set of analyses compares the associations between overall, child, and elderly poverty. Figure 3.7 shows that child poverty is very highly associated with overall poverty ($r = .95$). Because these two are almost perfectly correlated, it is difficult to argue that child poverty is a unique or distinct social problem. Just like the association between women's and overall poverty, children's fate is reflected in the patterns of poverty for the entire population. Countries that prevent poverty overall are quite successful at keeping child poverty low. Those countries that have high child poverty, especially the United States, are very likely to have high overall poverty. Also, it is not as if child poverty departs radically from overall poverty in the United States. In the upper right corner of figure 3.7, U.S. child poverty levels are about what one would expect from our high overall poverty.

Figure 3.8 demonstrates that elderly poverty is also associated strongly with overall poverty ($r = .61$). Interestingly, though the association is robust, the correlation is not nearly as strong as the correlation between overall and child poverty. Although the patterns in elderly poverty reflect the patterns in

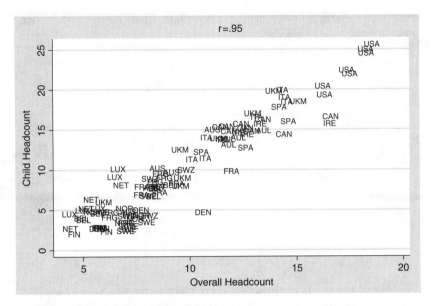

Figure 3.7.   The Association between Child and Overall Headcount
Poverty ($r = 0.95$)

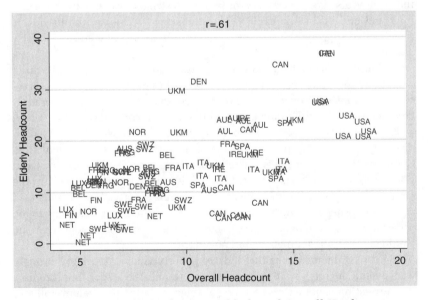

Figure 3.8.   The Association between Elderly and Overall Headcount
Poverty ($r = 0.61$)

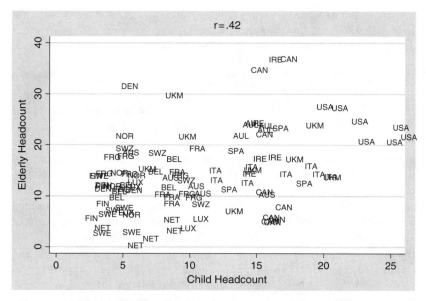

Figure 3.9.   The Association between Elderly and Child Headcount
Poverty (r = 0.42)

overall poverty, there are some departures. Given their levels of overall
poverty, the United Kingdom (UKM), Denmark (DEN), and Canada (CAN),
for example, posted much higher elderly poverty than would have been
expected. Therefore, elderly poverty diverges more from overall poverty,
but again, the prevailing pattern is that elderly and overall poverty are
associated. For both child and elderly poverty, one gets a good impression
of the patterns from examining overall poverty.

Figure 3.9 takes the analysis a step further and presents the association
between child and elderly poverty. These two are much less associated than
they are with overall poverty. The correlation (r = .42) is positive but is only
moderately strong. Some countries, for example, Canada and the Netherlands,
had years where child poverty was higher than would be expected from their
elderly poverty. Some others, for example, Denmark, Ireland (IRE), and the
United Kingdom (and Canada for other country-years), had years where elderly
poverty was higher than would be expected from their child poverty. Despite
all the attention on the U.S. case, it falls squarely in the upper right part of the
figure with high poverty for both children and the elderly.

One broad finding deserves to be emphasized here: there is no trade-off
between elderly and child poverty. The evidence clearly shows that child
and elderly poverty generally move in concert with each other and with a
country's overall poverty. Egalitarian countries with low overall poverty
tend to have low child and low elderly poverty. These results flatly contradict Preston's contentions. Countries do not accomplish lower elderly

poverty at the expense of higher child poverty, and child poverty does not worsen because of the pursuit of lower elderly poverty. The overriding pattern is a coherence among child, elderly, and overall poverty.

Trends in U.S. Child and Elderly Poverty

Much of the conventional wisdom about child and elderly poverty was based on data from the United States. Indeed, the perception of a trade-off has been strongest in the United States, and U.S. social scientists and commentators have done the most to promote the conventional wisdom. Thus, it is essential to revisit the trends in U.S. child and elderly poverty with a relative measure.

Figure 3.10 displays the trends in U.S. elderly poverty with the official and relative headcount measures. In every year, the relative measure of elderly poverty is much higher than the official measure.[42] As expected, the official measure underestimates elderly poverty. The relative measure shows that the elderly, in fact, experience very high levels of poverty. In 2000, the official estimate was 9.9%, while the relative estimate was 27.7. Figure 3.10 also shows the ratio of the rate of elderly poverty with the relative measure over the rate with the official measure. There is substantial historical variation in how much the relative estimates depart from the official estimates. In 1974, the relative measure estimated about 88% more elderly poverty than the official measure (a ratio of 1.88). In 2000, this ratio rose dramatically to 2.8. As a result, by 2000, the rate of elderly poverty would have been about 2.8 times greater with the relative instead of the official measure.

Figure 3.11 shows the trends in U.S. child poverty with the official and relative measure. Consistent with elderly poverty, the official measure

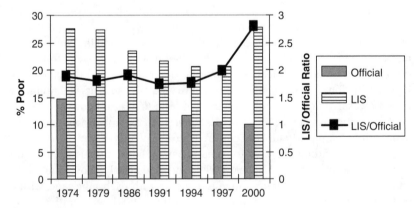

Figure 3.10.   A Comparison of Official and LIS Elderly Poverty in the United States, 1974–2000

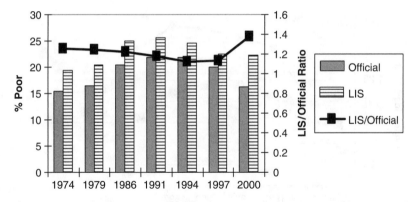

Figure 3.11.   A Comparison of Official and LIS Child Poverty in the United States, 1974–2000

underestimates child poverty. In 2000, the official estimate was 16.2%, while the relative estimate was 22.3%. Figure 3.11 also displays the ratio of the LIS rate over the official rate. Compared to elderly poverty, this ratio is smaller and fluctuates less over time. In 1974, the relative measure estimated about 25% more child poverty than the official measure. By 2000, the rate of child poverty would have been about 38% greater with the relative instead of the official measure.

As figures 3.10 and 3.11 reveal, the relative measure results in higher poverty than the official measure for both the elderly and children. These figures also reveal something about the trends in how child poverty compares to elderly poverty. Figure 3.12 displays the trends in the ratio of child over elderly poverty with the official and relative measure. The official measure charts a dramatic increase in the ratio of child to elderly poverty. This ratio rose from 1.05 in 1974 to a peak of 1.9 in 1997, and fell to 1.63 in 2000. According to the official measure, children were only about 5% more likely to be poor than the elderly in 1974, but were 90% more likely to be poor in 1997, and 63% more likely in 2000. This is the startling divergence between child and elderly poverty that so many have highlighted.

The relative measure provides a starkly different account: children were actually less likely to be poor than the elderly in the 1970s, with a ratio of only 0.7 in 1974 and 0.75 in 1979. Even with the relative measure, however, the ratios of child to elderly poverty increased in the 1980s. Children were more likely to be poor than the elderly from 1986 to 1997. Importantly, however, the ratios are significantly smaller with the relative measure: the ratio was only 1.07 in 1986 and rose to a peak of 1.19 in 1991 and 1994. Even in the early 1990s, children were only 19% more likely to be poor than the elderly. Importantly, the relative ratio declined precipitously in 1997 to 1.09

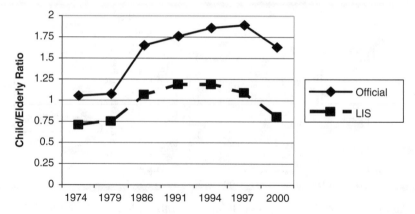

Figure 3.12.   A Comparison of Ratios of Child to Elderly Poverty with Official and LIS Measures in the United States, 1974–2000

and again in 2000 to 0.80. In sharp contrast to the official measure, the relative measure suggests that children were only 9% more likely to be poor in 1997 and actually about 20% less likely to be poor in 2000.

This comparison of the official and relative measure challenges the popular claim that child and elderly poverty have diverged in the United States. The elderly were clearly not less likely to be poor in the 1970s and in 2000. Even in the 1980s, the relative measure suggests that children were only slightly more likely to be poor. Ultimately, the relative measure provides evidence that the elderly and children are similar to, not divergent from, each other. Both groups are overrepresented among the poor.

Conclusion

This chapter describes the empirical patterns in poverty across and within affluent Western democracies with the relative headcount and intensity measures. One of the conclusions that should emerge is that many of our beliefs about the patterns in poverty may be mistaken. Upon closer inspection of the evidence, several widely held beliefs about patterns in poverty turn out to be myths. The comparisons of affluent democracies and the reexamination of the United States should provide a better understanding of poverty.

This chapter examines patterns in poverty along several dimensions. In subsequent chapters, I analyze the factors that explain these dimensions of poverty. Specifically, the remaining chapters treat 10 dimensions of poverty as dependent variables: overall headcount and intensity, working-age headcount and intensity, adult women's headcount and intensity, adult men's headcount and intensity, children's headcount, and the elderly headcount.

If social scientists seek to make scientific inferences and inform public policy, it is imperative that relative measures of poverty be integrated further. At present, the contribution of U.S. social science is probably limited by the reliance on the official U.S. measure. For example, the debate on poverty has probably been obfuscated by the concern that child poverty has worsened and elderly poverty has been conquered. As this chapter reveals, a careful reexamination of relative and official measures does not support such claims. While the social science of poverty has grown considerably over the past few decades, the field has underutilized advances in poverty measurement (especially within sociology). Too many studies and too much conventional wisdom rest solely on the official U.S. measure. Comparisons with relative measures demonstrate this is clearly problematic. It is noteworthy that in the 1990s, the social science of poverty cultivated increasingly sophisticated statistical models of poverty. Yet, while racing ahead with the latest analytical innovations, we often neglected the more fundamental issue of measurement. Plausibly, the study of poverty would benefit more by first scrutinizing the basic and primary methodological concern of measurement before proceeding with increasingly sophisticated statistical analyses of the causes and consequences of poverty. Rethinking measurement and scrutinizing basic descriptive empirical patterns should be prioritized as the first step in the analysis of poverty.

4

The Welfare State and Poverty

Perennially a contentious issue, the welfare state has recently come under a storm of criticism. Regarded for decades as egalitarian havens, the generous West European welfare states appear unsustainable and possibly even counterproductive. Many social democracies struggled with what were regarded as rigid, unproductive labor markets in the 1990s. Sweden, long considered the social democratic utopia, suffered a crisis of three straight years of negative economic growth, massive budget deficits, and high unemployment.[1] The Christian democratic continental European countries appeared stuck with high unemployment and underperforming economies. By contrast, the liberal, flexible, and efficient United States seemed to experience an unprecedented decade of robust economic expansion in the 1990s.

More specifically, the relationship between the welfare state and poverty has received tremendous skepticism. Critics variously claim that even the most generous welfare states fail to eradicate poverty; that the welfare state provides disincentives and leads to dependency, carries a middle-class bias, and is inadequate and inefficient.[2] In his history of U.S. poverty, Michael Katz lamented that poverty, hunger, and a lack of health insurance and housing remain unacceptably prominent, and further noted, "Neither public policy nor private enterprise has moderated the great forces that generate poverty in America."[3] The legal scholar Richard Epstein argued, "The strongest objection to welfare is the humdrum practical point that these programs, when administered by government, are not likely to work, especially in the long run."[4] Although France is often perceived to have more generous social policies than the United States, Monica Prasad writes, "French welfare policies actually end up benefiting the upper portions of the income distribution more than the lower.... The French model is in many ways no better than the American model at integrating those on the margins into the benefits of market capitalism."[5] In the United States, the mounting criticism culminated with the 1996 Personal Responsibility and Work Opportunity Reconciliation Act (popularly known as "welfare reform"), which both scientific studies and political rhetoric claim overwhelmingly vindicated social policy retrenchment.[6]

At the same time that these criticisms have been circulating, scholarly advances provide new opportunities to study the welfare state and poverty. While the welfare state's effectiveness appears increasingly tenuous, the potential for research on the welfare state and poverty has never been more secure. The building of comparative historical data sets on welfare states has reached a zenith. Further, as has been exhibited in chapters 1–3, measurement innovations and high-quality income data have greatly advanced the study of poverty. Finally, theoretical developments in the sociology of the welfare state have enabled increased sophistication in empirical analyses of the relationship between the welfare state and poverty.[7] Thus, scholars are now uniquely positioned to answer questions and validate claims that have been in the literature for decades.

This chapter shows the welfare state to be the principal and proximate influence on a nation's amount of poverty. The welfare state is a complex of social policies and programs that distribute economic resources disproportionately to a nation's vulnerable populations. Every nation has vulnerable populations, but welfare states differ in the extent to which they protect the vulnerable against economic insecurity. To establish the first part of institutionalized power relations theory, this chapter examines multiple measures of the welfare state and poverty, while controlling for factors that critics argue are more important to poverty. Building on past research, I explain the causal mechanisms by which the welfare state influences poverty. The analyses compare various specific features of the welfare state to explore their precise effects on poverty. Then, I examine the impact of welfare state regimes and the effects of the key welfare state features across regimes. Last, I test the historical stability of the relationship between the welfare state and poverty.

What Does the Welfare State Do?

A growing body of research has begun to investigate the relationship between the welfare state and poverty.[8] Given the contributions of previous scholars, the field is now at a point where one can construct a general explanation for the mechanisms between the welfare state and poverty. While past empirical research has contributed greatly, general explanations of how and why the welfare state should have large effects on poverty are rarely articulated. As I explain in chapter 1, the welfare state does three major things that shape poverty: manage risk, organize the distribution of resources, and institutionalize equality. The first two are fairly well established in the literature, though I revise the second. The third has been implicit in others' writings, and my aim is to call greater attention to it.

First, welfare states manage against risk.[9] Welfare states are collective insurance programs that protect people who have experienced a trigger event that leads to financial loss. In minimalist welfare states, poverty is more common because citizens are less protected against "risks" that occur normally or abnormally over the life cycle. Common risks include losing one's job, becoming a mother (especially a single mother), growing old, and experiencing a family transition like divorce or widowhood. Less common risks include becoming disabled and unable to earn a sufficient income because of a workplace accident. Perhaps most often mentioned, welfare states provide economic resources for the unemployed. Because unemployment is a fairly systemic feature of advanced capitalism, welfare states plan for the chance that a worker will lose her or his job, facilitate the saving of money to protect against this risk, and alleviate the costs or "scar effects" of unemployment.[10] Where welfare states are tightfisted and stingy, working adults depend more exclusively on labor market earnings and private insurance to evade the consequences of these risks. Hence, the poor are those that are more vulnerable to the occurrence of and harmed by the ramifications of disadvantaged statuses. Generous welfare states provide insurance for their citizens against these risks.[11]

Second, welfare states organize the distribution of economic resources. Welfare states shape how much income and wealth each household receives. Through governing the rules of exchange between workers, owners, and managers, or regulating currencies and business, or providing public goods like education and health care, or by facilitating transportation and communication or even simply by creating jobs, the welfare state is involved in all aspects of the distribution of economic resources.[12] Normally, this mechanism is understood as *redistribution*, as is illustrated by the studies of pre-fisc and post-fisc poverty described in chapter 2. But, this framing problematically neglects how welfare states, or states more generally, govern the accumulation of profits and income for the affluent as well as the poor. The imagery of redistribution artificially insinuates that there is a two-step process, where markets "naturally" distribute income and states subsequently redistribute that income.[13] As explained in chapter 2, however, no such two-step process exists. States are always involved in the allocation of income to workers, owners, and managers. As Walter Korpi explains, "The intervention of the state in the distributive processes in society is thus not limited to measures directed towards persons with publicly acknowledged needs."[14] States do not simply respond to what markets have initiated; states initiate, define, and constitute markets. Indeed, this claim is one of the central principles of economic sociology.[15] Rather than framing welfare states as narrowly about redistribution, it is far more justified to claim that welfare states shape distribution.

Third, welfare states institutionalize equality. Welfare states are shaped by and shape societal ideologies. That is, how societies normalize collective expectations about whether various economic distributions are appropriate and just.[16] Welfare states are negatively associated with poverty partly because they manage risk and organize the distribution of economic resources. But, welfare states also shape the very possibility of how much poverty is normatively allowed to exist in a society. So, societies with very generous welfare states are societies that collectively define egalitarianism as appropriate and just. Welfare states also create constituencies of beneficiaries that feed back into the political process that supports welfare states' existence and form. Welfare states reflect political struggle, but they also guide subsequent political struggle. Thus, welfare states contribute to the formation of citizens' interests and ideologies in the maintenance or expansion of welfare state programs. Through these interests and ideologies, societies collectivize and socialize the responsibility of averting poverty for their citizens.

Diverse Features of the Welfare State

In some ways, the majority of the sociology, history, and political science of welfare states has sidestepped the question of whether the welfare state reduces poverty. A wealth of research presumes the welfare state is beneficial and concentrates instead on what causes the welfare state. Many studies trace the history of social policy expansion or compare the causes of welfare generosity across countries.[17] If one takes for granted or assumes that all aspects of the welfare state reduce poverty, the only questions that remain are why some welfare states are more generous or developed more quickly than others.

One of the major contributions of this literature is to show that the welfare state has a diversity of specific features. Scholars interested in the causes of welfare states have studied pensions, unemployment programs, health insurance, child care, maternity leave, active labor market policies, public services, and a host of other aspects of the welfare state. Because research on the welfare state's causes has been so productive, studies of the welfare state's effects can now benefit from this literature's insights. In turn, to understand fully the welfare state's effects on poverty, we need to examine several specific features of the welfare state. This leads to two major issues.

First, scholars often debate the best general measure of the entirety of the welfare state's influence on social equality. Traditionally, analysts relied on measures of social spending, social welfare expenditures, or social security transfers. Until the 1990s, in fact, there rarely was any other way to measure the welfare state. For decades, analysts were satisfied examining widely available data on social spending, and an industry of researchers modeled historical welfare state expansion or cross-national differences with such measures. These measures quantitatively gauge the extensiveness of social policy or what was often called "welfare effort."[18]

However, by 1990, the tide had begun to turn. In his 1990 classic *The Three Worlds of Welfare Capitalism*, Gøsta Esping-Andersen offered a persuasive, well-received critique of the dominant style of analyzing the welfare state. He argued that the *quality* of welfare programs was actually more salient than the *quantity* of welfare effort. Among many other points, Esping-Andersen specifically wrote: "The existence of a social program and the amount of money spent on it may be less important than what it does," "Expenditures are epiphenomenal to the theoretical substance of welfare states," and "Welfare states may be equally large or comprehensive, but with entirely different effects on social structure."[19] These critiques went hand in hand with Korpi and Joakim Palme's contention that "encompassing" welfare states that uphold social citizenship rights for all universally— as opposed to those that guarantee basic economic security for those at the bottom—were more successful at reducing poverty.[20]

By the late 1990s, most welfare state scholars followed Esping-Andersen's focus on qualitative differences in the welfare state. In order to analyze the welfare state's effects, it was often considered inadequate to examine general spending measures. Many followed Esping-Andersen and advocated for his innovative new index of decommodification, which measured the extent to which workers did not have to sell their labor as commodities. For example, Korpi and colleagues used an index of the social rights of citizenship.[21] Several scholars advocated for measures of social wages: the amount of income a worker would receive if one were to stop working and rely solely on the state.[22] Recently, James Allan and Lyle Scruggs replicated and extended Esping-Andersen's original decommodification index and provided publicly available data for affluent democracies over time.[23] After much heated debate about how to measure the welfare state, one can now empirically compare the various general measures of the welfare state.

Second, beyond general measures, scholars suggest the distinctive value of at least two specific features of the welfare state. Both focus on the notion that what really make the most generous welfare states stand out are services. As Evelyne Huber and John Stephens argue about the most generous welfare states, the "public delivery of a wide range of welfare state services is the most distinctive feature."[24] Unfortunately, few prior studies have analyzed whether these specific features alleviate poverty.[25] Also, it would be equally valuable to compare their distinct influence relative to general measures of the welfare state.

Public health spending may be particularly salient.[26] Potentially, public health spending might capture the welfare state mechanisms outlined above: managing risk, organizing distribution, and institutionalizing equality. The lack of health insurance in many low-wage jobs often acts as a disincentive to labor market entry for low-income families in the United States, and many low-income families fall into poverty because they cannot manage expensive private health costs.[27] Because state-sponsored health care is expensive, it requires larger government budgets and higher taxes on households above the median. These higher taxes and large government budgets end up redistributing resources downward and, in the process, lower poverty after taxes and transfers.[28] By providing services to low-income households, public health care effectively distributes resources across the entire income distribution and, in turn, reduces poverty. Unlike unemployment insurance granted for previous employment, for example, health services are guaranteed universally as a citizenship right in most welfare states. As Huber and Stephens argue, "The redistributive effect of the free or subsidized provision of public services and goods should differ from, and be greater than, the redistributive effect of transfer payments."[29] Moreover, public health spending quantitatively tracks fundamental differences between encompassing and minimalist welfare states. Almost all welfare states publicly cover nearly 75% of total health costs, whereas the minimalist, high-poverty United States provides less than 50%. Health spending might be a quantitative means to understand the qualitative differences between encompassing and minimalist welfare states.[30]

Public employment may also contribute to poverty reduction. Public employment matters in terms of the civil servants who provide welfare services, and this gauges the extent of resources available to provide quality assistance for the poor.[31] Public employment also matters because it is a program to alleviate unemployment and provide entry into the labor market for groups vulnerable to unemployment and poverty, especially less skilled and young workers.[32] Policy analysts and scholars often advocate public employment because it provides work experience and income for the poor, enhances the upward mobility of the disadvantaged, and reduces gender inequality and women's poverty.[33] These virtues are often mentioned as justification for the prominent role of public employment in the U.S. welfare reforms of 1996.

Varieties of Types of Welfare States

The most recent generation of welfare state scholarship broadly contends that welfare states cluster into different types that are not necessarily directly comparable. These institutional clusters—usually called "regimes"—reflect the genetic historical legacies of social policy development and the state's particular institutionalized tradition of intervention into the market. The literature has experienced a proliferation of institutional typologies. Korpi and Palme divide countries along a targeting versus universalism continuum. Huber and Stephens break welfare states into the social democratic,

Christian democratic, Mediterranean, Antipodean, and liberal types. Peter Hall and David Soskice argue that countries can be collapsed into coordinated and liberal market economies. Even before these typologies, there were classic distinctions between residual and institutionalized welfare states, or civil, political, and social rights.[34]

That said, Esping-Andersen provided the most influential typology: socialist, liberal, and conservative welfare state regimes. The liberal regime is epitomized by the United States and typically includes Ireland, Australia, Canada, and the United Kingdom. The welfare state in this regime is based on free market and individualistic ideology and involves means-tested benefits targeted at the poor's basic security. The best example of the conservative regime is Germany, and often included are Switzerland, Austria, and France. This regime emphasizes social insurance (for unemployment, sickness, and old age) for male breadwinners and their families. This regime developed during authoritarianism and reflects a tradition of corporatism, Catholicism, and familialism. The Scandinavian countries more or less make up the socialist regime. This regime features universal welfare programs guaranteed to all citizens, extensive public employment systems, and generous family leave policies. With their high unionization and female labor force participation, socialist regimes are uniquely collectivist and egalitarian.

Esping-Andersen's typology profoundly reoriented scholarship away from universal explanations of social policy expansion and effects. Laying out this typology was the other major contribution of Esping-Andersen's *Three Worlds of Welfare Capitalism*,[35] and it is not an overstatement to say that much welfare state scholarship since has been a conversation with him. The various other typologies actually have a great deal in common with Esping-Andersen's schema. For my purposes, Esping-Andersen's work has generated two claims that are relevant to this analysis.

First, these regimes supposedly reflect core differences in the institutionalization of equality that *cannot* be captured by simply analyzing the quantitative levels of welfare effort. Purportedly, measures of welfare state features are inadequate for testing the fundamental differences between liberal, conservative, and socialist welfare state regimes. Esping-Andersen explicitly criticized the literature's focus on welfare effort and social policy.[36] Moreover, he argued vigorously that affluent democracies cluster into regimes that reflect complex and systematically interwoven relations between the state and economy.[37] According to his now widely held view, a focus on welfare effort neglects and obscures these deeper institutional sources of variation in social inequality. Analyzing welfare state regimes instead of specific welfare state features should ultimately yield a greater understanding of poverty and inequality.

Second, social policies are expected to have different effects across the three regimes. Because of different historically institutionalized traditions of social policy, the consequences for stratification should vary across regimes.[38]

Alexander Hicks and Esping-Andersen summarize this prevailing view: "The sociological conceptualization of welfare states is now dominated by the idea of distinct real-world models, thus rejecting the notion that they can be compared simply along a linear dimension—such as social spending levels."[39] As another example, Korpi and Palme argue that the universalist social policies of encompassing welfare states reduce poverty more effectively than targeted social policies of minimalist welfare states.[40] In his 1990 book, Esping-Andersen claims, "It is misleading to compare welfare states as merely 'more' or 'less' egalitarian. We discover, instead, entirely different logics of social stratification embedded in welfare-state construction."[41] In his 1999 book, *Social Foundations of Postindustrial Economies*, Esping-Andersen contrasts the effects of Scandinavian social democracy, focused on equalizing resources, against the liberal Anglo-Saxon welfare state, which selectively sponsors disadvantaged groups for mobility. He even explicitly claims that, in liberal regimes, "Market inequalities are unlikely to be affected much by social redistribution," and in socialist/social democratic regimes, "The distribution of resources and life chances should be additionally egalitarian, creating homogeneity not only within the working class, but also between the social classes."[42] Therefore, based on a careful reading of welfare state theorists, especially Esping-Andersen, one should expect the welfare state to have different effects on poverty across different welfare state regimes. Because social policies should have different effects on poverty across regimes, one should expect an interaction effect between regimes and the aforementioned features of the welfare state.

Welfare state regimes have been tremendously influential in the literature especially since Esping-Andersen's 1990 book. Despite this remarkable impact, it is even more striking that little research has tested the relevant implications for poverty (or even inequality). Very little research actually examines whether welfare state regimes influence poverty or whether welfare state programs have differing effects across regimes. Proponents of the regime view, like Esping-Andersen and Korpi, provide only descriptive evidence on the patterns in poverty across welfare state regimes.[43] To seriously engage these arguments, a more rigorous test is needed.

Historical Change or Stability?

Beyond exploring the effects of the welfare state for all of the past few decades, it would be valuable to scrutinize the period after 1990. It is widely understood that the period after 1990 was a particularly challenging era of welfare state retrenchment.[44] This most recent period has involved a weakening of organized labor and corporatism—two key bases of support for the welfare state.[45] Surveying welfare states, Stephens and colleagues remark, "Overall, then, by the late 1980s and early 1990s a picture of widespread cuts emerges, in some cases at least of considerable magnitude."[46] In their notably titled *Development and Crisis of the Welfare State*, Huber and Stephens summarize, "We find that roll-backs and 'restructurings' in welfare state programmes have been a universal phenomenon in the past two decades."[47] Even Esping-Andersen has lamented that welfare states were built to manage the risks of an earlier era and should not be as effective at risk management in postindustrial societies.[48] While the social democracies faced a series of economic crises that threatened their sustainability, the minimalist liberal United States, at least in the 1990s, seemed to produce both dynamic economic expansion and low unemployment and welfare recipiency. As a result, the classic trade-off between social protection and economic efficiency has seemed more immediate and acute.[49]

Of course, there has never been a shortage of skeptical critics of the welfare state. Yet, the criticism of welfare generosity has grown louder since 1990, as many claim that the long-term unsustainability of social democracy and corporatism finally became apparent.[50] While the literature mentioned above suggested that the welfare state reduced poverty prior to the 1990s, it remains highly debatable whether that relationship still held in more recent years. Nevertheless, few have tested the temporal stability of the welfare state's effects.

Testing the Welfare State's Effects

The following analyses test several features of the welfare state, the three welfare state regimes, and interactions between features and welfare state regimes and time.[51] First, I examine four general measures of the welfare state. *Social welfare expenditures* is the standard measure of overall, total spending on welfare cash and noncash transfers and welfare services as a percentage of the gross domestic product (GDP). *Social security transfers* includes state-sponsored cash and noncash transfers (but excludes services) for sickness, old-age pensions, family allowances, unemployment, workers' compensation, and other assistance as a percentage of GDP. *Decommodification* is measured with Allan and Scruggs's new index that recreates Esping-Andersen's original index.[52] This measure combines information on the percentage of the population covered, the length of qualifying periods for eligibility, and the replacement rates for three welfare programs: unemployment, sickness, and pensions. Data on decommodification are not available for Luxembourg and Spain, so those analyses include 16 countries. *Government expenditures* accounts for all government spending and outlays as a percentage of GDP. While decommodification represents Esping-Andersen's emphasis on qualitative distinctions, the other three are classic quantitative measures of welfare effort.[53]

Second, I evaluate two specific measures of welfare state services. *Public health spending* is measured as a percentage of a country's total health spending, public and private. This variable summarizes all public spending on health care, medicine, and public health and includes transfers, in-kind benefits, and services. *Public employment* is measured as a percentage of total civilian employment. This variable measures all civilian nonmilitary government employment as a percentage of all civilian employees.[54]

Last, I constructed a *welfare generosity index*, by averaging the standard scores (z-scores) of social welfare expenditures, social security transfers, decommodification, government expenditures, and public health spending.[55] As shown below, these four measures are the significant features of the welfare state. This index combines them into one variable, and becomes a fifth general measure of the welfare state. By combining the four significant features, I aim to measure the interconnectedness and combination of a host of social policies and welfare programs.[56] Although it is often valuable to focus on the precise effects of specific social policies, this index assesses the broader and more comprehensive generosity of the entire welfare state.

Beyond the general effects of the welfare state, I evaluate how the welfare state's effects might differ across two relevant contexts. First, I examine Esping-Andersen's schema of socialist, liberal, and conservative welfare state regimes.[57] In addition, Luxembourg and Spain are coded as conservative due to their traditional family relations and feudal or authoritarian legacies. I include binary variables for *socialist* and *liberal* regimes, while *conservative* is the reference. Further, I include the interaction of liberal and socialist regimes with the main welfare state features. Second, I investigate the welfare state's effectiveness over time. A dummy variable for the *post-1990* period is introduced, and interactions of that period with the welfare generosity index are included. Also, I created a linear measure of *year* and examined the interaction between year and the welfare generosity index. Appendix table A.1 lists each of the variables described here, their means and standard deviations, and their sources.

To make these welfare state measures more concrete, table 4.1 displays a few aspects of the welfare state for all countries for the latest year in the sample, grouped by welfare state regime. The first two columns are key features in the analyses below, and the last two columns are components of the decommodification index. As table 4.1 reveals, there are substantial cross-national differences in the generosity of the welfare state. Australia, Ireland, Spain, and the United States allocate less than 20% of their GDP to social welfare. By contrast, Denmark, France, Sweden, and Switzerland allocate more than 28%. The U.S. publicly covers less than 45% of total health care spending, and every other country covers more than 57% (16 cover more than 63%), with Denmark, Luxembourg, Norway, Sweden, and the United Kingdom covering more than 80% of health care costs. In Australia, an unemployed family of four will be insured at 65% of their former wages for a limitless time. In Switzerland, an unemployed family will be insured only for 30 weeks, but they will receive 82% of their former wages.

Table 4.1.   Selected Welfare State Features in Latest Year in Analyses for 18 Affluent Western Democracies

Regime, Country	Social Welfare Expenditures (% GDP)	Public Health Spending (% Total Health Spending)	Unemployment Insurance for Family of Four (Replacement %)	Unemployment Insurance Duration (Weeks)
Liberal				
Australia, 2001	18.0	67.9	67.1	No limit
Canada, 2000	17.3	70.9	76.2	38
Ireland, 2000	13.6	73.3	50.4	65
United Kingdom, 1999	21.3	81.0	54.5	26
United States, 2000	14.2	44.2	57.1	26
Conservative				
Austria, 2000	26.0	67.9	72.2	30
Belgium, 2000	26.7	71.7	59.0	No limit
France, 2000	28.3	75.8	62.5	130
Germany, 2000	27.2	75.0	71.3	52
Italy, 2000	24.1	73.4	49.1	26
Luxembourg, 2000	20.0	89.9	NA	NA
Netherlands, 1999	22.2	63.4	77.2	104
Spain, 2000	19.9	71.7	NA	NA
Switzerland, 2002	28.3	57.1	82.1	30
Socialist				
Denmark, 2000	28.9	82.5	66.0	208
Finland, 2000	24.5	75.1	67.6	100
Norway, 2000	23.0	85.2	72.5	156
Sweden, 2000	29.8	85.2	71.6	60

In Italy, the United Kingdom, and United States, an unemployed family will be covered only for 26 weeks at less than 58% of their former wages.

Though I discuss the other independent variables more in chapters 6 and 7, the models control for a host of factors that others have claimed are more important than the welfare state in affecting poverty: economic growth, unemployment, productivity, manufacturing employment, female labor force participation, the elderly population, and single motherhood. In the analyses that follow, all these variables are included, but they are discussed in detail in chapters 6 and 7.

As mentioned in chapter 1, more details on the statistical analyses are available in the appendix, including some sensitivity analyses.[58] For ease of interpretation, almost all of the statistical results are presented in figures focusing on the key findings.

Does the Welfare State Reduce Poverty?

Descriptive Patterns

Before proceeding with the analyses, I first display the basic associations between the welfare state and poverty. At this point, I show only the correlations between social welfare expenditures, perhaps the most generic welfare state measure, and a few dimensions of poverty.

Figure 4.1 shows a strong negative relationship between social welfare expenditures and the overall headcount measure of poverty ($r = -.65$). As countries devote a larger share of their economy to welfare, poverty declines steeply. For example, the Scandinavian social democracies of Finland (FIN) and Sweden (SWE), as well as continental European countries such as

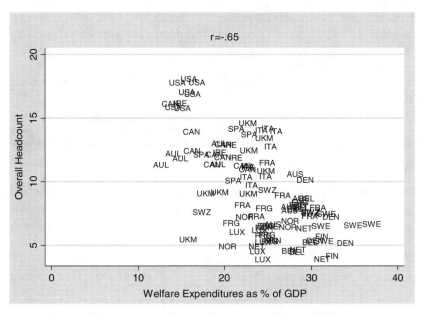

Figure 4.1. The Association between Social Welfare and Overall Headcount Poverty ($r = -.65$)

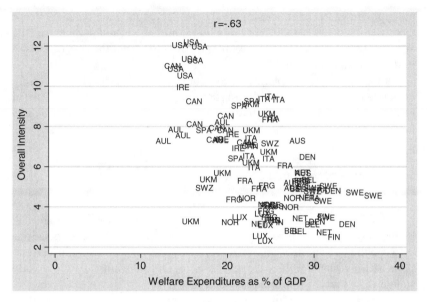

Figure 4.2.   The Association between Social Welfare and Overall Poverty
Intensity ($r = -.63$)

Belgium (BEL) and the Netherlands (NET), have high welfare expenditures
and low poverty. By contrast, the United States (USA), Ireland (IRE), and
Canada (CAN) have low welfare expenditures and high headcount poverty.
Some fall out of this pattern. For a few time points, Australia (AUL) had only
moderate poverty despite low social welfare expenditures. However, the
general pattern is quite strong.

Figure 4.2 displays a similarly robust negative relationship between
social welfare expenditures and overall poverty intensity ($r = -.63$). The
pattern is quite similar, with the United States and Scandinavia at the
extremes. As social welfare expenditures vary from roughly 10% to 35% of
GDP, overall poverty intensity correspondingly declines from about 12% to
3%. Even if one were to exclude the outlying United States, a clear negative
association prevails.

While these bivariate correlations do not prove a causal relationship, the
patterns certainly suggest a strong association that warrants careful scrutiny.
The remaining models explore this relationship and test if indeed the welfare state reduces poverty.

Models of Overall Poverty

The first set of models each includes one of the five general welfare state
features: social welfare expenditures, social security transfers, decommodification, government expenditures, and the welfare generosity index.

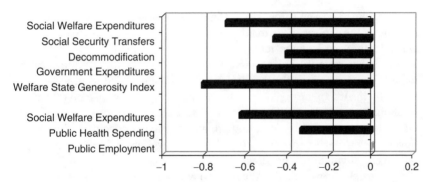

Figure 4.3.   Standardized Effects of Various Features of the Welfare State for Overall Headcount Poverty. [All bars are significantly different from zero ($p < .05$) except the shaded bar for public employment. See appendix table A.2 for details.]

Figure 4.3 shows the effects of each of these five general features. Each of the first five bars represents a separate model. For simplicity, I display only the standardized coefficients. The remaining details for each of these five models are displayed in appendix table A.2. Because these effects are standardized, one can compare the relative size of the effects of the diverse features of the welfare state. Also, these standardized effects are easy to interpret: how many standard deviations poverty would change if the welfare state feature changed one standard deviation.

In separate models, each of the five general features has a significant negative effect on overall headcount poverty. For a standard deviation increase in social welfare expenditures, overall headcount poverty should decline by about 0.7 standard deviations. For a standard deviation increase in social security transfers, decommodification, or government expenditures, overall headcount poverty should decline by about 0.48, 0.42, or 0.55 standard deviations, respectively (I return to the welfare generosity index in a moment). With any of these measures, the welfare state has a considerable effect. Social welfare expenditures appear to have a larger effect than the other features of the welfare state. If social welfare expenditures are increased one standard deviation—about 5.3% of GDP—overall headcount poverty should decline by about 2.6%. These models provide some suggestive evidence that the effect of decommodification is actually smaller than the effect of the more generic features of the welfare state. In contrast to Esping-Andersen and others who have argued that decommodification is a more pure measure of the welfare state, these analyses suggest that old-fashioned general measures of welfare effort—like social welfare expenditures, social security transfers, and government expenditures—have greater predictive influence on poverty.

In addition to the general welfare state features, figure 4.3 shows the effects of the specific features of public health spending and public employment. The last three bars in figure 4.3 represent one model where I control for the generic measure of welfare effort, social welfare expenditures, and add the two specific measures. As figure 4.3 displays, public health spending has a significant negative effect on poverty while public employment is positively signed and insignificant. For a standard deviation increase in public health spending, overall headcount poverty is expected to decline by about 0.35 standard deviations. Social welfare expenditures have a larger effect, but public health spending appears to have a specific influence on poverty even net of this measure of general welfare effort. Interestingly, public employment has no effect at all.

Figure 4.3 also reveals that the index of welfare generosity has a very large negative effect on overall headcount poverty. Recall that the welfare generosity index combines the five specific features that have significant effects: social welfare expenditures, social security transfers, decommodification, government expenditures, and public health spending. Its standardized effect is actually larger than any of the five component measures of the index. For a standard deviation increase in the welfare generosity index, overall headcount poverty is expected to decline by about 0.82 standard deviations. This turns out to be the largest effect of any of the welfare state features. So, I retain this welfare state measure in analyses of various dimensions of poverty that follow. Finally, it is worth noting that none of the five general welfare state measures has significant positive effects. There is no support for concerns that the welfare state counterproductively increases poverty.

Figure 4.4 displays the same analyses for overall poverty intensity. The results are quite consistent. All four general features have a significant negative effect on poverty intensity. Social welfare expenditures appears to have the largest effect among the first four general features of the welfare state, and contrary to Esping-Andersen, decommodification has a smaller effect. Public health spending has a specific negative effect, even controlling

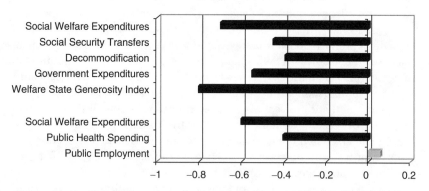

Figure 4.4.   Standardized Effects of Various Features of the Welfare State for Overall Poverty Intensity. [All bars are significantly different from zero ($p < .05$) except for the shaded bar. See appendix table A.3 for details.]

for social welfare expenditures, while public employment is insignificant and positively signed again. As with overall headcount poverty, the welfare generosity index has the largest effect. For a standard deviation increase in the welfare generosity index, overall poverty intensity is expected to decline by about 0.81 standard deviations. Thus, the analyses of overall poverty intensity confirm the robustness of the findings for overall headcount poverty and further support my claim that the welfare state has a substantial negative influence on poverty.

One way to illustrate the magnitude of the influence of the welfare state on poverty is to counterfactually simulate what would happen to a country's poverty level if a substantial change in welfare generosity occurred. Figure 4.5 displays this counterfactual simulation for overall headcount poverty. I display Sweden and the United States because of their position at the extremes in figures 4.1 and 4.2. I present the actual values and the simulated values as if Sweden reduced its welfare generosity index one standard deviation and the United States increased its index one standard deviation.[59] If both countries took a step toward average welfare generosity, the United States and Sweden would have poverty levels that are much closer than their actual values. Instead of the highest level of overall headcount poverty rate of 17.1% in 2000 in the United States, it would be about 14%. This would put the United States close to Australia's headcount poverty rate and below that of Ireland and Spain in the most recent cross section of the Luxembourg Income Study (LIS). Throughout the period, the U.S. headcount poverty rate would have exceeded 15% only in 1991—a level it always exceeded in actual values. If Sweden retrenched its welfare generosity one standard deviation, its headcount poverty rate in 2000 would be 9.5% instead of its actual 6.5%. Instead of having the sixth-lowest

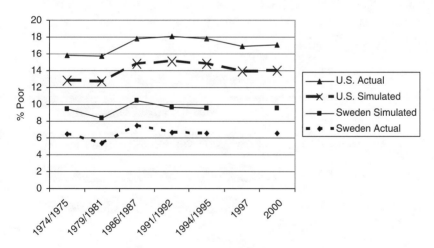

Figure 4.5.   Actual and Simulated Overall Headcount Poverty: United States (+1 Standard Deviation in Welfare Generosity) and Sweden (−1 Standard Deviation in Welfare Generosity)

headcount poverty rate in the most recent cross section of the LIS, Sweden would have the eighth highest headcount poverty (eleventh lowest of 18). Clearly, a change in welfare generosity could amount to a substantial change in the level of poverty.

Models of Poverty for Demographic Subgroups

Despite its powerful impact on overall poverty, it is possible that the welfare state is less beneficial for certain demographic groups. Indeed, some have criticized the welfare state because it benefits men more than women or favors the elderly over children. One enduring concern has been that the welfare state only redistributes between working-age adults and nonworking individuals, rather than actually helping working-age adults.[60] Figure 4.6 addresses these critiques, displaying the standardized effects of the welfare generosity index for poverty among several demographic subsamples of the population (in separate models for each group).

Clearly, the welfare state is beneficial for *all* of these groups. For a standard deviation increase in welfare generosity, headcount poverty among children, the elderly, adult men, adult women, and working-age adults should all decline by at least 0.62 standard deviations. Many of the commonly perceived biases of the welfare state fail to materialize. The standardized effect of welfare generosity appears to be larger for children than for the elderly, larger for adult women than for adult men, and larger for working-age adults than for the elderly.[61] One should probably not overstate the claim that some coefficients are really much larger than other coefficients. Nevertheless, these results provide strong evidence against views that the welfare state favors the elderly over children, men over women, and the elderly over working-age adults. The correct interpretation is that welfare generosity

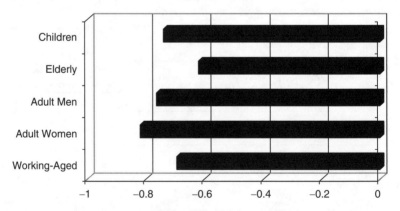

Figure 4.6.   Standardized Effects of the Welfare Generosity Index for Various Dimensions of Headcount Poverty. [All bars are significantly different from zero ($p < .05$). See appendix table A.4 for details.]

benefits all. There is no support for the common perceptions that it dispro-portionately favors the elderly or men.

Welfare State Regimes

As discussed above, Esping-Andersen's typology of welfare state regimes has dominated much of the welfare state literature since 1990. Regarding pover-ty, the claims have been made that (1) welfare regimes reflect core differences in the institutionalization of equality that cannot be captured by simply analyzing the levels of welfare generosity and that (2) welfare generosity is expected to have different effects across the three regimes. The next analyses test Esping-Andersen's claims, first, by assessing whether the socialist—conservative—liberal typology explains poverty; second, by examining whether any interregime differences can be explained by the welfare gener-osity index; and third, by examining whether the effect of the welfare generosity index differs across regimes.

Figure 4.7 displays the mean levels of overall headcount poverty and poverty intensity across each of the three welfare state regimes. Consistent with Esping-Andersen, the levels of poverty are arrayed from the more egalitarian socialist regimes to the moderately equal conservative regimes, to the most unequal liberal regimes. Thus, on a basic descriptive level, the patterns in poverty correspond to Esping-Andersen's "three worlds of wel-fare capitalism." This is the kind of evidence that has commonly been offered in the welfare state regime literature. Clearly, however, such descrip-tive patterns are not sufficient to assess all of the claims about welfare regimes and poverty. In order to do so, it is essential to estimate a model while controlling for other influences on poverty.

Figure 4.8 displays these analyses for overall headcount poverty. Because these models include binary (0, 1) independent variables for socialist and

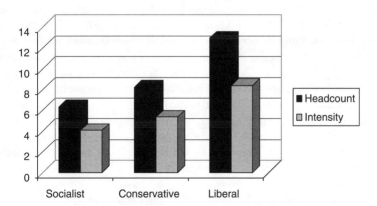

Figure 4.7.   Mean Levels of Overall Headcount Poverty and Poverty Intensity across Welfare State Regimes

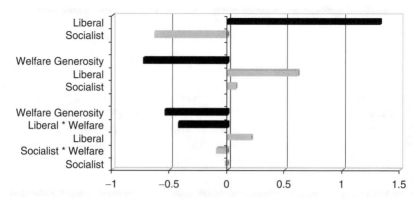

Figure 4.8.   Standardized and Semi-Standardized Effects of Welfare Regimes and Welfare Generosity for Overall Headcount Poverty. [The dark bars are significantly different from zero ($p < .05$). The shaded bars are not significantly different from zero. See appendix table A.5 for details.]

liberal welfare state regimes, I calculate only semistandardized coefficients for the binary variables and compare them with standardized coefficients for the continuous independent variables. The first two bars test the effects of socialist and liberal regimes, with conservative regimes as the reference. Liberal regimes have about 1.3 standard deviations more headcount poverty than do conservative regimes, which corresponds with the patterns in figure 4.7. But, surprisingly, socialist regimes are not significantly different from conservative regimes. Hence, liberal regimes have much more poverty, but there is no robust difference between, for example, continental Europe and Scandinavia.

The next three bars show that when the welfare generosity index is added to the model, the effects of socialist and liberal regimes become insignificant. Thus, differences in the welfare generosity index *entirely* account for any interregime differences in overall headcount poverty. The third set of bars show that the effect of the welfare generosity index mostly does not differ across regimes. The interaction between socialist regime and welfare generosity is insignificant, as are the main effects of socialist and liberal regime. Surprisingly, welfare generosity interacts significantly, and negatively, with liberal regime. Welfare generosity has an even more powerful antipoverty effect in liberal regimes, which tend to have higher levels of poverty. Because Esping-Andersen argued that liberal regimes were particularly ineffective at achieving egalitarianism, this hardly supports his account. Therefore, overall headcount poverty is best explained by simply examining the welfare generosity index, and it is not particularly essential to incorporate welfare state regimes into the analysis.[62]

Figure 4.9 presents results for overall poverty intensity, which are entirely consistent with the analyses of overall headcount poverty. Liberal regimes have significantly more poverty intensity than do conservative regimes, but

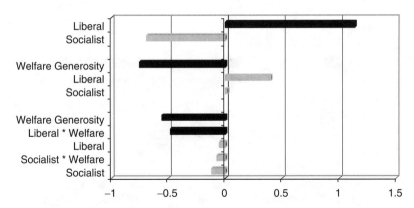

Figure 4.9.   Standardized and Semi-Standardized Effects of Welfare Regimes and Welfare Generosity for Overall Poverty Intensity. [The dark bars are significantly different from zero ($p < .05$). The shaded bars are not significantly different from zero. See appendix table A.5 for details.]

the difference between socialist and conservative regimes is not significant. All the regime differences can be explained by the welfare generosity index. Last, welfare generosity significantly interacts only with liberal regimes. In sum, the analyses do not support the claims of Esping-Andersen, and the broader welfare state regime literature, regarding welfare state regimes and poverty.

Historical Change or Stability?

It could be that what is driving these powerful welfare state effects is the residue of a bygone era. Some suspect that the welfare state was far more effective in the past and that it has become much less effective at reducing poverty in recent years. These concerns are addressed in figures 4.10 and 4.11 for headcount poverty and intensity, respectively. First, I analyze whether poverty was different in the post-1990 period after controlling for welfare generosity, and whether the effects of welfare generosity differed after 1990. Second, I treat year as a linear trend and test whether there has been a change over time such that poverty has increased linearly and welfare generosity's effect was different over time.

Figure 4.10 shows that the 1990s did not experience significantly different overall headcount poverty. The effect of the post-1990s period is positively signed but is not significantly different from zero. Moreover, the effect of welfare generosity did not change in the 1990s, because the interaction term is insignificant (and negatively signed, suggesting that, if anything, the welfare state became more effective after 1990). The coefficient for the interaction of year and welfare generosity is also insignificant. Year is positively

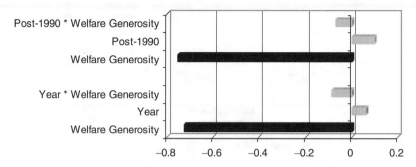

Figure 4.10.   Standardized Effects of Historical Time and Welfare
Generosity for Overall Headcount Poverty. [The dark bars are significantly
different from zero ($p < .05$). The shaded bars are not significantly
different from zero. See appendix table A.6 for details.]

signed, suggesting that overall headcount poverty has increased over time,
but the effect is insignificant. Thus, arguments that the 1990s ushered in a
changed relationship between the welfare state and poverty are not supported. The welfare state has not become less effective over time—the relationship appears to be stable.

Figure 4.11 displays similar results for overall poverty intensity. Welfare
generosity has a stable effect that has not changed after 1990 or over time.
There has not been a significant change in the level of poverty after 1990 or
linearly over time. The relationship between the welfare state and poverty
is historically stable. Perhaps the most noteworthy conclusions about the
relationship between welfare generosity and poverty are its durability and
stability over time.

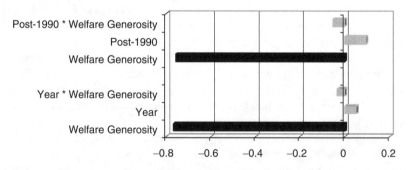

Figure 4.11.   Standardized Effects of Historical Time and Welfare Generosity for Overall Poverty Intensity. [The dark bars are significantly different
from zero ($p < .05$). The shaded bars are not significantly different from zero.
See appendix table A.6 for details.]

Conclusion

This chapter demonstrates the welfare state's powerful impact on poverty with multiple measures of the welfare state and poverty. The analyses reveal that five features of the welfare state effectively reduce poverty: social welfare expenditures, social security transfers, decommodification, government expenditures, and public health spending. For a standard deviation increase in social welfare expenditures, for example, overall headcount poverty and poverty intensity should decline by more than 0.7 standard deviations. The combined index of welfare generosity has even larger effects. For a standard deviation in welfare generosity, the two overall poverty measures should decline by roughly 0.8 standard deviations. To be clear, these are substantial effects. Interestingly, public health spending adds a specific negative effect on poverty, even controlling for social welfare expenditures.

There are at least two surprises regarding specific welfare state features. Following Esping-Andersen, many proclaim that qualitative differences in the welfare state, as exemplified by decommodification, are more important than old-fashioned quantitative welfare effort measures. Yet the results contradict this claim for poverty. Decommodification appears to have a smaller effect on poverty than traditional welfare effort measures. While decommodification has significant negative effects, social welfare expenditures, social security transfers, and government expenditures have more powerful effects. It is possible that decommodification might be more consequential to *inequality* by stabilizing workers' incomes through sickness insurance and unemployment compensation. Nevertheless, generous transfers and services are more consequential for integrating those that otherwise would be socially excluded (e.g., the elderly, children, and others out of the labor force). Because these groups are much more vulnerable to poverty, broader measures of welfare generosity appear to be most effective at integrating them into society. Ultimately, traditional, general measures of welfare effort have greater predictive validity for poverty. This is surprising because so much has been written about the purported theoretical superiority of decommodification compared to traditional measures.[63]

A second surprise regards the insignificance of public employment. Many push for public employment as a strategy to combat poverty. In her well-received book on U.S. poverty, *It Takes a Nation*, Rebecca Blank "propose[d] a reconfigured system of public assistance that moves us away from large-scale cash support and toward a more work-focused system."[64] Public employment, rather than direct cash transfers to the poor, appears to be more politically popular in the United States. As mentioned above, much of the 1996 U.S. welfare reform was predicated on pushing poor women into work. Despite the momentum for public employment, it strikingly has no relationship with poverty. After controlling for social welfare expenditures, the analyses provide no evidence that countries could expect less poverty if public employment was expanded. Though welfare services generally seem to help reduce poverty, public employment appears to be a much less effective antipoverty strategy.

There is no evidence that welfare state regimes have independent effects on poverty net of levels of welfare generosity. There is only contrary evidence that welfare generosity has different effects across regimes. While regime differences in poverty initially appear in the descriptive patterns, such descriptive patterns are not sufficient evidence. All of the regime differences can be explained by the welfare generosity index.[65] Because the regime differences become insignificant after including the welfare generosity index, this index explains variation in poverty better than the historically institutionalized differences across welfare state regimes. Also, because the interactions of the welfare state features and regimes are mostly insignificant, there is little evidence that social policies operate differently across regimes. Only one of the interaction effects is significant, and that was the unexpected finding that welfare generosity may be even more effective in liberal regimes. Ultimately, the simpler models without welfare regimes are preferred over the more complicated models with welfare regimes. The results in this chapter raise questions about the value of Esping-Andersen's typology for understanding poverty. Given Esping-Andersen's influence and the massive scholarly tradition of documenting welfare state typologies, these results are quite surprising.

For both overall headcount poverty and poverty intensity, the 1990s period did not have significantly different patterns of poverty. Also, poverty levels did not change linearly over time. The welfare generosity index did not have different effects in the 1990s, nor did the effects change over time. It is more appropriate to use simpler models without temporal complications rather than models that incorporate time or interactions with time. These findings challenge the view that the 1990s ushered in a different period for welfare states, or that the welfare state has become less effective over time. In the 1990s, generous welfare states continued to reduce poverty effectively.

In sum, the welfare state is a stable and powerful poverty-reduction mechanism. The many vocal critics of the welfare state are premature, and probably mistaken, in claiming that the welfare state is ineffective at reducing poverty. Regardless of the era or regime, welfare generosity is robustly predictive of a country's poverty. Consistent with the institutionalized power relations theory laid out in chapter 1, the welfare state should be prominently at the center of any explanation of poverty.

Chapter 5 builds on these results and develops the second part of the institutionalized power relations theory of poverty. Because the welfare state has such a powerful influence, it is worthwhile to explore backward in the causal process. What underlies these differences in welfare generosity? Do the causes of welfare generosity have effects on poverty, even net of welfare generosity? Chapter 5 concentrates on Leftist collective political actors, partly because so much welfare state research has demonstrated their influence as causes of welfare states. Although the welfare state has a direct and powerful effect on poverty, I explore whether Leftist collective political actors, in particular, have an indirect and fundamental effect. The welfare state and Leftist collective political actors could combine to reduce poverty, and/or Leftist collective politics could channel through the welfare state to reduce poverty. Together, chapters 4 and 5 develop the institutionalized power relations theory that forms the backbone of the book.

5

The Politics of Poverty

In the mid-1990s, the Left returned to power in both Sweden and the United Kingdom. For supporters of generous welfare states, these elections seemed promising. In both, the Left followed governments that had been outspoken about dismantling the welfare state. Margaret Thatcher's efforts were more visible, in what Donald Sassoon called "the most radical administration in twentieth-century Britain."[1] But even Sweden's conservative Moderate Party leader Carl Bildt had expressed contempt for "the sacred structures of the cherished model," of egalitarian capitalism.[2] Yet, beneath the surface of Leftist victory, there were salient differences between Sweden and the United Kingdom.[3]

In 1994, the Swedish Social Democrats (SAP) won the election after three years of center-right governance led by the Moderate party and Bildt. A few years later, the Labor Party gained control of the government in the United Kingdom. Labor followed an era of conservative Tory dominance of nearly two decades, led by Thatcher and John Major. In Sweden, the SAP had been out of power only since 1991 and for less than 10 of the past 60 years. In the United Kingdom, the Tories had controlled government twice as long as Labor since World War II. Since the late 1970s, when Labor was last in power, unionization had declined from nearly 50% of the labor force to less than 30%. During Thatcher's and Major's regimes, women never comprised more than 10% of parliament. By contrast, unionization actually increased in Sweden in the 1980s and continued to hover above 75%. By the 1990s, women had risen to roughly a third of parliamentary seats in Sweden.

Wrapped up in these dynamics, Sweden practiced a proportional representation electoral system where each party gained seats proportionate to its
percentage of national votes. The United Kingdom had a single-member-
district simple-plurality system where parties need to win a local district to
gain a seat. As a result, the more-centrist "New" Labor led by Tony Blair
gained complete control of government in the United Kingdom after winning
a simple majority of local seats. By contrast, the SAP in Sweden had to form
coalitions with the Greens and former Communists after winning about 45%
of the national electorate. These differences speak to systemic variations in
the extent and nature of Leftist politics across affluent Western democracies.

Do these political dynamics influence poverty? Is it simply a question of
whether the Left has won the most recent election or does one need a
constellation of social democratic institutions? More impartially, does the
Left matter *at all* to the entrenched inequalities of capitalism? In the process
of addressing these questions, we are faced with a debate that had endured
for more than a century. At least since Marx, activists and intellectuals have
deliberated over the potential for Leftist politics to reduce the economic
deprivation brought on by industrialization. Throughout the twentieth century, poverty advocates proposed political organization as an effective
means to combat poverty.

Nevertheless, the scholarly community has often been skeptical that
Leftist politics, whether in Sweden, the United Kingdom, or elsewhere,
can actually help the poor. Many studies fail to find evidence that Leftist
political mobilization alleviates inequalities generated by markets.[4] For
example, in his influential study of "union threat effects," Kevin Leicht
concludes, "Unions are, at best, selectively effective at raising the earnings of unorganized workers."[5] Despite finding that labor market institutions (e.g., unions) reduce earnings inequality, Michael Wallerstein
decisively rejects the hypothesis that governing socialist, social democratic, or labor parties reduce wage inequality.[6] Others argue that unionization, strikes, and Leftist parties mainly benefit the most advantaged of
the working class but do little for the bottom half and the "outsiders"
without well-protected jobs.[7] Such skepticism is found even within the
core of the intellectual and political Left. As the poverty activist Michael
Harrington lamented 50 years ago,

> The poor are politically invisible. It is one of the cruelest ironies of
> social life in advanced countries that the dispossessed at the bottom of
> society are unable to speak for themselves. The people of the Other
> America do not, by far and large, belong to unions, to fraternal organi-
> zations, or to political parties. They are without lobbies of their own;
> they put forward no legislative program. As a group, they are atomized.
> They have no face; they have no voice.[8]

One strand of thinking, Walter Korpi calls it Leninist, claims that capitalism is so deeply exploitative of workers that no reform can substantially alter

its essential inequalities.[9] For more than a century, certain factions of the Left have argued that electoral victories and formal politics are a false mirage of success.

The most influential version of the skeptical Left—though it is inappropriate to call it Leninist—is provided by Frances Fox Piven and Richard Cloward.[10] In their deservedly classic books *Poor People's Movements* and *Regulating the Poor*, Piven and Cloward argue that the formal organization of Leftist movements hinders their effectiveness in securing economic equality and lessening poverty. Piven and Cloward specifically argue that bureaucratic organizations blunted the militancy and compromised the potential success of the civil rights, welfare rights, unemployed workers', and industrial workers' movements. While others view formal political organizations as a strength, they contend that the internal oligarchy and integration with external elites of these formal organizations weakened the influence of Leftist movements. Opposing pluralist views of the effectiveness of institutionalized interest groups, they argue that disruptive, militant protest causes the government to expand the welfare state and redress poverty while formal political institutions accomplish very little.[11]

Thus, despite a history of intellectual enthusiasm for Leftist politics as a strategy to combat poverty, careful research has often failed to find a link. It is quite possible that the victories for Labor in the United Kingdom and the SAP in Sweden yielded few real benefits for those at the bottom of the income distribution. Theorists of poverty often have some vague sense that political organization could help the poor, but it may be idealistic to claim that social equality can result from political victories. Even among those sympathetic to the Left and the poor, there is disagreement about how effective political action is within formal institutions versus protest that rebels against those formal institutions. Possibly, social inequality is so entrenched that Leftist collective political actors cannot really make a difference.

This chapter revisits this long-standing debate about Leftist politics and poverty. I begin by outlining the contributions and limitations of power resources theory, a key starting point for the study of politics and poverty. Next, I articulate how institutionalized power relations theory moves beyond power resources theory, and then provide an empirical evaluation of the causal hypotheses derived from institutionalized power relations theory. Ultimately, I aim to both theoretically and empirically advance the understanding of the economic consequences of politics and the political causes of poverty. This chapter builds on chapter 4 in developing the institutionalized power relations theory. Broadly, the analyses demonstrate that Leftist politics does influence poverty. The effects are mostly channeled through the welfare state and only partly combine with the welfare state. Leftist politics fundamentally influences a society's amount of poverty, but the welfare state remains the proximate and direct influence on poverty.

Power Resources Theory

The best place to start in building a theory of how Leftist collective political actors shape poverty is power resources theory. Though power resources theory is primarily a theory of the welfare state, it offers a general explanation for the politics of the distribution of economic resources in advanced capitalist democracies.[12] In the past few decades, power resources theory has probably been the leading theory of the welfare state.[13] Nevertheless, there are limitations to power resources theory, so it should be used to commence, not conclude, theorizing the politics of poverty.

Power resources theory begins with the realistic premise that political power is very unequally distributed in a capitalist democracy. Business, owners, and managers have far more power because they control the means of production and thus control the primary delivery of economic resources to the population. Because business possesses greater wealth, it also has more resources to deploy in politics.[14] Metaphorically, business can be thought of as an iceberg of power. The majority of the power of business lurks below the surface and does not need to be visible to present a threat. At any time, business can create economic instability, which undermines the parties holding office, and can therefore influence elections. Business can also flex its muscles in the political arena by deploying resources strategically to tilt elections in its favor. Business does not need to always exert power in these ways, because everyone knows they have it. The threat, coupled with a business-friendly ideology common in affluent democracies—something business actively cultivates—is sufficient to encourage and legitimate business-friendly policy. Ultimately, the default organization of markets becomes favorable for business, which enables the exploitation of workers and results in the subsequent economic insecurity for the broader population.

Business has an interest in maintaining this default organization, and so exerts its influence to maintain a minimalist welfare state and low levels of government regulation. Of course, business is often supportive of government intervention to enhance profits and facilitate opportunities and subsidies for profit making. But, this is ignored when business advocates a broad free-market orientation for workers. In this default position, the working class and the poor have very little political power.

To alter power relations, the working class and poor must bond together and attract some of the middle class. Then, this bonding can be mobilized into class-based political action in the workplace and elections. As Evelyne Huber and John Stephens explain, "The struggle over welfare states is a struggle over distribution, and thus the organizational power of those standing to benefit from redistribution, the working and lower middle classes, is crucial."[15] Workers can strike and interrupt the ability of business to make profits. Moreover, the working class and poor allied with parts of the middle class can form and support Leftist political parties. Though labor unions are the immediate manifestation of working-class mobilization, Huber and Stephens emphasize that "political parties perform the crucial mediating role."[16] When in office, these parties can push for an expansion of the welfare state to protect workers and the poor and guard against the economic insecurity that is inherent in capitalism.[17] Thus, collective political actors representing the working class pressure the state in order to institutionalize egalitarianism.

The Limitations of Power Resources Theory

Power resources theory provided a deep contribution to the study of politics, inequality, and the welfare state. For decades, power resources theory has proven valuable for understanding many of the key debates that animate this book. However, in recent years, the weight of the criticisms of power esources theory has begun to accumulate. In order for our understanding of the politics of poverty to advance, we must acknowledge and address the limitations of power resources theory. I articulate the limitations of power resources theory by way of advancing institutionalized power relations theory.

Underlying power resources theory is a materialist interest-based rational choice explanation.[18] The interests of business lead to profit seeking and exploitation of workers. In the state, business is interested in free markets as it regards protections for workers. The interests of the working class and poor translate directly into Leftist politics. While there is room in power resources theory for questions of how and why the working class becomes mobilized, the interests of the working class and poor are never really questioned. Power resources theory presumes that workers and the poor act in their rational economic interest to support welfare state expansion, and that business acts in its interest to support profits and exploitation. The dilemma is that much social science research has moved beyond such a strict materialist interest-based account. Certainly, we should acknowledge that the working class and business can have divergent interests in the marketplace and state. However, it has become much more difficult to rely on an *exclusively* interest-based account.

Indeed, ideology may be equally as important as interest in accounting for political support for a generous welfare state and reduced poverty.[19] In *Why Welfare States Persist*, Clem Brooks and Jeff Manza show that mass policy preferences—public opinion about social policy and egalitarianism—substantially influence welfare state generosity.[20] Deeply embedded in national values are stable norms about welfare states, and there are national differences that cannot be accounted for by the class distribution. The rich literature on class voting shows that there is still a great deal of class voting: the poor and working-class women are often more likely to vote Leftist, and managers and high-income people are more likely to vote Rightist. But, the relationship is far from deterministic. The working class and poor often do not vote even though doing so is in their economic interest. When they vote, a sizable minority vote for parties opposed to a generous welfare state. Indeed, there is persuasive evidence that white working-class men in the United States have voted overwhelmingly for Republicans since at least 1996.[21] Moreover, professionals are one of the most supportive classes of Leftist parties, and because professionals tend to be affluent, voting Leftist is against their strict economic interest.[22] So, one cannot simply read party preferences from the economic interests of class locations. Ideology has a similarly large role to play. When the working class or affluent do not vote in the expected direction, it is not because of their interests, but rather because they have different ideological values about the welfare state. Moreover, much of the reason that the working class and poor support a generous welfare state is not because they have strategically calculated which party will benefit them materially. Rather, it is because they view Leftist parties as more consistent with their values.[23] When the working class supports the Left—and it does not always do so—it is not simply because the working class fears poverty or acts out of a sense of insecurity of falling into poverty.

A related dilemma is that power resources theory presents a picture of an independent game where politics involves separate negotiations at each election.[24] Though there is little dispute about the stability of cross-national differences between generous and minimalist welfare states, power resources theory implies that each election presents a real chance for welfare states to expand or contract. It is almost as if each election is a new negotiation between the power resources of capital and labor. Indeed, in a series of recent articles, Korpi and Joakim Palme argue that the decline of Leftist class politics has led to substantial welfare state cutbacks in Europe.[25] Social policies have purportedly been retrenched as working-class political organizations have declined. Because there is no evidence of increased poverty over time or a decline in the effectiveness of the welfare state, as shown in chapter 4, this study casts doubts on these claims. Hence, one of my key departures from power resources theory regards claims that recent working-class disorganization has led to welfare retrenchment and cuts in what Korpi refers to as social citizenship rights.[26]

In contrast to the image of a game, welfare state politics is better characterized as path dependent.[27] Welfare state and poverty politics are deeply institutionalized, and past political conflict and settlements feed back into contemporary politics.[28] Welfare politics very much reflects the rules of the electoral arena, stability between power relations, previous historical settlements, and, importantly, each country's traditional commitment to egalitarianism. Welfare politics are more about habit, normative expectations, bureaucratic inertia, and institutionalized rules than about a game of struggle and conflict with each election. Relatedly, the politics of welfare and, as a result, the politics of poverty are as much about constituencies of welfare beneficiaries as about class politics these days. As Jason Beckfield, Martin Seeleib-Kaiser, and I have shown, the size of the elderly population has as large a positive effect on welfare generosity as unionization or Leftist parties.[29] This is not to suggest, as some "new politics of the welfare state" scholars do, that parties have become irrelevant. Rather, the point is that power resources theory underappreciates the new bases and coalitions that support welfare generosity and Leftist parties (including the elderly, constituencies of beneficiaries, etc.), because it is so focused on the old bases and coalitions of workers.[30]

Unfortunately, like many Leftists, power resources theory harbors a rather romantic and unrealistic image of civil society. One of the central factors in power resources theory has always been the ability of workers to disrupt production. Strikes and labor militancy, in many ways *anti-* institutional politics, have gotten a lot of attention. Yet, strikes are simply too few, far between, and politically impotent in contemporary society.[31] Thus, power resources theory is constrained with its focus on a bygone era of manual working-class mobilization. It is more important to examine the role of institutional political action that has little of the romantic imagery of strikes in the streets.

Finally, as others have pointed out, the most important limitation is that power resources theory has always underappreciated race and gender.[32] Because it centers its argument on class politics, race and gender have always been considered marginal influences. In response, feminist scholars of the welfare state have compellingly critiqued the blindness of power resources theory to gender hierarchies.[33] As any careful observer of welfare and poverty politics in the United States would attest, race and gender are essential to the failure to accomplish more generous social policies. For example, Jill Quadagno's persuasive history of U.S. policy, *The Color of Welfare*, demonstrates how profoundly racial divisions and the exclusion of women and minorities shaped assistance to the poor, single mothers, the elderly, and the disabled.[34] In his convincing study *Why Americans Hate Welfare*, Martin Gilens demonstrates that much of the American reluctance to support welfare and help the poor can be explained by animosity toward racial minorities.[35] In one example, Gilens shows that survey attitudes about helping the poor significantly depend on whether the survey question features a black or a white poor person. Given the cumulative contributions of such scholars, it has become untenable to argue that class is the dominant source of welfare states. Gender and race are not secondary, but are probably equally salient to the mobilization of support for welfare generosity and the politics of poverty. By remaining centralized on class, power resources theory presents an incomplete account.

The Power Constellations Approach

In recent years, many scholars informed by power resources theory have sought to address these limitations. Perhaps the most significant attempt to revise and amend power resources theory is Huber and Stephens's power constellations approach.[36] In their rigorous and compelling book *Development and Crisis of the Welfare State*, these authors provide a mix of qualitative and quantitative evidence to demonstrate how parties drove the expansion of the welfare state since the 1960s. Their incisive account was clearly a step in the right direction to redress power resources theory's limitations. Yet, I would briefly point to five differences between the power constellations approach and institutionalized power relations theory.

First, the power constellations approach continues to centralize class, despite nods to the role of nonclass factors. For example, Huber and Stephens write, "At the core of our theory is the class-analytic frame of the power resources theory...thus, the organizational power of those standing to benefit from redistribution, the working and lower middle classes, is crucial."[37] The way power resources theory has been amended has been mainly to add a new variable for the alternative explanation (e.g., adding variables for female labor force participation or the elderly population). But, these variables rarely take on central roles in interpretations of results or case study narratives. In my account below, I treat all members of what I call latent coalitions for egalitarianism as similarly relevant.

Second, the power constellations approach neglects the political action of those excluded from employment and especially the poor themselves. For example, Huber and Stephens marginalize the political relevance of the unemployed: "Our conceptualization of classes here excludes people without connection to the process of production....[P]recisely because [the underclass] lacks skills and connection to the process of production, it also lacks organization and power and thus is acted upon rather than being an actor in shaping the welfare state."[38] In the power constellations approach, the key actors remain the working class and lower middle class. For example, Huber and Stephens treat voter turnout as a control variable. Institutionalized power relations theory treats voter turnout as an important manifestation of how many poor people actually participate in the formal electoral arena. Indeed, voter turnout might matter to poverty as much as Leftist parties and unions. I contend that the poor also have political agency, and that the coalitions in support of welfare generosity and egalitarianism include the affluent such as professionals.

Third, the account of Huber and Stephens gives political parties the dominant role in the development of the welfare state. While I appreciate the impact of parties, my account below emphasizes other political institutions as equally consequential. For example, they treat "veto points" (e.g., parliamentary or presidential systems) as a control. Instead, I highlight the substantial influence of at least one veto point: proportional representation systems. Thus, institutionalized power relations theory recognizes other political institutions as equally consequential to parties. By contrast, the power constellations approach emphasizes parties as most important to the initial rise and development of welfare states.

Fourth, Huber and Stephens argue that parties have recently become much less important to welfare politics. Although their account is that political parties once played a crucial role in the initial development of the welfare state, party control of government has purportedly become less consequential after the mid-1970s. Huber and Stephens argue that the differences between parties have narrowed and that new political dynamics drove welfare states in the 1980s and 1990s. In contrast, I argue that parties continue to be quite consequential to welfare politics, even in recent decades. To summarize the previous two points, the power constellations approach of Huber and Stephens says parties were paramount in the initial development of the welfare state but have become less relevant in recent decades. My institutionalized power relations theory contends that parties were one of several key political actors initially, but still continue to be salient.

Finally, the power constellations approach, especially as applied in empirical studies of poverty and inequality, departs in several regards from my strategies. In particular, Huber and Stephens analyze poverty *before* taxes and transfers as something separate (see chapter 3), in turn explain the welfare state as *redistribution* rather than *distribution* (see chapter 4), and do not specify the *channeled* and *combined* causal relationships (see below). Ultimately, although the power constellations approach was a compelling response to critics of power resources theory and a pivotal contribution, my institutionalized power relations theory aims to be distinct.

Institutionalized Power Relations Theory

Institutionalized power relations theory is deeply influenced by power resources and power constellations theories. As mentioned in chapter 1, my account explicitly builds on the contributions of those theories. Consistent with power resources theory, this book accepts the realistic premise that political power is very unequally distributed in a capitalist democracy. Those who support the poor face long odds and an unfriendly political environment. Thus, power resources theorists are correct to emphasize that those opposed to social equality have a default advantage in the electoral arena. Still, my aim is for institutionalized power relations theory to be a step beyond even the cogent revisions to power resources theory. Institutionalized power relations theory is intended to take seriously the criticisms of power resources theory, while advancing scholarship and thinking about the politics of welfare states and equality.

A core claim of institutionalized power relations theory is that the politics of poverty is driven by *latent coalitions for egalitarianism*. These coalitions are constituted by diverse classes, and though the poor tend to support such coalitions, the coalition is largely nonpoor.[39] Prominent in these coalitions are the working class, and the formal organizations of labor unions that often represent those workers. But, equally valuable are professionals, policy intellectuals, and institutional entrepreneurs that populate state bureaucracies and the administration of collective political actors. These latent coalitions are motivated as much by ideological commitments as by strict material interests. Probably the majority of these coalitions are not vulnerable to falling into poverty. Thus, these latent coalitions are often driven by normative expectations and guided by cultural frames about protecting their citizenry and including all in a state of general socioeconomic equality.

As mentioned in chapter 1, I call these coalitions "latent" because a firm commitment to poverty alleviation is rarely explicitly what brings them together. These latent coalitions are often accidental or at least unanticipated partners in support of welfare programs that end up helping the poor. Few people go to the voting booth with a paramount desire to alleviate poverty in society. Instead, these latent coalitions end up advancing economic egalitarianism as a secondary consequence of political power. Moreover, these latent coalitions often gain and are able to institutionalize this power largely for reasons that have little to do with an explicit commitment to alleviating poverty.

In that vein, Peter Hall and David Soskice have shown in *Varieties of Capitalism* that even business can be a member of these latent coalitions for egalitarianism in the presence of a coordinated market economy.[40] Thus, institutionalized power relations theory acknowledges and incorporates recent challenges to the traditional two-class model of politics pitting labor against capital.[41] Moreover, key constituents of these coalitions include women and women's organizations, many of whose politics do not simply and necessarily reflect a direct economic interest in welfare generosity. Less central to power resources theory, but pivotal to my account, are the constituencies of beneficiaries of welfare programs. One of the most loyal supporters of these coalitions are the elderly, whose economic security rests on welfare programs like public pensions and socialized health care. Although the elderly, business, and single mothers might appear to have little in common, latent coalitions for egalitarianism crystallize around the support of such diverse classes. The elderly and business are often key components of the latent coalitions that establish generous welfare states that alleviate single-mother poverty. For example, the elderly in the United States may politically mobilize for Social Security and Medicare, and this ends up contributing to a more generous welfare state, which consequently ends up helping single mothers avoid poverty. Thus, business, women, and constituencies of beneficiaries may come together in unanticipated coalitions. Indeed, these groups might be essential components, right alongside the poor and working class, in building political support for welfare states and social equality.[42]

The critical manifestations of these coalitions are the Leftist collective political actors participating in the formal political arena. This point helps to illustrate how the latent coalitions are not simply civil society, because civil society disconnected from the state is unlikely to influence poverty.

Institutionalized power relations theory explicitly marginalizes noninstitutional actors. Like the power constellations approach of Huber and Stephens, I contend that those who are normal members and participants in the formal political arena are the collective actors that stand to alleviate poverty. This is because the welfare state is the primary and proximate causal influence on poverty. Because the welfare state is absolutely central to shaping the amount of poverty in society, only collective political actors that can and do influence the welfare state are ultimately consequential to the poor. Though civil society and anti-institutional politics may have a place in the background, most such political action ends up having few effects on the poor. Because the sort of dissensus politics that Piven and Cloward call attention to is so rare, and institutionalized party politics are routine, political action directly connected to the state ends up being far more consequential. In short, it is the formal politics of Leftist collective political actors operating inside and around the state that is most important to shaping poverty.

The politics of poverty is institutionalized in a second way. The imagery of games, struggle, and contestation that animated power resources theory tended to overemphasize each election and did not represent the politics of poverty very well. Rather, the amount of poverty in society is a deeply path-dependent phenomenon.[43] Elections and political parties mainly have an effect on poverty in the long term. It takes cumulative political power, mounting over historical time, for poverty to be reduced. Rather than viewing each election as an opportunity to reduce poverty and inequality, welfare generosity is locked in place and only slowly evolves toward or away from egalitarianism. Even if parties strongly in favor of or opposed to the welfare state take power, these parties are constrained by the traditions and established expectations that preceded their power. Moreover, electoral rules that have a long-term bias in favor of Leftist parties may have greater influence than the immediate returns from a Leftist electoral victory. Ultimately, once egalitarianism is established, welfare programs are generous and mature, and poverty is low, it is quite difficult for those opposed to egalitarianism to reverse the status quo. Conversely, in a policy environment where welfare generosity has not historically been established, it is very difficult to reduce poverty with immediate electoral victories.

As is clear above, institutionalized power relations theory rests on the assumption that ideology is equally salient to interest in driving Leftist collective political actors, welfare generosity, and poverty.[44] Because so many constituents of the coalitions for egalitarianism are not directly vulnerable to poverty, one could conclude that ideology may be even more important than interest. It is important to acknowledge that, consistent with power resources theory, the original development of the welfare state and adoption of social policies may have been heavily influenced by the interests of the working class and poor. Yet, in this era of mature, institutionalized welfare states, it is more realistic to focus on the confluence of interest and ideology. As Brooks and Manza explain, public opinion about egalitarianism results from the long-term feedback from generous social policies and exerts a significant influence on the stability and continued generosity of welfare programs.[45] Often, ideology is a more appropriate concept for thinking about the motivations of latent coalitions for egalitarianism because I contend that race and gender are as equally influential as class. Racial and gender divisions and belief systems often undermine the coalitions for egalitarianism by eroding support for Leftist parties. Because Leftist parties are powerful actors for expanding the welfare state and alleviating poverty, these divisions serve to weaken the latent coalitions for egalitarianism. Often these racial and gender divisions have nothing to do with economic interest, and rest more on ideological beliefs about the subordination of women or racial/ethnic minorities. For example, when working-class white men vote Republican even though the Democrats might better fit their economic interests, racial and gender ideologies may be weakening the latent coalition for egalitarianism.[46]

Pulling together these arguments, institutionalized power relations theory implies two possible causal relationships between Leftist collective political actors and poverty: *channeled* and *combined*.[47] Both imply that the latent coalitions for egalitarianism manifest visibly in strength of Leftist collective political actors and these Leftist politics are interrelated with the welfare state. According to institutionalized power relations theory, most of the influence of these latent coalitions for egalitarianism implicates the welfare state.

Channeled Effects

One possible causal relationship between Leftist collective political actors and poverty is that Leftist politics triggers welfare state expansion, which subsequently reduces poverty. In this causal chain, Leftist politics channels through the welfare state to alleviate poverty. This relationship would be demonstrated if Leftist politics had a significant negative effect on poverty, but this effect became insignificant when welfare generosity was included in the model. Essentially, we would observe that the welfare state fully mediates the effect of Leftist politics on poverty. As a result, the sole utility of Leftist politics for poverty reduction would be to act as a vehicle for expanding the welfare state.

Part of this causal chain is already established empirically. Countless studies demonstrate that Leftist politics affect welfare generosity.[48] Unions, Leftist and Labor parties, socialist movements, and even voter mobilization all are positively associated with welfare state development.[49] For example, Huber and Stephens highlight the effects of Social Democratic parties in parliament for the development of the welfare state.[50] Such accounts build on the assumption that social movement organizations and interest groups can and do influence public policy.[51] As challenger groups, Leftist politics can mobilize power resources to provoke an expansion of the welfare state, which in turn reduces poverty and social inequality. For example, Kenneth Andrews provides a vivid account of this dynamic in the civil rights movement's impact on the war on poverty in Mississippi in the 1960s. Andrews finds that membership levels of Mississippi Freedom Democratic Party and the National Association for the Advancement of Colored People, the number of black candidates for electoral office, the percentage voting for Lyndon Johnson, and local government employment influenced county-level funding for community action programs—which plausibly resulted in less poverty.[52]

If the entire influence of Leftist politics is channeled through the welfare state, the centrality of welfare generosity for poverty reduction would be further supported. If welfare generosity mediates all of the effects of the Leftist collective political actors, one could conclude that the welfare state is still the crucial and proximate cause of poverty reduction. In turn, analyzing the effect of Leftist collective political actors would be secondary in institutionalized power relations theory, but the already established importance of Leftist politics for the welfare state would be augmented.

Combined Effects

A second plausible causal relationship between Leftist politics and poverty is that Leftist politics and the welfare state have combined effects on poverty. While chapter 4 established that the welfare state reduces poverty, it could be that Leftist politics have an additional effect on poverty net of the welfare state. If Leftist politics and welfare generosity both significantly affect poverty, and the effects do not mediate each other, one could infer that both are relevant. Further, if such models more effectively account for the variation in poverty, a causal explanation of combined effects would be preferred.

The combined effects account rests on a social democratic model that synthesizes labor market institutions, encompassing social policies, and consistently strong Left political parties. In this explanation, social equality rests on the interconnections between these various facets of social democracy. For example, Huber and Stephens claim that poverty is lowest when coordinated market economies with strong labor market institutions combine with social democratic welfare states.[53]

Part of the combined effects causal account emerges from the literature on labor market institutions. In this scenario, it would almost be as if Leftist politics reduce poverty in the labor market before and separately from the welfare state. Societal-based Leftist politics, such as unionization and labor market institutions, could be especially important in addition to state-based political parties. For decades, labor market sociologists and economists have argued that organized worker mobilization reduces economic inequality and raises workers' earnings.[54] Some have shown that labor market institutions can explain differences between affluent democracies in the levels and inequality of wages.[55] Relatedly, several scholars argue that as determinants of inequality, labor market institutions are much more important than the welfare state. For example, Bjorn Gustafsson and Mats Johansson find that while welfare transfers have no effect at all, unionization significantly reduces income inequality.[56] Wallerstein argues that labor market institutions such as wage coordination, unionization, and collective bargaining arrangements are more important than any other variable for earnings inequality.[57] Others conclude that the organized mobilization of the poor themselves will change the power distribution in society and lead to a process of redistribution separate from the welfare state.[58]

Despite this extensive literature, scholars have not fully established that labor mobilization, or Leftist politics more generally, filters down to the very bottom of the income distribution and benefits the poor as well as the working class. While many suggest that strengthening unions will help poor people, few serious empirical tests have examined whether this is actually the case.[59] As mentioned at the beginning of this chapter, several studies on this very question have ended up quite skeptical about the potential for Leftist politics to really help the poor. Thus, the evidentiary base for the combined account is more tenuous than for channeled account. In turn, it is less clear that Leftist politics actually combines with the welfare state to reduce poverty.

Testing the Effects of Leftist Politics

Measures of Leftist Politics

To test the arguments emanating from institutionalized power relations theory, I assess the effect of six measures of Leftist collective political actors. The relative power of Leftist politics can take the form of mobilization and capacity. The capacity of Leftist politics is the extensiveness of organizational resources or institutionalized relationships—what Bruce Western calls "congealed power."[60] Mobilization involves activating people toward an organization's mission—for example, getting out the vote or capturing positions of policy-making authority. Thus, Leftist politics matters both when Leftist parties win elections and when they pose an imminent threat to power holders. The analysis I present here simply considers both as potential strengths and does not attempt to determine which is relatively more important. Because the various measures of Leftist politics are highly associated with each other, I model one measure at a time. Therefore, I do not test which measure of Leftist politics is most important. Rather, I simply test whether each measure has a significant effect net of controls, and how this effect channels through or combines with welfare generosity.

First, included is a classic measure of organized labor: *union density*, the extent of unionization or the percentage of total civilian employees that are union members.[61] Second, I include *current left government*.[62] This is measured as Left seats as a proportion of seats held by all government parties. Third, as a step beyond current party governance, I examine the long-term, historical partisan control of government. I include *cumulative left government*, measured as cumulative Left seats out of total government seats since 1946. This variable tabulates the Left seats as a proportion of seats held by all government parties in each individual year and then sums these proportions for all years since 1946. Fourth, I consider *cumulative women in the legislature*, which is a cumulative average since 1946. This variable measures seats held by women as a percentage of total seats in parliament. Fifth, *voter turnout* is calculated as the percentage of the electorate that voted in the most recent election.[63]

Finally, I assess *proportional representation (PR) system*. This variable is coded 1 for a PR system of elections, .5 for modified PR, and 0 for a single-member district simple plurality electoral system.[64] This is a key rule of the electoral arena because PR systems tend to substantially favor Leftist parties.[65] PR systems allocate seats in the legislature according to the share of votes a party receives in the national election (even if that share is small). For example, a far-Left socialist party would probably get zero seats in a single-member district system because they would be unlikely to win the plurality of any one district. Yet, in PR, socialists would get seats commensurate with their national vote—even if that vote was only 5–10% of the electorate. As a result, center-Left parties have a much greater incentive to ally with far-Left parties, and true Leftists end up being much more relevant.

Welfare State and Control Variables

Because chapter 4 demonstrated that the welfare state is a central predictor of poverty, and because it could play a role in a channeled or combined causal relationship, I include the *welfare generosity index* developed in the previous chapter. Again, this measure scales the standard scores of social welfare expenditures, social security transfers, decommodification, government expenditures and public health spending.[66]

In all models and as in the previous chapter, I control for key economic and demographic influences on poverty: economic growth, unemployment, productivity, manufacturing employment, female labor force participation, the elderly population, and single motherhood. As mentioned in chapter 4, these variables are discussed more in chapters 6 and 7.

Do Leftist Politics Influence Poverty?

Descriptive Patterns

Before moving on to the analyses, I display the basic associations between the various measures of Leftist politics and poverty. To simplify the presentation, I only show overall headcount poverty.

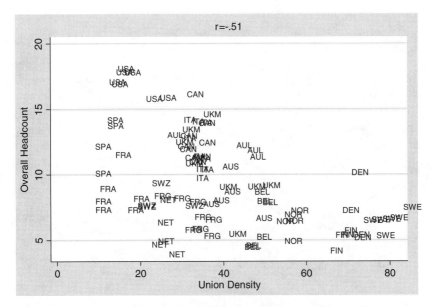

Figure 5.1.   The Association between Union Density and Overall
Headcount Poverty (r = −.51)

Figure 5.1 demonstrates a strong negative association between union
density and overall headcount poverty (r = −.51). Countries with higher
levels of unionization among employed workers tend to have lower levels of
poverty. Spain (SPA) and the United States (USA) exhibit high poverty and
low unionization, and the Scandinavian countries maintain low poverty and
very high unionization. The graph includes some outliers—such as France
(FRA) and the Netherlands (NET), with low unionization and low poverty—
but otherwise the association is quite strong.[67]

Figure 5.2 displays a moderate negative relationship between current
Leftist government (proportion of government seats held by the Left) and
overall headcount poverty (r = −.35). Many of the countries that are wholly
governed by Left parties (a proportion of 1.0) have quite low poverty, whereas many of the countries with no presence of Left parties in the government
(a proportion of 0) have high poverty. Moreover, because the proportion
fluctuates between less than .2 and more than .8, there is a negative slope.
In this descriptive sense, there appears to be a moderate association between
current Left government and poverty. Yet, one should also note that
countries like Italy (ITA), Ireland (IRE), Spain, and the United Kingdom
(UKM) had Leftist governments at points but still had high poverty.

Figure 5.3 shows a stronger negative relationship between cumulative
Left government and poverty (r = −.55). This measure tabulates the historical Leftist control of government since 1946 and so provides a longer term
perspective than the current Left government measure in figure 5.2.

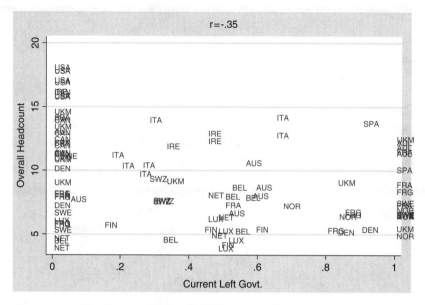

Figure 5.2.   The Association between Current Left Government
and Overall Headcount Poverty ($r = -.35$)

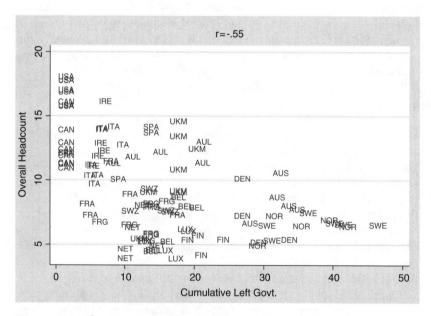

Figure 5.3.   The Association between Cumulative Left Government
and Overall Headcount Poverty ($r = -.55$)

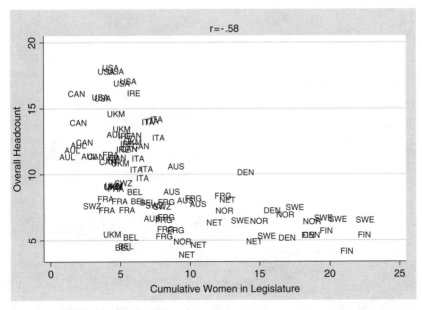

Figure 5.4.   The Association between Cumulative Women in Legislature and Overall Headcount Poverty ($r = -.58$)

Interestingly, the cumulative measure has a much stronger relationship. The United States and Canada (CAN) have never had a true Leftist government since World War II, while Ireland, Italy, and France have only had a few years of true Leftist party rule. All of these countries had higher poverty, while countries like Norway (NOR), Sweden (SWE), and Austria (AUS) have had many years of Leftist rule and low poverty.

Figure 5.4 provides evidence of a strong negative association between women's cumulative presence in the legislature and poverty ($r = -.58$). As the average percentage of women in the legislature has historically risen, poverty tends to be lower. Because gender quotas in legislatures really have only existed in countries with strong Leftist party traditions, the patterns are similar to the patterns for cumulative Left government.[68] The United States and Canada occupy one end of the continuum, while Scandinavian countries with a significant female presence and low poverty occupy the other end.

Figure 5.5 shows a negative association between voter turnout and poverty ($r = -.43$). Many countries legally require citizens to vote, so several countries exhibited near complete voter turnout. Such countries with high voter turnout like Belgium (BEL) tend to have lower poverty. Other countries, like the United States, have high poverty and lower turnout. There are many exceptions to this pattern. Switzerland (SWZ) has low poverty and low turnout, Australia (AUL) and Italy have high turnout and

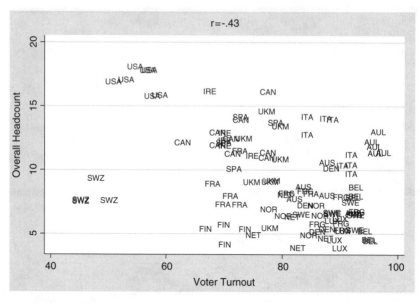

Figure 5.5.   The Association between Voter Turnout and Overall
Headcount Poverty ($r = -.43$)

moderate poverty, and Canada, Ireland and the United Kingdom have moderate to high turnout and high poverty. However, there is generally a negative
slope.

Finally, figure 5.6 reveals a nuanced, but very strong negative relationship
between a PR system and poverty ($r = -.63$). Because most countries have
either a PR system or a single-member-district simple-plurality system, the
countries cluster at 0 and 1. Countries without a PR system tend to have
higher poverty than do countries with a PR system. France, Italy, and Australia have mixed systems and have moderate to high poverty. Indeed, the
average overall headcount poverty is lowest in PR systems (7.74), highest in
single-member simple-plurality systems (13.18), and in between in mixed
systems (10.85). That said, the effects of PR systems should not be over-
blown. Alberto Alesina and Edward Glaeser imply that PR systems have an
almost deterministically negative influence on poverty.[69] My evidence
shows a strong negative association, but it still does not really substantiate
their claims because there is historical variation in poverty. Countries without PR systems, especially Canada and the United Kingdom, actually had
low poverty in some years. Moreover, some countries with PR systems,
especially Ireland and Spain, have had very high poverty in recent years.
While a PR system is associated with lower poverty, it is unrealistic to argue
that such an electoral system guarantees low poverty or even Leftist party
dominance.

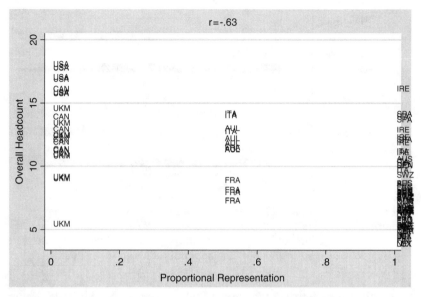

Figure 5.6.   The Association between a PR System and Overall
Headcount Poverty ($r = -.63$).

Models of Overall Poverty

The following analyses test whether Leftist politics have any effect on poverty and, if so, the nature of the relationship. For each measure of Leftist
politics, I continue the practice from chapter 4 of displaying the standardized coefficients. Because these figures are slightly more complex, please
let me clarify. Each figure contains two sets of bars, with one set for overall
headcount poverty and one set for overall poverty intensity. The first bar
within each set displays the effect of a measure of Leftist politics *without*
controlling for welfare generosity. The second and third bars in each set are
the effects of Leftist politics and welfare generosity in the *same* model. If the
second bar remains significant, the effect *combines* with welfare generosity
to reduce poverty. If the first is significant, but the second is insignificant,
the effect *channels* through welfare generosity. If the first and second are
both insignificant, the measure of Leftist politics simply does not influence
poverty.[70]

Figure 5.7 shows that union density has a significant negative effect for
both overall headcount poverty and poverty intensity. The first bar for each
of the two sets displays a respectable significant standardized coefficient.
Specifically, for a standard deviation increase in union density, overall
headcount poverty is expected to decline by about 0.45 standard deviations,
and poverty intensity is expected to decline by about 0.46 standard deviations. A standard deviation difference in union density roughly corresponds

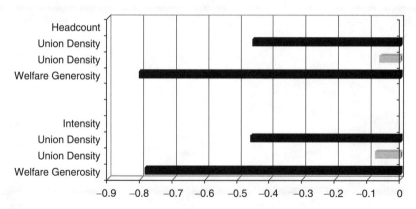

Figure 5.7.   Standardized Effects of Union Density and Welfare Generosity for Overall Headcount and Intensity Poverty. [The dark bars are significantly different from zero ($p < .05$). The shaded bars are not significantly different from zero. See appendix table A.10 for details.]

to the difference between the United States versus Canada or Italy. Using these estimates, if the United States had unionization rates comparable to Canada or Italy, the overall headcount poverty would be about 1.65% lower.

Union density provides evidence that Leftist politics indeed have a negative influence on both measures of poverty. However, all of the effects are channeled through welfare generosity. This is shown by the second and third bars in each set of models in figure 5.7. For both dependent variables, union density becomes statistically insignificant and the standardized coefficient drops below -0.1. In the same model, welfare generosity has large, significant negative effects (approximately $-.8$). Because union density is initially significant in the first models but becomes insignificant when controlling for welfare generosity, union density's effects do not combine with welfare generosity. Rather, union density channels through the significant effects of welfare generosity to reduce poverty.

Figure 5.8 shows that current left government fails to have a significant effect on overall headcount poverty or poverty intensity. For both dependent variables, its effect is not significantly different from zero in the first bars (without welfare generosity in the model). Also, it does not have an effect once welfare generosity is added to the model (in the second bars). Thus, there will be no change to poverty if the government is currently controlled by a Leftist party. In short, one cannot expect significantly less poverty to result immediately from an electoral victory for Leftist parties.

Figure 5.9 examines cumulative left government, which, unlike the previous measure, involves the long-term control of government. Before adding welfare generosity, cumulative Left government has a significant negative effect on poverty. For a standard deviation increase in cumulative Left government, overall headcount poverty and poverty intensity are expected

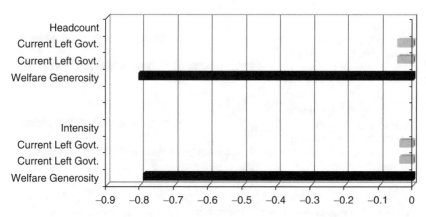

Figure 5.8.   Standardized Effects of Current Left Government and Welfare Generosity for Overall Headcount and Intensity Poverty. [The dark bars are significantly different from zero ($p < .05$). The shaded bars are not significantly different from zero. See appendix table A.11 for details.]

to decline by about 0.44−0.43 standard deviations. A standard deviation in cumulative Left government amounts to about 11 years of Left party rule since 1946, and this effect translates to slightly more than 1.6% lower headcount poverty. The significant effects of cumulative Lefty party power are channeled through welfare generosity, however. When welfare generosity is added to the model, it has a large and significant effect but cumulative left government's effect is less than half as large and becomes statistically insignificant. Thus, the effect of cumulative left party power is channeled through welfare generosity.

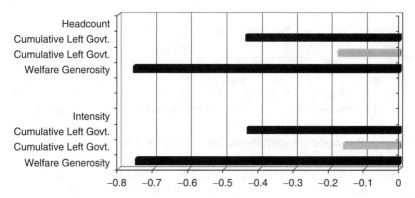

Figure 5.9.   Standardized Effects of Cumulative Left Government and Welfare Generosity for Overall Headcount and Intensity Poverty. [The dark bars are significantly different from zero ($p < .05$). The shaded bars are not significantly different from zero. See appendix table A.12 for details.]

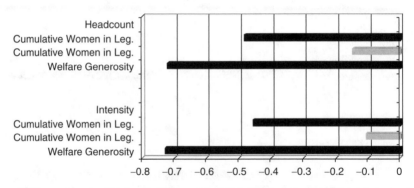

Figure 5.10.   Standardized Effects of Cumulative Women in Legislature and Welfare Generosity for Overall Headcount and Intensity Poverty. [The dark bars are significantly different from zero ($p < .05$). The shaded bars are not significantly different from zero. See appendix table A.13 for details.]

Figure 5.10 demonstrates that the cumulative average percentage of women in the legislature has a significant negative effect on overall headcount poverty and poverty intensity. For a standard deviation increase in the cumulative average of women in the legislature, overall headcount poverty is expected to decline by about 0.48 standard deviations and overall poverty intensity is expected to decline by about 0.46 standard deviations. A standard deviation in the cumulative average of women in the legislature is 5.3%, so this effect is equivalent to 1.8% lower headcount poverty. The effect of cumulative women in the legislature, however, is channeled through welfare generosity. When the welfare generosity index is added to the second models, the effect of the cumulative average percentage of women in the legislature becomes insignificant and welfare generosity has a large negative effect.

Figure 5.11 shows that voter turnout has a significant negative effect for overall headcount poverty and poverty intensity. For a standard deviation increase in voter turnout, overall headcount poverty is expected to decline by about 0.26 standard deviations and overall poverty intensity is expected to decline by about 0.29 standard deviations. Voter turnout's standard deviation is 12.7%, and this translates to about 1% lower headcount poverty. Yet, for both overall headcount poverty and poverty intensity, voter turnout's effect is channeled through the welfare generosity index. When that index is added to the second models, voter turnout becomes insignificant.

Figure 5.12 shows that having a PR system, the last measure of Leftist politics, leads to less poverty. For a standard deviation in how much the electoral system is a PR system (roughly, moving from a single-member-district simple-plurality system to a mixed system or from a mixed to a PR system), overall headcount poverty is expected to decline by about 0.57 standard deviations and poverty intensity is expected to decline by

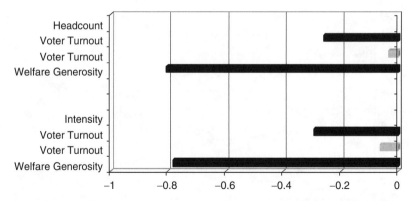

Figure 5.11.   Standardized Effects of Voter Turnout for Overall Headcount and Intensity Poverty. [The dark bars are significantly different from zero ($p < .05$). The shaded bars are not significantly different from zero. See appendix table A.14 for details.]

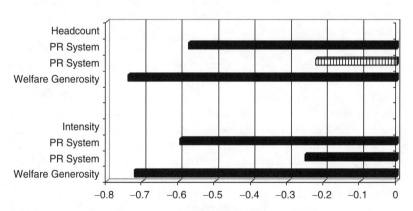

Figure 5.12.   Standardized Effects of Proportional Representation (pr) System for Overall Headcount and Intensity Poverty. [The dark bars are significantly different from zero ($p < .05$). The hatched bar is nearly significant ($p < .10$). See appendix table A.15 for details.]

about 0.60 standard deviations. The PR system variable has the largest effect of any of the measures of Leftist politics. If a country moved from a mixed to a full PR system (one standard deviation), headcount poverty would be about 2% lower. While I noted that PR systems do not deterministically lock in egalitarianism and Leftist elections, PR systems do have a powerful effect.

Even more interesting, PR system is the only measure of Leftist politics that *combines* with welfare generosity to significantly reduce both measures of poverty. Although the effect of PR system is less than half as large once the welfare generosity index is added to the second models, it remains significantly negative for poverty intensity and near significantly negative for headcount

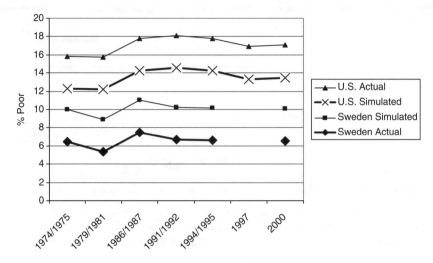

Figure 5.13.   Actual and Simulated (± 1 Standard Deviation for Welfare Generosity and PR system) Overall Headcount Poverty: United States and Sweden

poverty. Therefore, PR systems partly combine with and partly channel through the welfare state to reduce poverty.

As in chapter 4, I illustrate the magnitude of the effects of these institutionalized power relations theory variables on poverty with a counterfactual simulation. In this simulation, I concentrate on the welfare generosity index and PR system because PR system is the Leftist politics variable that remains most significant with welfare generosity in the model. As in chapter 4, I compare the actual and simulated values of Sweden and the United States. I present the simulation as if Sweden reduced its welfare generosity index and its PR system one standard deviation each and the United States increased its welfare generosity index and PR system one standard deviation (i.e., both United States and Sweden would have a mixed PR system). As figure 5.13 displays, the United States and Sweden would have poverty levels that are much closer—even closer than the simulation in chapter 4 (see figure 4.5). Instead of the highest level of overall headcount poverty at 17.1% in 2000, the United States would have a headcount of 13.5%. This would put the United States just above Australia's headcount and below Ireland and Spain in the most recent cross section of the Luxembourg Income Study (LIS). Throughout the period, the U.S. headcount would have never have exceeded 14.53%. If Sweden's welfare generosity index and PR system were reduced one standard deviation, its headcount in 2000 would be 10% instead of its actual 6.5%. Instead of having the sixth lowest headcount in the most recent cross section of the LIS, Sweden would have higher headcount poverty than Germany—the eighth highest of the 18 affluent democracies.

Conclusion

The most important conclusion from this chapter is that Leftist politics *do* greatly reduce poverty. Five of the six measures have significant negative effects on poverty, despite controlling for economic and demographic factors. In the latter period of the twentieth century, Leftist politics were triumphant in reducing the economic deprivation of industrialized democracies. The balance of political power clearly affects the poor.

Mostly, the influence of Leftist politics on poverty is channeled through the welfare state. Four of the five significant measures of Leftist politics are significant initially but become insignificant once welfare generosity is included in the model. As many welfare state scholars have documented, Leftist politics trigger an expansion of the welfare state. As chapter 4 demonstrates, this welfare state expansion reduces poverty. The welfare state remains the proximate and paramount influence on poverty, while Leftist politics mostly are a fundamental cause of poverty. These results demonstrate that Leftist politics matters to poverty, but mostly indirectly by triggering welfare generosity.

Although there is broader evidence for the channeled explanation, I find some specific evidence for the combined effects account. Proportional representation (PR) systems are the component of Leftist politics that have the largest effects before and after controlling for welfare generosity. Much of the influence of PR systems channels through the welfare state, as demonstrated by its smaller standardized coefficient in the second models (figures 5.7–5.12). Yet, the effect of PR system remains significant even controlling for welfare generosity. Though this chapter broadly supports the argument that the import of Leftist politics for poverty reduction is channeled through the welfare state, PR systems combine with the welfare state. Ultimately, the best way to model institutionalized power relations theory is by retaining both PR systems and welfare generosity as important influences on poverty.

The findings in this chapter generally support institutionalized power relations theory and at least partly qualify power resources theory. Consistent with institutionalized power relations theory (and the power constellations approach), I find that the long-term cumulative Leftist control of government is more consequential than is current Left government. Immediate electoral victories, something highlighted as a part of the class struggle game in power resources theory, are simply not consequential to poverty (as shown by the insignificance of current Leftist government; see figure 5.8). Relatedly, the results demonstrate the powerful path-dependent processes of generous welfare states. PR systems have the largest effect of the Leftist politics measures. That this rule of the game is so consequential provides more support for institutionalized power relations theory than power resources theory or even the power constellations approach. Additionally, nonclass collective actors matter at least as much as the working class in supporting the coalitions for egalitarianism. Cumulative women in the legislature and voter turnout both have very large significant negative effects on poverty. It is difficult to absorb these factors into traditional power resources theory, and their salience demonstrates the value of the more encompassing institutionalized power relations theory. Certainly, material interest and rational calculations may matter for voter turnout, Leftist parties, and women in the legislature. But, it is more likely that a broad ideology and collective expectation of egalitarianism are influential in these electoral outcomes.

These measures of Leftist politics are institutionalized and formal political actors operating in and around the state. Although this chapter does not prove the futility of dissensus politics, it does contradict Leftist skepticism of formal politics. Institutionalized formal political actors have great capacity to influence poverty, and the pessimistic mistrust of formal political institutions by some Leftist thinkers appears to be unjustified. While the U.S. Democratic Party is probably a weaker advocate for the poor than the true Leftist parties of Western Europe, a variety of other Leftist politics have been very effective in reducing poverty. Unions and Leftist parties may have weaknesses, but they still accomplish poverty reduction.

It is certainly possible that the radical Left matters to poverty, as it bubbles up to the surface and influences poverty. But, it is probably not by the sort of dissensus politics advocated by Piven and Cloward. Rather, far-Leftist parties can pull more center-Leftist parties toward greater egalitarianism through coalitions in PR systems. In PR systems, a communist or Green party might be a necessary partner for Leftist governance. Even though this gives far-Leftist parties some influence, it is still in an institutionalized formal political arena, not through protests in the streets. In the end, a comprehensive and effective strategy to reduce poverty should concentrate on formal, institutionalized Leftist politics.[71]

In summary, this chapter documents the important role of Leftist collective political actors as sources of poverty reduction. Thinkers across the disciplinary and political spectrum often assert that poverty is an unfortunate by-product of economic and demographic factors. By contrast, this analysis demonstrates that poverty is also the consequence of the power and institutions within the formal politics of affluent Western democracies. More specifically, the results show that during the latter period of the twentieth century, the strength of Leftist collective political actors was mostly channeled through but partly combined with the welfare state to reduce poverty. Though the welfare state remains the paramount and proximate influence on poverty, a full understanding of the causes of poverty in affluent Western democracies should recognize the important role of Leftist collective political actors.

6

The Poverty of Liberal Economics

Tours of poor communities are a recurring spectacle of American political history. John Kennedy, Lyndon Johnson, Robert Kennedy and Joseph Clark, and Paul Wellstone all utilized tours to draw attention to American poverty. Mimicking their pageantry, in the summer of 1999, President Clinton conducted a four-day, six-state tour of poor communities.[1] Throughout, Clinton promised opportunity for corporations who invest in poor neighborhoods. Ceremoniously, he unveiled a new Walgreen's in East St. Louis, promoted the Bank of America's $500 million "catalyst fund" that would make equity investments in poor areas, and attended the annual meeting of a corporate-sponsored vocational education center in Los Angeles.[2]

Many commentators doubted the sincerity of what one critic called "Clinton's Cosmetic Poverty Tour."[3] Senator Paul Wellstone lamented, "I can't help but be skeptical." James Patterson, a historian of antipoverty movements, said, "I don't think this is terribly exciting news." The renowned poverty scholar Christopher Jencks remarked, "One of the ways I preserve my mental health is to read as little as possible about Bill Clinton."[4] Having been a staff lawyer on Robert Kennedy's tour and having resigned as one of Clinton's assistant secretaries of the Department of Health and Human Services to protest the 1996 welfare reforms, Peter Edelman was uniquely critical. He argued that Clinton "should stop referring to them as 'pockets' of poverty. Persistent poverty is endemic in cities and rural areas and is increasingly present, if less visibly so, in suburbs."[5] Because Clinton did not conduct the tour until his seventh year in office, coupled with the lack of substance and financial commitment to his proposals, his tour left many poverty advocates and scholars disappointed.

Reflecting the historical legacy of U.S. social policy, however, an equally noteworthy feature of Clinton's tour was the devotion to liberal economics. At every stop, Clinton emphasized the need for private sector and market-oriented initiatives. In Pine Ridge, South Dakota, Clinton sought $980 million in tax credits to stimulate $6 billion in private investment for businesses to create jobs in poor areas.[6] In Hazard, Kentucky, Clinton stressed, "This is a time to bring more jobs and investment and hope to the areas of our country that have not fully participated in this economic recovery." In East St. Louis, Clinton's chief economic adviser, Gene Sperling, explained, "The goal is not to ask people to make charitable contributions, but to make companies take a second look in our own backyard where there could be profitable business opportunities while also helping rebuild communities that have been left behind." In Clarksdale, Mississippi, while visiting the Waterfield Cabinet Company factory that had recently been rescued from bankruptcy, Clinton proclaimed, "This is a good business opportunity here."[7] In Watts, California, Clinton emphasized the necessity of raising the human capital and education levels of poor people. Clinton's suggestions were labeled "an alternative approach," but really were a mix of older market initiatives, including empowerment zones, community development financial institutions, and enterprise communities.[8] All of these initiatives highlight and depend upon corporate profits as a major incentive for investment in poor areas. Throughout his tour, Clinton offered exclusively liberal economic solutions to poverty.[9]

Clinton's agenda in many ways mirrored the main intellectual currents in the social science of poverty. Indeed, it is not unreasonable to suggest that liberal economics is the dominant social scientific explanation for poverty. Throughout recent research, public policy, and conventional wisdom, liberal economics is used to account for trends in U.S. poverty and cross-national and historical variation in poverty.[10] Though most classical liberals rarely analyzed poverty explicitly, their ideas and arguments implicitly underlie much poverty scholarship, and popular polemics on poverty—for example, Charles Murray's *Losing Ground*—often rest solely on a simplistic rendition of the principles of liberal economics.[11] As I show below, liberal economics cuts across the political spectrum. Liberal economics is so deep-seated in contemporary thinking about poverty that it is found in both the intellectual Left and Right.

While liberal economics exerts great influence, systematic evaluations of the approach have rarely been undertaken. In particular, few have articulated the core precepts of the liberal economic explanation of poverty, demonstrated its coherence, and subjected it to empirical scrutiny.[12] In this chapter, I first review the core elements of the liberal economics of poverty by identifying strands in classic and contemporary liberals. Also, I review recent empirical social science and policy developments that display its contemporary manifestations. Second, I operationalize each of the tenets of liberal economics and conduct an empirical analysis of affluent Western democracies. In the process, I compare the performance of liberal economics to institutionalized power relations theory. Ultimately, based on these results and others' findings, I critique liberal economics and advocate for institutionalized power relations theory as a superior explanation of poverty.

The Liberal Economic Account

By labeling liberal economics this way, I mean to explicitly acknowledge that liberal economics does not represent all of economics, economists, or economic approaches to poverty. Rather, I am referring to a set of implicit, core assumptions that underlie much public policy, conventional wisdom, and social science research. These core assumptions cohere with each other, but are somewhat severable—some scholars support a few of the precepts more than the others.

Despite a tradition of economic commentary on poverty, a mature liberal economic theory of poverty has rarely been articulated.[13] In turn, detailing the liberal economics of poverty involves identifying a set of commonalities that underlie social science theory and research. Based on such an effort, liberal economics can be distilled to a set of four theoretical precepts: harmonious progress, free market capitalism, human capital and worker productivity, and supply and demand. Arguing that liberal economics can be reduced to four precepts is possible only because of its intention to be a simple and generalizable explanation that applies across historical and cultural contexts.[14] This sweeping universality and generalizability is a major source of the extensive influence of liberal economics in the social sciences.

Harmonious Progress

Among the deeply held beliefs in liberal economics is a faith in the general harmony of interests of a progressing economy. In short, what is good for the nation is good for the nation's poor.[15] Though liberal economic proponents might concede that prosperity sometimes benefits employers more than employees or the affluent more than the poor, prosperity is expected to benefit all. To reduce poverty, the clear solution is to help the economy grow and to let harmonious progress take hold.[16] This contention reflects the discipline of economics' long-standing and prevailing concern with the preconditions for and the maintenance of economic growth. In turn, economic growth remains the focal point of liberal economics in explaining national levels of poverty.

More specifically, liberal economics contends that with a rising tide of economic prosperity, the amount of poverty in society will decrease.

Because of the optimistic confidence of classical liberal economists like John Stuart Mill in the power of economic growth and industrialization, the prediction naturally followed that poverty would one day be eliminated.[17] When discussing how economic growth transformed society, Friedrich Hayek acknowledged "dark spots in society" that were slow to experience a rising standard of living, but he also emphasized, "There was probably no class that did not substantially benefit from the general advance."[18] Liberal economists have even extended this claim to assert that economic growth reduces relative deprivation as well as absolute deprivation.[19] As Milton Friedman claims, "The economic progress achieved in the capitalist societies has been accompanied by a drastic diminution in inequality."[20] Thus, economic growth is commonly identified as the dominant strategy to combat both absolute and relative poverty.

Many contemporary researchers emphasize the primacy of economic growth for alleviating poverty as well.[21] David Ellwood and Lawrence Summers even go so far as to conclude, "Economic performance is the *dominant* determinant of the poverty rate."[22] Others argue that although economic growth had a smaller effect on poverty in the 1970s and 1980s than in earlier decades, the relationship was strong again in the 1990s. Robert Haveman and Jonathan Schwabish write, "Strong economic growth and high employment may again be the nation's *most* effective antipoverty policy instrument."[23] A widely publicized U.S. Census Bureau report concluded that the strong economy was mainly responsible for the late-1990s drop in official U.S. poverty and post-welfare reform decline in recipiency.[24] In a recent state-of-the-art test, Craig Gundersen and James Ziliak conclude, "Aggregate business cycle and economic growth do, in fact, 'lift all boats.'...A strong macroeconomy at both the state and national levels reduces the number of families with incomes below the poverty line and the severity of poverty."[25]

As one of the most visible intellectuals studying poverty (and previously a clear critic of liberal economics), Rebecca Blank provides an illustrative case of liberal economic belief in economic growth. In the mid-1990s, Blank was one of the more persuasive skeptics of liberal economic faith in growth. In her 1997 book, *It Takes a Nation*, Blank wrote, "Economic growth is not likely to be effective in the near future in reducing poverty....Poverty is harder to address through broad-based economic growth policies now than thirty years ago."[26] Yet, only *three* years later, after serving in the Clinton administration, Blank completely reversed her position. She wrote: "A strong macroeconomy matters more than anything else," and "the first and most important lesson for anti-poverty warriors from the 1990s is that sustained economic growth is a wonderful thing."[27] The very first line of Blank, Sheldon Danziger, and Robert Schoeni's book *Working and Poor* reads: "Fluctuations in the economy have a strong effect on the extent of poverty and well-being among low-income families."[28] Although Blank has often been a supporter of generous welfare programs,[29] her policy recommendations in what was labeled "A New Agenda for Fighting Poverty" in *It*

Takes a Nation prioritize a growing economy. Thus, even among economists that might appear more nuanced, one finds a devoted liberal economic commitment to harmonious progress.

Overall, much scholarship emphasizes economic growth's power to reduce poverty. This precept underlies the specific arguments of liberal economics about worker productivity and the supply and demand of labor. Further, the emphasis on harmonious progress in liberal economics has key implications for government intervention and the welfare state. Thus, the paramount role for economic growth guides the remaining three precepts.

Free Market Capitalism

Liberal economics holds that the most effective system for ensuring prosperity is a free market. Because prosperity and economic growth are the best mechanisms to combat poverty, free market capitalism is purportedly the best system for reducing poverty in the long term.[30] Classical liberals emphasized the efficacy of competitive market mechanisms and had a general distrust of government intervention.[31] The free market was strongly preferred, and liberals routinely expressed skepticism about government programs to ameliorate social problems. In describing the United States, for example, Friedman emblematically argues that free markets have caused remarkable improvement in life and that, "[g]overnment measures have hampered, not helped, this development."[32] When confronted with the specific problem of poverty, liberal economists often maintain this preference for the free market. Some scholars go even further and argue that free market capitalism reduces inequality and poverty. Even though much empirical research has shown otherwise since, Friedman claimed, "Capitalism leads to less inequality than alternative systems of organization and that the development of capitalism has greatly lessened the extent of inequality.... Among the Western countries alone, inequality appears to be less, in any meaningful sense, the more highly capitalist the country is: less in Britain than in France, less in the United States than in Britain."[33]

Beyond the general criticism of government intervention, the welfare state has been the object of vigorous criticism. Of course, many contemporary liberal economists, especially "neoliberals," are fully aware of how states can affect affluence and poverty. However, these thinkers are usually normatively opposed to governments and welfare states. Typically, liberal economists contend that the drawbacks of government intervention outweigh the potential benefits for poverty. Although many liberal economists concede that the welfare state might initially reduce poverty, most contend that in the long term it actually worsens and deepens poverty. Though present in contemporary debates, this thinking is actually as old as the welfare state itself.[34] Purportedly, the welfare state is counterproductive and inefficiently hinders the free market from achieving its full potential. David Ricardo argued at the beginning of the nineteenth century that we should cut back government assistance to the poor and teach the poor to be independent. As Ricardo summarized, "No scheme for the amendment of the poor laws merits the least attention, which has not their abolition for its ultimate object."[35] In recent years, there has been no shortage of liberal economic thinkers arguing for a reduced welfare state.[36] In fact, James Galbraith suggests that the classic preference for free markets and the reduction of the welfare state is probably a majority view in the economics profession.[37] Liberal economic critics of the welfare state argue that generous welfare programs have direct and indirect effects that actually increase poverty.

Directly, welfare generosity encourages dependency and longer poverty spells.[38] Thus, the welfare state might have positive effects on poverty. Indirectly, welfare generosity provides an incentive for unemployment and labor force nonparticipation (e.g., early retirement or single-earner couples).[39] Also, many scholars contend that the generous welfare states of large Western European governments contribute to labor market rigidity and inefficiency and hence limit economic performance.[40] If the welfare state encourages unemployment and labor force nonparticipation and reduces economic growth and productivity, the poverty-reducing effects of the welfare state might be counterbalanced. If these economic variables have large effects on poverty, the welfare state could be so counterproductive that it actually indirectly increases poverty.

Several studies evaluating the 1996 U.S. welfare reform seem to support these liberal economic criticisms of the welfare state.[41] For instance, a study by the Rockefeller Institute found that two-thirds of the people who left New York's welfare rolls found work.[42] Political rhetoric echoed these findings. President Clinton called welfare reform a "whole happy scenario."[43] Celebrating New York's successful reform, Mayor Rudy Guiliani said, "Today marks a milestone of replacing the culture of dependency in New York City with the culture of work and employment."[44]

Even more intriguingly, this liberal economic view has influenced many economists who otherwise function as public intellectual critics of rising social inequality. After its economic crisis in the early 1990s, even the progressive labor economist Richard Freeman and colleagues characterized the generous Swedish welfare state as "nearly impossible for the country to afford," "unsustainable," and "dysfunctional."[45] Paul Krugman displays implicit liberal economic skepticism for welfare programs in his widely read book on the declining fortunes of middle- and working-class Americans, *The Age of Diminished Expectations*. Analyzing historical trends in U.S. poverty, Krugman writes, "Neither generosity nor niggardliness seems to make much difference to the spread of the underclass."[46] Krugman goes on to argue that Lyndon Johnson's war on poverty was ultimately unsuccessful at reducing poverty. While citing Murray's book *Losing Ground* (a well-known conservative attack on welfare), Krugman specifically claims, "Despite sharp increases in aid to the poor between the late 1960s and the mid-1970s, poverty remained as intractable as ever, and the underclass that is the most visible sign of poverty grew alarmingly."[47] Given Krugman's vocal criticism of neoliberalism and because he is so influential among the intellectual Left, it is relevant to point out that most research on U.S. social policy contradicts Krugman. On another occasion, Krugman attributed "Eurosclerosis" to Europe's rigid welfare state institutions that prevent the free market creation of "jobs, jobs, and jobs."[48]

Overall, liberal economics holds that free markets are more effective for cultivating economic growth and, as a result, combating poverty. While these first two precepts are widely agreed upon by economists, their appeal may be less robust in other social sciences.[49] By contrast, the next two are conventional wisdom in poverty research across the social sciences and in public policy.

Productivity and Human Capital

Liberal economics has long stressed that if a worker is more productive, his or her earnings will rise and the likelihood of poverty will diminish.[50] On a national level, the average worker productivity should predict the amount of poverty in the labor force (and hence population).[51] Further, enhanced productivity reduces poverty indirectly by boosting the economic growth of a nation. Thus, liberal economic efforts to reduce poverty have often fixated on raising the productivity of workers. The predominant mechanism utilized to raise productivity (both within and outside of liberal economics) has traditionally been human capital—the skills, training, and education invested in a person.[52] Thus, liberal economics typically advocates raising human capital, through training and education, in order to raise productivity and as a result decrease poverty.[53]

In a rare comment related to poverty, Adam Smith explained the inequalities of employment solely as a function of productivity, human capital variables, and hardships of particular employment—naturally more grueling, physically intensive, or intellectually demanding work would pay higher wages.[54] Lamenting the growth of the class of unskilled laborers and the poor, Alfred Marshall argued that a nation should "[d]iminish the supply of labour, incapable of any but unskilled work; in order that the average income of the country may rise faster still . . . . Education must be made more thorough." Linking the education of poor children to their chances at social mobility, Marshall argued on behalf of increasing the productivity of the children of poor families: "The children of unskilled workers need to be made capable of earning the wages of skilled work." Marshall argued specifically that children of unskilled laborers should be encourage to develop economically productive skills, which at that time meant becoming artisans and craftsmen.[55]

More than the other precepts, the emphasis on productivity, and relatedly on education and human capital, is shared beyond the boundaries of economics and into other disciplines. Sociological theories of stratification have long held that productivity and human capital are the key mechanisms for social mobility, and hence prevent workers from being poor. By valuing training and human capital, Kingsley Davis and Wilbert Moore's classic functionalist explanation of inequality is broadly consistent with the liberal economics of poverty.[56] Status attainment researchers emphasize the role of education and productivity in avoiding poverty. While rejecting hypotheses about a "vicious cycle of poverty" across generations, Peter Blau and Otis Duncan wrote, "Education exerts the strongest direct effect on occupational achievements."[57] Subsequent mobility researchers emphasized that education secures socioeconomic attainment and prevents the intergenerational transmission of disadvantage.[58] Various studies in this tradition have concluded that education is essential for avoiding the intergenerational transmission of poverty.[59] By emphasizing the importance of education, human capital, and productivity for an individual's attainment, sociological traditions of inequality research share much with liberal economics.

The liberal economic emphasis on productivity and human capital has a long history in U.S. social policy as well.[60] The strategy of equipping the poor with human capital was central to Lyndon Johnson's war on poverty. In their classic book *Inequality*, Jencks and colleagues explained that the war on poverty emphasized expanding education and equalizing skills: "Many people imagined that if schools could equalize people's cognitive skills this would equalize their bargaining power as adults. In such a system, nobody would end up very poor."[61] Michael Katz also points out that Johnson's plan was modeled partly on "Mobilization for Youth," a New York program aimed at combating delinquency by lifting poor minority youth over the barriers to mobility.[62] In fact, two of the four key parts of Johnson's plan were job training and education for the poor. In his well-known study of the black family, Daniel Moynihan argued that the poor performance of African-American youths on educational tests signaled a greater likelihood of poverty.[63] Finally, much of the 1996 welfare reform focused on job training and education. Where welfare reform has been unsuccessful, human capital has often been the explanation for the inability of the poor to find work. John C. Weicher of the Hudson Policy Institute remarked, "If you can read and write only at a third-grade level, the economy has to get extremely strong for there to be a market for you at the minimum wage or any wage."[64]

Thus, emerging from liberal economics, a long history of scholarship and policy prioritizes education, human capital, and productivity for alleviating poverty. Especially among Leftist economists, there has been a nearly unwavering faith in the expansion of education as a solution for poverty.[65] David Gordon explains, "Many if not most economists argue publicly that if the government does anything in this area [poverty reduction], it should concentrate on upgrading the education and skills training of those with relatively low earnings."[66] To decrease the likelihood that an individual worker will be poor, it is broadly accepted that investing in human capital and raising the marginal productivity of the worker are very effective.[67] On the whole, efforts to raise the human capital and productivity of the poor have been one of the most widely supported ideas in the social sciences.

Supply and Demand

Like any other economic outcome, liberal economists have long asserted that national levels of poverty adhere to the laws of supply and demand in the labor force. Manifestly, poverty is considered a function of the national rates of unemployment.[68] Ricardo explained that unemployment increases the likelihood of poverty directly for the unemployed because they have no income. Ricardo also theorized that unemployment indirectly increased unemployment by lowering of wages for those still in the workforce—as the greater supply of unemployed reduces the demand for the employed.[69] Linked to the earlier precept on worker productivity, liberal economists argue that unproductive workers do not meet market demands for skilled labor and end up unemployed.[70] Thus, the poor lack the human capital to be productive as both the demand for more productive workers and the supply of less productive workers increase. Liberal economists have historically argued that to alleviate poverty, unemployment must be reduced.[71]

Many contemporary economists stress that the first and greatest priority for reducing poverty is to lower unemployment and to encourage job opportunities of the poor.[72] In their study of poverty across the U.S. states, Gundersen and Ziliak found, "A one-percentage-point decrease in the unemployment rate leads to a 4.5% decline in the short-run poverty rate."[73] Isabel Sawhill reviewed the scholarship linking poverty and unemployment and basically concluded that Ricardo's assessment of direct and indirect effects still applies today.[74] In many studies, unemployment is identified as more influential for poverty than is any other factor.[75] For example, Richard Hauser and Brian Nolan argue that unemployment is more important than social policy in explaining trends in poverty in Western Europe.[76]

While more complex and contextual than liberal economics, even William Julius Wilson's influential sociological research ultimately concludes that unemployment and joblessness are the dominant sources of concentrated inner-city poverty.[77] Partly as a result, sociologists often focus on unemployment and earnings as key determinants of poverty.[78] For example, Walter Korpi argues that mass unemployment is the greatest threat to Western European equality.[79] Numerous studies focus on unemployment or underemployment as measures of the economic changes that cause poverty.[80] Across the social sciences, unemployment is viewed as one of the most important causes of poverty.

Testing the Liberal Economic Model

To summarize, the liberal economic model involves four precepts—each of which can be stated as hypotheses. First, economic growth has a negative effect on poverty. Second, government intervention into the free market increases poverty. Third, increased productivity and human capital reduce poverty.

Fourth, unemployment increases poverty. This model represents a coherent, albeit severable, set of explanations for poverty in affluent democracies.

The remainder of the chapter empirically evaluates liberal economics. Surprisingly, despite the widespread influence of liberal economics, relatively few rigorous tests of it have been undertaken. Even rarer have been tests that analyze countries besides the United States.

Measuring Poverty

Some readers of this evaluation may object to the relative measurement of poverty. While chapter 2 offered a general justification for relative measures, it is worthwhile to consider whether relative poverty is appropriate for testing liberal economics. Most of the support for liberal economics has come from studies with the official U.S. measure of poverty. Because the official U.S. measure is often considered to be an absolute measure, one could argue that liberal economics really is a model for absolute poverty. Of course, characterizing the official measure as an absolute measure is highly debatable if one takes a realistic look at its problems (see chapter 2). Nevertheless, a test with relative poverty could be considered less relevant.

There are three reasons this argument is mistaken. First, liberal economists often actually conceptualize poverty as a relative phenomenon. Two classical liberal economic theorists were very clear in arguing that poverty is relative. In *The Wealth of Nations*, Adam Smith defined poverty relatively:

> Whatever the custom of the country renders it indecent for creditable people, even of the lowest order, to be without. A linen shirt, for example, is, strictly speaking, not a necessary of life. The Greeks and Romans lived, I suppose, very comfortably, though they had no linen. But in present times, through the greater part of Europe, a creditable day-labourer would be ashamed to appear in public without a linen shirt, the want of which would be supposed to denote that disgraceful degree of poverty, which, it is presumed, no body can well fall into without extreme bad conduct. Custom, in the same manner, has rendered leather shoes a necessary of life in England. The poorest creditable person of either sex would be ashamed to appear in public without them.... In France, they are necessaries neither to men nor to women.... Under necessaries therefore, I comprehend, not only those things which nature, but those things which the established rules of decency have rendered necessary to the lowest rank of people.[81]

In a careful study of Smith's writings, Geoffrey Gilbert concludes that Smith defined poverty as relative economic position and that material goods mattered because they influenced social status or one's standing in social interaction.[82] Gilbert further explains that Smith characterized poverty in terms of psychic pain, social isolation and relative inferiority: "Thus poverty, as addressed by Smith in 1759, did not subject the individual to hunger, malnutrition, disease, lack of clothing or shelter; rather, it shamed him through a pained awareness of his inferior position in the social scale."[83] Perhaps more strikingly, in *The Constitution of Liberty*, Hayek wrote, "Poverty has, in consequence, become a relative, rather than an absolute concept....Most of what we strive for are things we want because others already have them."[84] Even though many contemporary economists use the official U.S. measure, when pressed to define poverty, they often fall into the same reasoning as these classic liberal economists and define poverty as a relative concept.[85] When conducting analyses of other countries, economists (who, of course, vary in their support for liberal economics) overwhelmingly rely on relative measures.[86]

Second, liberal economic justifications for using the official U.S. measure suggest that convenience and convention are the real reason for its use. Rather than methodologically and theoretically justifying the official U.S. measure, or any absolute measure, scholars typically defend it on the grounds that it is readily available. For example, in his study of the connection between economic performance and official U.S. poverty, Freeman acknowledges in a footnote, "The official poverty rate is an imperfect indicator." However, he also claims, "The alternative measures of poverty show a similar pattern of change over time and similar differences among groups. Thus, little is lost by using the official rate in analysis."[87] Unfortunately, many have shown that the second claim is simply false.[88] As I showed in chapter 3, the extent of and trends in poverty are not at all similar with the official measure compared to a relative measure.

Third, there is ample historical evidence that the official U.S. measure resulted from an unbalanced predisposition for liberal economics. The official measure probably biases the results to be unrealistically supportive of liberal economics. In her history of poverty research, Alice O'Connor convincingly demonstrates that the original choice of the official U.S. measure, and the subsequent scholarly focus on absolute poverty, was a political choice to complement the preexisting emphasis on economic growth and to find an easily achievable target for winning the "war on poverty."[89] O'Connor explains that leading economists in the Johnson administration sought a "politically workable definition or concept of poverty," and this led to the focus on absolute deprivation. Indeed, those economists set aside their own long-standing concerns with persistent income inequality because of the political desire to avoid discussion of redistribution.[90] O'Connor emphasizes that this focus on absolute deprivation "would lend itself to the growth-centered strategy they were proposing."[91] Essentially, policy makers had a prior commitment to economic growth, free markets, productivity, and unemployment and, as a result, subsequently sought a measure that would fit this liberal economic agenda.

Rather than following the conventional use of the official U.S. measure, it would be better to provide a theoretical and methodological case for measuring poverty, and then evaluate the causal sources of poverty. If liberal economics provides a successful model of poverty, it should explain poverty when poverty is operationalized objectively—not in a way that is biased in favor of a predetermined liberal economic model. Ultimately, as I argue in chapter 2, it is best to use a relative measure of poverty. Thus, an analysis of relative poverty can serve as an appropriate evaluation of the effectiveness of the liberal economic model.

Nevertheless, for the sake of argument, I also present an analysis of absolute poverty toward the end of this chapter. As I explained in chapters 2 and 3, there are many problems with absolute measures. Yet, to give liberal economics an even better chance of being a useful theory of poverty, I empirically evaluate absolute poverty as well. In this analysis, I analyze a cross section of the 18 countries from the Luxembourg Income Study (LIS) at one point in time—the preferred approach of Lane Kenworthy, one of the leading advocates for this absolute measure of poverty.[92] Also, I do so because comparisons of absolute poverty over time are even more problematic.

Measuring Liberal Economics

In the analyses that follow, I present the most supportive results for liberal economics. In other words, I try to give liberal economics its best chance of being confirmed. For each of the liberal economic precepts, several measures were considered. In other research, I displayed the various possible ways to measure each liberal economic precept.[93] Here, I exclusively show the most supportive operationalization. I should add that these models do not include some of the control variables that were featured in previous chapters: manufacturing employment, female labor force participation, the elderly population, and single motherhood. I compare those variables' influence against liberal economic variables in chapter 7. Again, I present the models without those controls in an attempt to present the most supportive evidence for liberal economics. Adding these controls weakens the evidence for liberal economics (and strengthens the case for institutionalized power relations theory).

First, I assess the harmonious progress of economic expansion with *economic growth*, measured as the three-year moving average of the real annual rate of change in gross domestic product (GDP), in purchasing power parity (PPP) dollars. Second, I measured the extent of the government's intervention into the free market with the *welfare generosity index* developed in chapter 4. Because liberal economics contends that welfare generosity might be counterproductive at higher levels and/or might have declining rates of return, the models also include *welfare generosity index squared*. If this squared term has a negative effect, this implies that welfare generosity becomes less effective at higher levels. I also considered a variety of possible measures that might track government intervention into the market without being a nuanced indicator of the welfare state, including government revenue as a percentage of GDP. However, none of these alternative measures was more supportive of liberal economics. Third, I measure *productivity* as the GDP (in PPP) per civilian employee, with the previous year's values in real

1995 U.S. dollars. In analyses available upon request, several measures of educational attainment—including the adult average years of schooling and the percentage of the adult population with or without a secondary degree— were considered, but none of these alternatives provided supportive evidence of liberal economics. Fourth, I measured the supply and demand of workers as contemporaneous *unemployment*. This variable measures the percentage of the labor force that is currently without employment. In addition to these liberal economic variables, I include the second most important institutionalized power relations variable, *proportional representation* (PR). Showing this variable's and welfare generosity's effects allows me to compare the performance of liberal economics against institutionalized power relations theory.

Does Liberal Economics Explain Poverty Better Than Institutionalized Power Relations Theory?

Descriptive Patterns

As with chapters 4 and 5, I begin by displaying the basic associations between the liberal economic variables and poverty. To simplify the presentation, I show only overall headcount poverty. Because chapter 4 gave so much attention to the association between the welfare state and poverty, I do not show that plot here (see figures 4.1–4.4).

Figure 6.1 shows that there is a relatively weak negative association $(r = -.17)$ between economic growth and overall headcount poverty. The association is in the expected negative direction, but compared to the associations with the welfare state or Leftist politics, for example, the correlation is much weaker. Several countries that experienced high levels of economic growth, including Luxembourg (LUX) and earlier years for Germany (FRG), did experience lower poverty. Yet, at the same time, Ireland (IRE) and Canada (CAN) had high growth and high poverty, while Belgium (BEL), Finland (FIN), and Sweden (SWE) had years of low (or even negative) growth and low poverty. Although there is an association between economic growth and poverty, the association is not strong.

Figure 6.2 shows that the association between productivity and poverty is in the opposite of the direction expected by liberal economics. The correlation is not particularly strong $(r = .29)$ and is surprisingly positive. Countries like Germany and the Netherlands (NET) have low to moderate poverty and lower productivity, while the United States (USA) and Italy (ITA) have higher poverty and higher productivity. There are certainly exceptions to this pattern; for example, Luxembourg has high productivity and low poverty. Thus, the broader pattern is only a moderate positive association.

Figure 6.3 demonstrates a moderate positive association between unemployment and poverty $(r = .30)$. This confirms liberal economic claims about

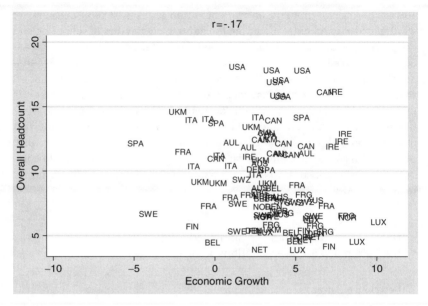

Figure 6.1.   The Association between Economic Growth and Overall
Headcount Poverty ($r = -.17$)

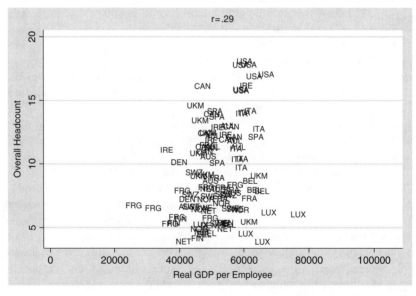

Figure 6.2.   The Association between Productivity and Overall
Headcount Poverty ($r = .29$)

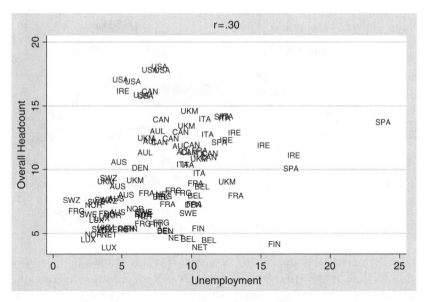

Figure 6.3.   The Association between Unemployment and Overall
Headcount Poverty ($r = .30$)

the link between the supply and demand of workers and the level of poverty.
When unemployment was high, for example, in Spain (SPA) or Ireland,
poverty tended to be much higher. When unemployment was lower, for
example, in Switzerland (SWZ) or Germany in the earlier years, poverty
was low. Again, there are outliers, like the United States with its low unemployment and high poverty and Finland with its higher unemployment and
low poverty. Yet, the general pattern is moderately positive, which is consistent with liberal economics.

Beyond the cross-sectional patterns, one could examine trends in poverty
over time and see if they correspond to trends in economic growth, productivity, and unemployment. The period around 1990 for Canada and the
United States provide useful examples.[94] This comparison is instructive
because the countries are similar in many regards, which somewhat controls
for other factors. Moreover, this period should show liberal economics'
relevance because a rather notable world recession in the early 1990s should
have triggered changes in poverty.

In 1987, Canada experienced solid economic growth of 2.94%, followed
by a contraction of −.75% in 1991 and a strong expansion of 3.91% in 1994.
Unemployment rose from 8.9% in 1987 to 10.3% in 1991, and remained at
10.4% in 1994. During this time, productivity grew modestly but steadily
from $43,593.40 to $44,026.31 to $45,482.58 (per employee). According to
liberal economics, poverty probably should have risen from 1987 to 1991 and
fallen in 1994. Despite these changes, overall headcount poverty barely

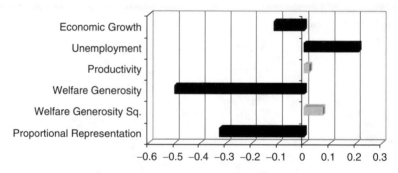

Figure 6.4.   Standardized Effects of Liberal Economic and Institutionalized Power Relations Theory Variables for Overall Headcount Poverty. [The dark bars are significantly different from zero ($p < .05$). The shaded bars are not significantly different from zero. See appendix table A.18 for details.]

moved from 11.36% in 1987 to 10.96% in 1991 to 11.26% in 1994. The decline from 1987 to 1991 is unexpected given the contraction in economic growth and rising unemployment, and the increase in 1994 is unexpected given the strong economic growth and rising productivity.

In the United States, the economy grew substantially (4.62%) in 1986 and moderately (2.72%) in 1994, yet was stagnant (0.59%) in 1991. Over those three time points, unemployment steadily declined from 7% to 6.8% to 6.1%, and productivity steadily rose from $55,188.58 to $56,448.53 to $57,729.75 (per employee). According to liberal economics, growth should have reduced poverty in 1986 and 1994 but failed to reduce it in 1991, while declining unemployment and rising productivity should have steadily alleviated poverty. Like Canada, however, there was hardly any change in poverty rates. The overall headcount rose from 17.8% in 1986 to 18.1% in 1991, while unemployment and productivity should have pushed it in the opposite direction. When the economy expanded in 1994, poverty declined only a tiny amount to 17.8%. Thus, upon close inspection, these countries, which should have experienced changes in poverty around the early 1990s recession, barely experienced any change at all. The link between liberal economics and poverty was very tenuous in Canada and the United States.

Models of Overall Poverty

In figure 6.4, I test if liberal economic variables influence poverty and how their influence compares to institutionalized power relations variables. As figure 6.4 shows, economic growth and unemployment have significant effects in the expected direction for overall headcount poverty. Interestingly, productivity fails to have a significant effect on overall headcount poverty, and its coefficient is even positively signed. For a standard deviation increase in economic growth, overall headcount poverty is expected to decline by about 0.12 standard deviations. For a standard deviation increase in unemployment, poverty is expected to increase by 0.21 standard deviations.

Though these two liberal economic variables have a significant effect, the more evident result in figure 6.4 is the continuing powerful negative effects of the institutionalized power relations variables: welfare generosity and PR. These findings confirm what was shown in chapters 4 and 5, and it is valuable to mention three additional points for the purposes of this chapter. First, this demonstrates that there is absolutely no evidence that broader government intervention into the free market has any counterproductive poverty-increasing effects. As mentioned above, there is simply no general measure of state intervention that could be utilized to show a significant positive effect for overall headcount poverty. Second, welfare generosity squared does not have a significant effect. Thus, there is no evidence that there is a declining rate of return to welfare generosity or that high levels of welfare generosity are counterproductive. Third, the effects of the institutionalized power relations variables are far more powerful than the effects of economic growth and unemployment. Even if one summed the absolute values of the standardized effects of economic growth and unemployment (0.12 + 0.21 = 0.33), their collective influence is far smaller than the collective standardized effects for welfare generosity and PR (0.50 + 0.32 = 0.83). Thus, even though there is some marginal benefit to a growing economy and declining unemployment, the influence of welfare generosity and a PR system is far more consequential for overall headcount poverty. Because liberal economics prioritizes harmonious progress and the supply and demand over social policy, these results challenge its propositions.

Figure 6.5 provides similar results for overall poverty intensity. Economic growth has a significant negative effect, unemployment has a significant positive effect, and productivity is insignificant. For a standard deviation increase in economic growth, poverty intensity is expected to decline by about 0.13 standard deviations. For a standard deviation increase in unemployment, poverty intensity is expected to grow 0.22 standard deviations. The combined effect of these variables (0.35) is far smaller than the collective standardized effects for welfare generosity and PR (0.83). Also important, welfare generosity squared does not have a significant effect. Therefore, the results contradict liberal economics. A country can expect much greater progress in reducing poverty by expanding the welfare state and moving to a PR system than by enhancing the business cycle. Economic growth and unemployment matter to poverty, but they matter far less than institutionalized power relations.

These results, in short, answer the question heading this section with a resounding no. Liberal economics does not explain poverty better than institutionalized power relations theory. As a further illustration of this point, I counterfactually simulate the values of overall headcount poverty for Sweden and the United States. This simulation mimics the simulations from chapters 4 and 5 (see figures 4.5 and 5.13), but in this case, I calculate poverty as if

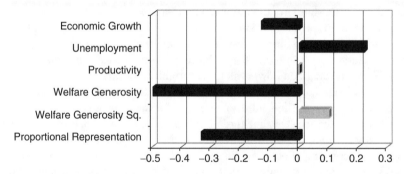

Figure 6.5.   Standardized Effects of Liberal Economic and Institutionalized Power Relations Theory Variables for Overall Poverty Intensity. [The dark bars are significantly different from zero ($p < .05$). The shaded bars are not significantly different from zero. See appendix table A.18 for details.]

Sweden's economy performed one standard deviation worse and the U.S. economy performed one standard deviation better. Thus, in both cases, I estimate poverty with a one standard deviation change in economic growth and unemployment to illustrate the combined impact of these liberal economic variables. The reader should recall that changing welfare generosity and the PR system one standard deviation resulted in a significantly narrower gap between low poverty Sweden and the high poverty United States (see figure 5.13).

By contrast, figure 6.6 reveals that even if the U.S. economy performed much better and Sweden's economy performed much worse, the gap in

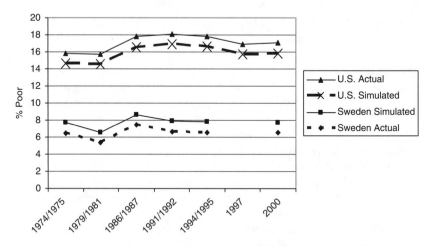

Figure 6.6.   Actual and Simulated (± 1 Standard Deviation for Economic Growth and for Unemployment) Overall Headcount Poverty: United States and Sweden

poverty between the two would not significantly change. For example, in 2000, the United States would still have an overall headcount poverty rate (15.8%) more than twice as high as Sweden's (7.7%). Recalling the patterns in chapter 3, the United States would still have higher overall headcount poverty than every affluent democracy except Ireland.

To be clear, these counterfactual simulations would involve rather unrealistically outstanding economic performance for the United States and very weak economic performance for Sweden. In 2000, this would imply the United States experienced economic growth of 6% and unemployment of less than 0.25%. Sweden's economic growth would have been only 2.5% and unemployment would have been more than 9.3%. Yet, even with such historically extraordinary economic performance, poverty would barely change. These simulations reveal just how ill-conceived U.S. policy is regarding poverty. The United States often emphasizes economic growth and unemployment as mechanisms to combat poverty above all else. But, as this simulation shows, even with record-breaking economic performance, the United States would still be an outlier for its extremely high levels of poverty.

Models of Working-Age Adult Poverty

Another reasonable test of liberal economics might be to examine how the liberal economic model performs for working-age adult poverty. Plausibly, this demographic subgroup should experience the greatest returns from economic performance. If the economy grows and unemployment declines, working-age adults are the most likely to experience lower poverty. Thus, this analysis may provide a more "liberal" test of liberal economics.

Figure 6.7 reveals the same significant variables for working-age adult headcount poverty. Productivity continues to be insignificant and positively

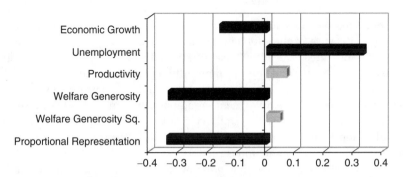

Figure 6.7.   Standardized Effects of Liberal Economic and Institutionalized Power Relations Theory Variables for Working-Age Adult Headcount Poverty. [The dark bars are significantly different from zero ($p < .05$). The shaded bars are not significantly different from zero. See appendix table A. 8 for details.]

signed. This shows that even among working-age adults, as human capital, skills, and productivity increase, there is no clear return to in terms of lower poverty. Economic growth significantly reduces and unemployment significantly increases working-age adult poverty. Consistent with my claim that working age adults provides a more supportive test of liberal economics, the standardized effects of these variables are larger than they were for overall poverty. For a standard deviation increase in economic growth, working-age adult headcount poverty is expected to decline by about 0.16 standard deviations. For a standard deviation increase in unemployment, working-age adult headcount poverty is expected to rise 0.33 standard deviations.

Thus, it is clear that economic performance benefits working-age adults more than the overall population and that liberal economics is a better model of working-age adult than overall poverty. Yet, there are two crucial qualifications. First, welfare generosity still has the second largest effect in the model, with a standardized effect of 0.34. Though welfare generosity has a smaller effect for working-age adults than for the overall population, working-age adult poverty will decline more substantially with a change to welfare generosity than with a change to economic growth or unemployment. Moreover, the largest effect in the model actually belongs to PR, the other institutionalized power relations variable. Thus, the institutionalized power relations variables continue to be more important than the liberal economic variables, even for working-age adult poverty. Second, it is important to keep in mind that poverty is always less common among working-age adults than among children and the elderly. Poverty is simply a less widespread concern for working-age adults than it is for other more vulnerable demographic subgroups. While this provides a more supportive test of liberal economics, it is also a less representative assessment of who is vulnerable to poverty.

Models of Absolute Poverty

As one final test, I examine how well liberal economics explains absolute poverty. Because of the problems of the cross-national standardization of absolute measures of poverty, I examine a model of the 18 affluent Western democracies at only one point in time. Although I examined a host of alternatives, I only present a simple model of the four key independent variables: economic growth, unemployment, productivity, and welfare generosity. Including welfare generosity squared or PR does nothing to change the results, and both would be insignificant. Because there are only 18 cases, I present this more parsimonious model.

Figure 6.8 demonstrates that *none* of these four variables significantly affects absolute poverty. It is interesting that economic growth appears to have a slightly larger effect than welfare generosity in this model (–.29 vs. –.23). But none of the coefficients in this model is even close to statistically significant. Moreover, even if this effect of economic growth was significant, it would still be about half as large as the effect of welfare

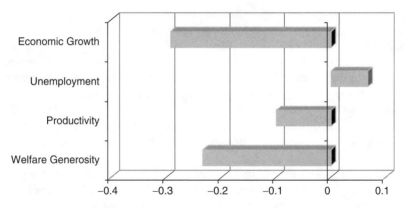

Figure 6.8.   Standardized Effects of Liberal Economic and Institutionalized Power Relations Theory Variables for Absolute Poverty in 18 Affluent Western Democracies. [All bars are not significantly different from zero. See appendix table A.16 for details.]

generosity for relative overall headcount poverty in figure 6.4. So, these insignificant effects are not that large substantively. Also, even with a measure of absolute poverty, there is simply no evidence that welfare generosity counterproductively increases poverty. Ultimately, even in this model set up to favor liberal economics, there really is no supportive evidence.[95]

Conclusion

This chapter sets out to evaluate the liberal economic explanation of poverty. Moreover, it compares how effective liberal economics is relative to institutionalized power relations theory of poverty. After reviewing the classical foundations and contemporary manifestations of liberal economics, I empirically scrutinized how well it explains poverty in affluent democracies since the late 1960s. Ultimately, this chapter is highly critical of liberal economics. Liberal economics does not provide nearly as effective an explanation of poverty as institutionalized power relations theory. Although economic growth and unemployment do influence poverty, the welfare state is far more influential.

The first liberal economic precept, that the harmonious progress of economic growth benefits the poor, was weakly confirmed by the empirical analysis. Economic growth has significant negative effects for overall headcount poverty, overall poverty intensity, and working-age adult headcount poverty. The effect of economic growth, however, is relatively small. For a standard deviation increase in economic growth, poverty is expected to decline by only about 0.15 standard deviations. These analyses refute

Blank's claim, quoted above, that "[a] strong macroeconomy matters more than anything else." Economic growth matters, but not nearly as much as the welfare state or PR systems. Indeed, relying on economic growth as the main mechanism to fight poverty—as the United States often does—is sort of like leaving a manual transmission car in first gear and trying to go faster. You can keep pushing the gas pedal, and revving the engine, but unless one switches to a higher gear, your speed increases only modestly. Much like this, unless the United States switches gears toward a much more generous welfare state, even accelerated economic growth can reduce poverty only modestly.

The second precept held that government intervention into the free market should produce more poverty. Specifically, liberal economics contends that welfare programs are ineffective and counterproductively increase poverty by providing incentives to avoid work or continue in longer poverty spells. In this way, liberal economics stands in direct opposition to institutionalized power relations theory. The analyses, however, contradict this liberal economic precept. Welfare generosity, as was already shown in chapters 4 and 5, has a very large negative effect on poverty. Moreover, welfare generosity squared never has a significant effect. So, there is also no evidence that higher levels of welfare generosity are counterproductive or even have diminishing returns.[96] Because no alternative measure of general government intervention can produce a positive effect on poverty, this confirms the central institutionalized power relations theory: the welfare state is very effective for reducing poverty.

This finding illustrates one of the more dubious features of U.S. poverty and welfare research. Implicitly, if not explicitly, most of the U.S. literature on poverty reflects the assumptions of the liberal economic model regarding welfare programs. Unfortunately, U.S. poverty researchers have had an unbalanced infatuation with trying to detect welfare disincentives and dependency.[97] In the process, considerably less attention has been devoted to comparative analyses of welfare states, and the more salient and clearly beneficial effects of welfare for poverty reduction have been neglected. This preoccupation with hunting for and highlighting small marginal disincentives has led U.S. poverty research not so much to have the wrong answers as to let the debate be dominated by the wrong questions.[98] A positive step for U.S. poverty research would be to reduce the disproportionate focus on dependency and disincentives and instead debate the more crucial matter of the welfare state's centrality to explaining variation in poverty across affluent democracies.

The third precept is not supported because productivity never has a significant effect on poverty. Liberal economics, and indeed, much of the social sciences, has long argued that raising the education, skills, human capital, and ultimately productivity of the workforce is an effective strategy for fighting poverty. One should keep in mind, however, that productivity rose nearly every year in all affluent democracies, and yet poverty did not decline as a result. If one supplements the analysis with measures of educational attainment instead of productivity, the results would not be any more supportive of liberal economics. It is striking that the one social policy—expanding education—that has had the most widespread appeal among liberal economists cannot be clearly linked with macro-level variation in poverty. Despite her claims about economic growth, Blank makes an important point in explaining that it is mistaken to conclude that today's less skilled workers are somehow less prepared for jobs.[99] Of course, college-level education has long been linked to social mobility and greater earnings for workers.[100] How human capital and productivity explain poverty beyond this categorical distinction, however, remains unclear. A simple lack of productivity or preparation is probably not the dominant cause of poverty. Given that scholars remain unclear about the role of education and skills for the majority of workers who lack college degrees, it is odd that education is usually our first proposal for fighting poverty.

The fourth liberal economic precept, that unemployment rates predict poverty, was supported by this analysis. It is true that when the supply of workers exceeds the demand for labor, poverty tends to increase. Unemployment has a positive significant effect on poverty, an effect that is larger than economic growth, and an effect that is larger for working-age adult poverty. Yet, what is clearer is that this relationship is still not very strong. Welfare generosity always has a larger effect on poverty than unemployment. Many countries had high unemployment and low poverty or, like the United States, low unemployment and high poverty. Moreover, many of the U.S. poor simply do not fit the profile of displaced workers lacking a niche in the labor market. As Blank explained, the majority of U.S. poor households in the 1990s contained employed people.[101] Recently, Andrew Fullerton, Jennifer Moren Cross, and I have shown that, in the United States, since the 1970s, there have always been more than three to four times as many people in working poor households as in poor households where no one is employed.[102] While there is some evidence that the poor work fewer hours than the nonpoor and that fewer poor work full time, the simple link between employment and escaping poverty is quite tenuous.[103] In fact, among low-income single parents, work behavior has increased over time yet their economic security has not improved.[104] Further, on a macroeconomic level, U.S. unemployment has cycled up and down but has not shown a long-term relationship consistent with trends in poverty.[105] Finally, given that the elderly and children are more likely to be poor than working-age adults, unemployment is simply not determinative.

This chapter analyzes and critiques the liberal economics of poverty. Liberal economics is anchored in classical theory, prominent in current research and popular in policy debates. Across the social sciences, much of the poverty literature basically reflects liberal economics. Despite this deep and broad influence, my analyses reveal the limitations of liberal economics. In recent decades, the liberal economic model only loosely fits

7

Structural Theory and Poverty

On a very clear day, Chicago residents can look southeast and see three decaying monuments to America's Golden Industrial Age: the Gary Works U.S. Steel Plant, the Inland Steel Plant, and the Standard Oil Refinery. At their peak in the early 1960s, these three plants employed more than 50,000 people. Today, they operate at a fraction of their former greatness, symbolizing the decline of Lake County, Indiana, and the deindustrialization of hundreds of communities across America's Rust Belt. In just three decades, good-paying manufacturing jobs that once provided a living wage for thousands of Lake County families have vanished, replaced mostly by unstable, low-paying service sector jobs, jobs in the underground economy, or no jobs at all.

Fortified by a strong base of manufacturing jobs in the early 1960s, the heart of Lake County in Gary was a haven for middle- and working-class families down the shore of Lake Michigan from Chicago. By the 1990s, much had changed. Gary had become the prototype of the modern America ghetto, where joblessness, poverty, drugs, and crime intermingle to create a pattern of community disorganization.[1] The percentage of people receiving Aid to Families with Dependent Children rose from 1.8% in 1960 to 8.9% in 1993, and the unemployment rate skyrocketed from 6% in 1968 to 16.3% in 1982. The flight of jobs and population was startling as well. In 1979, more than 201,847 were employed in Lake County. Only seven years later, 146,469 people were employed. In the early 1960s, Gary had a murder rate similar to the United States as a whole, with approximately 10 murders for every 100,000 people. After 1990, murder rates climbed sharply as Gary became the U.S. murder capital three times between 1994 and 1997. In 1994, for example, Gary had a rate of 90.3 murders per 100,000. In other words, nearly 1 in every 1,000 of Gary's residents was murdered in 1994.[2] Underlying these social problems was the impoverishment of tens of thousands of Gary's families.

This dramatic transformation and related social problems, which unfolded in only a few decades, reflected an intense concentration of inner-city poverty. It is this particular manifestation of poverty that has been the central concern of sociological poverty researchers over the past few decades. To make sense of what has variously been referred to as "the underclass," "the truly disadvantaged," "ghetto poverty," and "the jobless poor," sociologists have developed what can be called structural theory. Because this literature has been so central to sociological poverty research, and because of the impact and visibility of some poverty sociologists, structural theory tends to be the leading explanation among sociologists studying poverty.

Structural theory contends that macro-level labor market and demographic conditions put people at risk of poverty, and cross-sectional and temporal differences in these structural factors account for variation in poverty. Groups, cities, and countries disadvantageously affected by structural factors tend to have more poverty. Thus, structural theory is a compositional explanation: the more people in vulnerable demographic or labor market circumstances, the more poverty exists. In this sense, structure refers to the set of labor market opportunities and/or demographic vulnerabilities that explain the population's rate of poverty.[3] For the case of Lake County, structuralists might point to the county's deindustrialization, as manufacturing jobs declined from 102,000 in 1960 to 37,000 in 1997. Or, structuralists might highlight the rise of single parenthood, because female-headed families rose from 16.1% of all families in 1970 to 39.7% in 1990.

Structural theories have a long history in the social sciences and are perhaps best exemplified by William Julius Wilson's influential books *The Truly Disadvantaged* and *When Work Disappears*.[4] Like most structural theories, Wilson showed how labor market and demographic factors, like the loss of manufacturing jobs and the rise of single motherhood, disadvantage the urban poor. Of course, Wilson's model was not designed to explain cross-national variation and more precisely focused on concentrated inner-city African-American poverty in the United States. However, Wilson's work demonstrates the value of structural theory and provides a foundation to examining how structural factors affect poverty.

The historian Alice O'Connor explains that structural theories have actually existed for decades and originated at least in the 1960s with the work of scholars like Kenneth Clark, Gunnar Myrdal, and Lee Rainwater.[5] These structural theorists were talking back to liberal economics and its faith in harmonious progress. Perhaps most notably, Michael Harrington contended that the poor lived in an invisible "Other America" that was "immune" to, and even displaced by, economic progress.[6] John Kenneth Galbraith challenged the "conventional wisdom" that the poor would benefit from economic growth, because the poor were marginalized in labor markets.[7] Labor market segmentation theorists argued that the poor and African Americans were stuck in secondary labor markets and uniquely disadvantaged by massive transitions from agriculture to industry to service, from rural to urban to suburban, and from Fordism to post-Fordism.[8]

Contemporary structural accounts maintain these concerns. Historians like Thomas Sugrue in *The Origins of the Urban Crisis* have documented how structural factors shaped urban poverty in the late-twentieth-century decline of Detroit.[9] While illuminating the local experiences of the poor, ethnographers like Elijah Anderson and Katherine Newman often contextualize poverty within structural conditions like the decline of manufacturing jobs and the rise of single motherhood.[10] In a related literature, stratification analysts demonstrate that structural factors shape economic inequality, attainment, and mobility.[11]

Structural explanations are appealing, in part, because they unite demography and labor markets in one sociological model. Such models oriented a great deal of sociological research on poverty in the 1990s.[12] Several well-read collections and visible conferences on poverty essentially were working with an underlying structural theory.[13] Faced with mounting demographic and labor market structural changes to what was previously (if mythically) perceived as a stable Western Europe, structural theory conveyed a new sense of urgency. The power resources theorist Gøsta Esping-Andersen even claimed that postindustrial structural changes were producing new social risks that welfare states were not equipped to manage.[14]

Despite its popularity in sociology and the other social sciences, however, little research has examined whether structural theory can account for variation in poverty across affluent Western democracies. This chapter addresses this absence by evaluating five structural factors: manufacturing employment, agricultural employment, female labor force participation, the elderly population, and children in single-mother families. Hence, this chapter provides a systematic evaluation of the structural theory of poverty and compares structural theory to institutionalized power relations theory and liberal economics.[15] This chapter builds on research on poverty as well as research on macro-level variation in inequality, because many consider relative poverty and inequality similar phenomena and many others have linked structural factors to inequality.[16] Interestingly, despite its popularity in sociology, the existing evidence for structural theory is really quite mixed.

Key Factors in Structural Theory

Manufacturing Employment

In their pioneering book *The Deindustrialization of America*, Barry Bluestone and Bennett Harrison defined "deindustrialization" as the widespread, systematic disinvestment in a nation's core manufacturing industries.[17] While much debate has occurred on deindustrialization's causes, Bluestone and Harrison were equally concerned with its consequences.[18] Scholars have shown that deindustrialization contributed to a restructuring of labor relations and what Harrison and Bluestone called "The Great U-Turn" of rising income and earnings inequality since the early 1970s.[19] Many subsequent studies link deindustrialization with rising inequality. For example, Albert Chevan and Randall Stokes find that, among a host of changes, deindustrialization was the largest cause of the dramatic rise in family income inequality in the United States.[20] That said, others claim that the link between deindustrialization and inequality remains unclear.[21]

The focus on inequality has somewhat overshadowed the connection between manufacturing and poverty—a connection that Bluestone and Harrison fully recognized.[22] Because manufacturing provides secure, well-paid jobs, the less skilled poor are especially vulnerable to the consequences of deindustrialization. Wilson's research on inner-city poverty highlighted the role that manufacturing jobs played for African-American men and their families, and how the disappearance of that work disadvantaged poor neighborhoods. Wilson wrote about how "changes related to the mass production system in the United States," "industrial restructuring," and "structural shifts in the distribution of industrial job opportunities" powerfully contributed to the rise of jobless poverty in inner-city neighborhoods.[23] Subsequent scholarship suggests that deindustrialization in the United States increased poverty in cities for less skilled workers and families.[24] However, as with inequality, some doubt manufacturing's impact. For example, in his award-winning book *Poverty and Place*, Paul Jargowsky argues, "All things considered, the early emphasis of researchers on manufacturing may have been misplaced." Jargowsky explains that deindustrialization cannot really explain inner-city and African-American poverty, although perhaps it can be linked with poverty for the less educated.[25] Thus, despite the accumulation of studies linking deindustrialization to rising inequality and poverty, many remain unpersuaded by the effects of deindustrialization.

Agricultural Employment

Nobel Laureate Simon Kuznets theorized that inequality would rise with development as labor shifted from the more equal agricultural sector to the relatively more unequal modern and urban industrial sectors.[26] Consistent with this, researchers have found that across developing and developed societies, agricultural employment is associated with less inequality.[27] Recently, however, researchers have produced a different set of results for developed societies.[28] In the postindustrial era, inequality is actually higher in the agricultural sector. Reflecting a traditional agrarian social structure, affluent democracies with high agricultural employment tend to have greater inequality. In a recent study of affluent democracies, Arthur Alderson and Francois Nielsen find that agricultural employment is the strongest influence on rising income inequality. Agricultural employment's effect is twice as large as the next most important influence on inequality (unionization), more than four times larger than the effect of the welfare state, and nearly 14 times as large as the effect of female labor force participation. Manufacturing employment, by contrast, is not even statistically significant.[29]

Just like income inequality, agriculture has attracted attention in structural accounts of poverty. In his classic book *The Other America*, Harrington described the plight of migrant and seasonal farm workers, writing, "Perhaps the harshest and most bitter poverty in the United States is to be found in the fields."[30] Some research has examined the connection between agricultural employment and poverty and inequality in the rural United States.[31] For example, Duncan contends that rural U.S. poverty has declined for several decades because of the decay of an exploitative farm labor system.[32] Given the findings on inequality, agricultural employment may significantly increase poverty as well.

Female Labor Force Participation

As it pertains to income inequality, female labor force participation has been the source of mixed findings and uncertain conclusions. Some studies conclude that female labor force participation increases inequality.[33] These authors suggest that female labor force participation inflates the bottom of the earnings distribution, amplifies the relative advantage of high-income households, and is conflated with rising single motherhood. However, studies of rising U.S. inequality, which control for single parenthood, contrast with those conclusions.[34] For example, Nielsen and Alderson find that female labor force participation reduced income inequality across U.S. counties in 1980 and 1990.[35] Yet, still others remain skeptical that female labor force participation has more than modest effects.[36]

Poverty researchers broadly conclude that female labor force participation reduces poverty on a micro level.[37] For example, studies variously show that employment helps women exit welfare and escape poverty, decreases poverty and inequality, and reduces child poverty.[38] While we cannot always extend micro level findings to the macro level, it is plausible that female labor force participation influences comparative historical variation in poverty.[39] It could be that female labor force participation expands to redress the loss of family income with rising single motherhood and declining manufacturing employment. Given the findings for inequality, it is plausible that countries with greater female labor force participation will have less poverty.

The Elderly Population

Several analysts claim that the growing elderly population represents a demographic strain that will increase inequality. Many studies document the increasingly high inequality within the elderly, and high inequality between the working-age and elderly populations.[40] At the same time, there has been little evidence that the percentage of the population elderly is positively associated with income inequality. For example, Bjorn Gustafsson and Mats Johansson found that the size of the elderly population does not have a significant effect on inequality across affluent democracies.[41]

Structuralists, like Harrington, have long been concerned with elderly poverty in the United States.[42] However, recent debates have been dominated by the perception that the elderly have become much less likely to be officially poor or experience economic hardship—especially in comparison to children.[43] As I showed in chapter 3, that perception is largely mistaken. By critiquing the official U.S. measurement and replacing it with relative poverty, we see that both the elderly and children are much more likely to be poor than are working-age adults.[44] So, it is reasonable to suspect that the size of the elderly population is positively associated with poverty. At the same time, it remains unclear whether large elderly populations contribute to poverty once one considers how much the welfare state moderates poverty over the life cycle.[45]

Children in Single-Mother Families

Probably the most studied structural factor is single motherhood. Studies show that single motherhood contributed to the rise in inequality in the United States.[46] There is little doubt that U.S. single-mother families are more likely to be poor, and this contributes to poverty trends.[47] Indeed, single motherhood has always featured prominently in structural accounts.[48] for example, the rate of female-headed families is positively associated with poverty across U.S. cities and counties.[49]

Several micro-level cross-national studies suggest that single-motherhood contributes to poverty, especially for women and children.[50] Karen Christopher and colleagues demonstrate that single-mother families are more likely to be poor in most affluent democracies.[51] At the same time, however, macro-level cross-national variation in single motherhood does not clearly correspond to variation in poverty.[52] Possibly, single motherhood might not explain poverty, but rather, what explains poverty are the differences in how much welfare states ensure the economic security of single-mother families.[53] Further, other structural factors—especially female labor force participation—may offset the effect of single motherhood, and studies should control for these to guard against a potentially spurious association.

Testing Structural Theory

The analyses below evaluate five structural variables measured in the current year. First, *manufacturing employment* is measured as industrial employees as a percentage of the labor force. Second, I include *agricultural employment* as a percentage of the labor force. Third, *female labor force participation* is measured as the percentage of the female population between 15 and 64 years of age. Fourth, the *elderly population* is measured as the percentage of the population that is 65 or more years of age. Fifth, I include *children in single-mother families* as a percentage of the population. The Luxembourg Income Study (LIS) provides estimates of the percentage of children in single-mother families. I multiplied these estimates by the percentage of the population who are children. This standardization harmonizes this variable's denominator with the denominators of the dependent variables and the other structural variables. Thus, this measurement has several advantages and gives the single motherhood variable the best opportunity to explain poverty.[54]

In addition to these structural variables, I include the liberal economic variables from chapter 6: economic growth, productivity, and unemployment. Also included are the two most important measures of institutionalized power relations theory: the welfare generosity index and proportional representation. Thus, this chapter compares structural theory to liberal economic theory and institutionalized power relations theory and tests structural theory net of these other influences on poverty.

Does Structural Theory Explain Poverty?

Descriptive Patterns

From the 1960s to the end of the twentieth century, all affluent democracies experienced deindustrialization.[55] For example, Germany declined from nearly 50% of its labor force employed in manufacturing to less than 30%, Sweden fell from about 40% to 23%, and the United States declined from about 33% to just more than 22%. Sweden and the United States had less manufacturing employment throughout the period, but Germany (the most industrialized affluent democracy in the 1960s) actually underwent a more rapid decline. Plausibly, this deindustrialization contributed to cross-national and historical patterns in poverty.

Figure 7.1 displays the moderate negative association between manufacturing employment and overall headcount poverty ($r = -.22$). This figure reveals substantial cross-national as well as historical variation in manufacturing. For example, the United Kingdom (UKM) is represented with both high and moderate amounts of manufacturing employment. Not surprisingly, the level of poverty corresponds negatively to the levels of

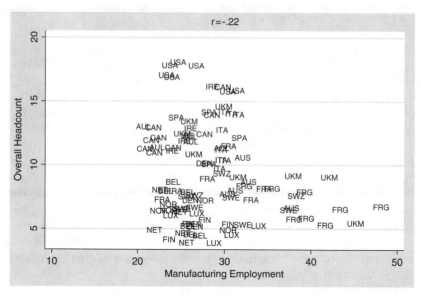

Figure 7.1.   The Association between Manufacturing and Overall
Headcount Poverty ($r = -.22$).

manufacturing. The very high levels of manufacturing in Germany (FRG),
especially prior to the 1990s, are reflected in low poverty. Also, recent years
for Australia (AUL), Canada (CAN), and the United States (USA) show lower
manufacturing and higher poverty.

As a sweeping historical change, the fall of agricultural employment
mirrored deindustrialization. For example, Germany and Sweden had nearly
10% agricultural employment in the 1960s, but both had fallen to less than
2.5% by 2000. The United States had already lost much of its agricultural
employment by the late 1960s, when it was only 4.4% of the labor force, but
it continued to decline to 2.5% in 2000. Agricultural employment was a
small percentage of the labor forces of these countries, but its substantial
decline might have alleviated poverty as the unequal traditional agrarian
social structures decayed.

Figure 7.2 demonstrates that there was only a weak positive association
between agricultural employment and overall headcount poverty ($r = .07$).
Consistent with the image of a traditional agrarian social structure, Spain
(SPA) and Ireland (IRE) stand out for having particularly high agricultural
employment and moderate to high poverty. But, several Scandinavian
countries also had moderate agricultural employment and very low poverty.
Interestingly, many of the countries with the highest poverty (e.g., the United
States) always had low agricultural employment. Thus, the association between agricultural employment and poverty is the weakest among the structural factors.

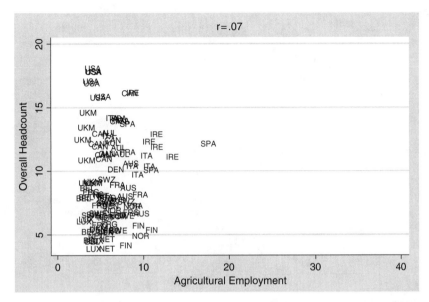

Figure 7.2.   The Association between Agriculture and Overall Headcount
Poverty ($r = .07$)

Since the 1960s, there has been a substantial rise in female labor force
participation in the affluent Western democracies. For example, Germany
increased consistently from less than 50% in 1960 to about 60% in 2000.
While the United States was actually below the supposedly "conservative"
Germany at about 40% in 1960, it rose quickly to almost 70% by 2000. Some
of the upward trends, especially in Scandinavia, have not been uniformly
linear. For example, Sweden rose from about 50% in 1960 to almost 80% in
1990 but actually fell to less than 70% in the late 1990s. Other countries, like
Germany and the United States, seemed to reach a plateau around 1990.
There is now much less variation in female labor force participation than
there was in the mid-1980s. Still, all nations experienced a fundamental
transition, and poverty may have followed suit.

Figure 7.3 shows a modest negative association between female labor
force participation and overall headcount poverty ($r = -.19$). Scandinavia
occupies the lower right corner of the graph with low poverty and high
female labor force participation. Spain, Italy (ITA), and earlier years of
Canada (CAN) and Ireland occupy the upper left corner with high poverty
and lower female labor force participation. There are notable outliers, like
the United States, with high poverty and recently high female labor force
participation. Yet, in total, there is a negative slope.

The elderly population grew significantly in affluent democracies over
the past few decades. For example, Germany's elderly population grew from
less than 11% in 1960 to more than 17% in 2000. Interestingly, in many

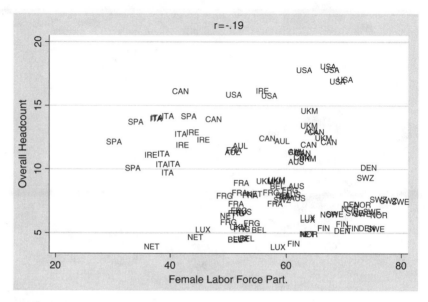

Figure 7.3.   The Association between Female Labor and Overall
Headcount Poverty ($r = -.19$)

affluent democracies, a peak was reached in the mid-1980s, and there has
actually been more stability than growth since. For example, Sweden
increased from less than 12% in 1960 to more than 17% in the mid-1980s
and has fluctuated but stayed at about that level. The United States increased
from less than 10% in 1960 to more than 12% in 1986 and has since
remained stable. Notably, the elderly remain a clear minority of most nations' populations, and their population sizes have remained relatively
stable since about 1990. Even though political rhetoric of graying societies
has probably exaggerated the problem, the aging of these populations does
present a challenge for their welfare states.

Figure 7.4 displays a striking negative association between elderly population and overall headcount poverty ($r = -.40$). This is fairly surprising
because most assume that growing elderly populations inflate the share of
dependents in families and society and lead to higher poverty. Instead, we
find that it is actually the generous Scandinavian welfare states, like Sweden
(SWE), that have the largest elderly populations and low poverty. By contrast, former British colonies tend to have smaller elderly populations and
higher poverty. I should emphasize, however, that this is merely the bivariate correlation. As I show below, controlling for welfare generosity changes
the story entirely.

According to the LIS estimates, single motherhood has grown in most
affluent Western democracies. For example, in Sweden, children in single
mothers as a percentage of the population rose from 2.3% in 1975 to about

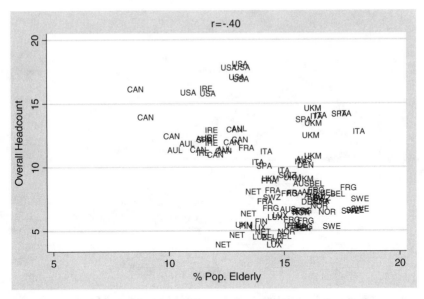

Figure 7.4.   The Association between Elderly Population and Overall Headcount Poverty ($r = -.40$)

3.6% in 1995, before falling to 3.3% in 2000. Germany grew from less than 1% in 1973 to almost 2% in 2000. The United States has always had very high levels, greater than 4%. Yet, the United States grew from that level in 1974 to more than 5% in 1994, and then stabilized at 4.2% in 2000. The United Kingdom was at only 1.4% in 1969. However, by 2000, the United Kingdom became the first country besides the United States to surpass 4%. A few countries exhibited trendless fluctuation rather than a rise. But, single motherhood grew in most of the countries.

Figure 7.5 confirms a strong positive association between single motherhood and overall headcount poverty ($r = .45$). The United States and the United Kingdom stand out for their high single motherhood and poverty. By contrast, Belgium (BEL) and Germany (at least in earlier years) had low single motherhood and low poverty. Although this correlation is the strongest of the structural variables, there is heterogeneity below the surface pattern. While many countries have very low rates of single motherhood, several of them (e.g., Italy and Spain) have higher poverty than do countries with high rates of single motherhood (e.g., Sweden and Norway [NOR]). Indeed, if one excludes the United States and the United Kingdom, this correlation falls all the way to a negligible .03. In other words, if one removes the very high single-motherhood United Kingdom and United States, there is really no association with poverty. Also, it is important to keep in mind the need to control for other factors in order to assess whether single parenthood actually causes poverty.[56]

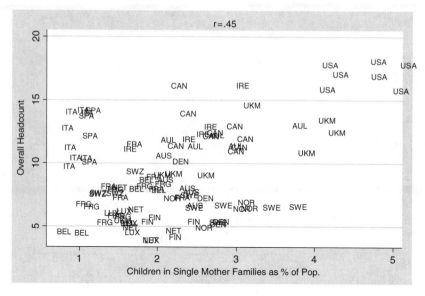

Figure 7.5.   The Association between Single Mothers and Overall
Headcount Poverty (r = .45)

Models of Overall Poverty

Figure 7.6 displays the standardized effects for the model of overall headcount poverty on structural, liberal economic, and institutionalized power
relations variables.[57] Four structural variables have significant effects:
manufacturing employment, female labor force participation, elderly population, and children in single-mother families. Agricultural employment is
not significant, but the remaining four have sizable effects. For a standard
deviation increase in manufacturing employment, overall headcount poverty is expected to decline by about 0.30 standard deviations. For a standard
deviation increase in female labor force participation, poverty should decline by 0.34 standard deviations. For a standard deviation increase in the
elderly population, poverty is expected to increase by 0.38 standard deviations. For a standard deviation increase in children in single-mother families, poverty should increase by 0.25 standard deviations. Given historical
trends, the decline of manufacturing, the increase in the elderly population,
and the growth of children in single-mother families have been partially
offset by the rise of female labor force participation. But, because the collective poverty-increasing effect of the first three is larger than the effect of
female labor force participation, the net effect of these historical structural
changes has been to increase overall headcount poverty.

These results demonstrate that structural theory is a far more useful explanation than is liberal economics. All four of these effects are considerably

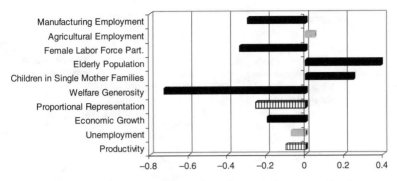

Figure 7.6.   Standardized Effects of Structural and Other Variables for
Overall Headcount Poverty. [The dark bars are significantly different from
zero ($p < .05$). The hatched bars are nearly significant ($p < .10$). The shaded
bars are not significantly different from zero. See appendix table A.21 for
details.]

larger than the effects of the liberal economic variables. Unlike in chapter 6,
only economic growth significantly reduces poverty—unemployment becomes insignificant with the inclusion of the structural variables. Also, the
effect of economic growth is smaller than any of the four structural variables.

Despite the salience of these structural variables, their effects are smaller
than the effects of the welfare generosity index. The welfare generosity index
has the largest effect by a considerable margin, a standardized effect of
−0.73. Also, proportional representation has a sizable standardized effect
of −0.25. One could argue that the collective sum of the absolute values of
the effects of the structural variables (approximately 1.26) is larger than
the collective effects of the institutionalized power relations variables (approximately −.98). However, that obscures how rising female labor force
participation has partially offset the poverty-increasing structural changes.
The welfare generosity index has the largest effect of any one variable, and
both institutionalized power relations variables remain significant. Yet, the
structural variables collectively have effects that are comparable to the institutionalized power relations variables.

Figure 7.7 provides similar results for overall poverty intensity. Four
structural variables have significant effects while agricultural employment
is insignificant. Again, the poverty-increasing structural changes of deindustrialization, growing elderly populations, and mounting single motherhood
have been partially offset by rising female labor force participation. These
structural variables, collectively and individually, have larger effects than
the significant liberal economic variables, economic growth and productivity. Again, the welfare generosity index has the largest effect of any one
variable. For example, the welfare generosity index's standardized effect
(−0.72) is more than twice as large as the next largest effect, elderly population (0.35). Also, proportional representation has a sizable effect that is

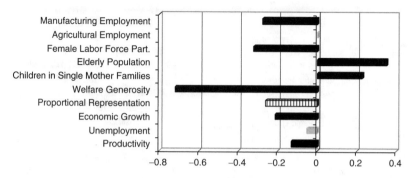

Figure 7.7.   Standardized Effects of Structural and Other Variables for
Overall Poverty Intensity. [The dark bars are significantly different from
zero ($p < .05$). The hatched bar is nearly significant ($p < .10$). The shaded bar
is not significantly different from zero. See appendix table A.21 for details.]

significant at the .10 level. Treating the structural variables as a group,
however, their collective influence is comparable to the influence of the
institutionalized power relations variables.

To illustrate the effect of the structural variables, I counterfactually simulate the values of overall headcount poverty for Sweden and the United
States. This simulation is similar to those in chapters 4–6 (see figures 4.5,
5.13, and 6.6). However, because rising female labor force participation has
partially offset the other structural changes, this simulation is somewhat
different. For Sweden, I calculate how much worse poverty would have
been if manufacturing employment had declined a standard deviation and
female labor force participation, the elderly population, and children in
single-mother families had increased a standard deviation. For the United
States, I calculate how much less poverty would have been if manufacturing
employment had increased a standard deviation, and female labor force
participation, the elderly population and children in single-mother families
had declined a standard deviation.

The simulation reveals that United States and Swedish poverty would
have been significantly closer had structural changes been different (figure
7.8). U.S. poverty would have been at 14.9% instead of its actual 17% in
2000. Sweden's poverty would have been about 8.7% instead of 6.5%. Thus,
these simulated structural changes could produce a real narrowing of the gap
between Sweden and the United States. Compared to figure 6.6 in chapter 6,
this simulation indicates that these structural variables are far more consequential than the liberal economic variables. Thus, structural theory appears
to have a lot more merit than the liberal economic model of poverty.

Although structural theory clearly is a useful explanation, it is important
to ask how consequential structural variables are relative to the key institutionalized power relations variables. Figure 7.9 reproduces the simulation
from figure 5.13. Comparing figures 7.8 and 7.9, structural theory does not

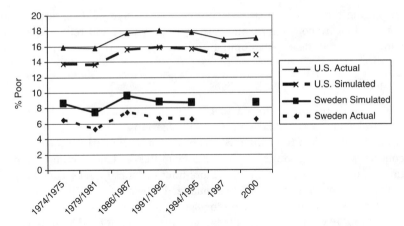

Figure 7.8.   Actual and Simulated Overall Headcount Poverty by Structural
Change: United States and Sweden

appear to be quite as powerful of an explanation as institutionalized
power relations theory. Both structural theory and institutionalized power
relations theory are useful. Both figures reveal a substantial narrowing of the
Sweden–United States poverty gap. Nevertheless, because the narrowing of
the gap is slightly more pronounced in figure 7.9 than in figure 7.8, perhaps
institutionalized power relations theory is a slightly more effective theory
than structural theory for explaining poverty across affluent democracies.
Ultimately, affluent democracies should be able to reduce poverty more by

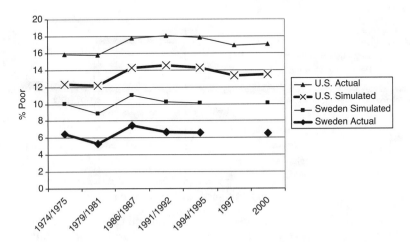

Figure 7.9.   Actual and Simulated (± 1 Standard Deviation for Welfare
Generosity and PR System) Overall Headcount Poverty: United States
and Sweden (Duplicate of Figure 5.13)

expanding the welfare state and shifting to a proportional representation system than by boosting manufacturing employment and reducing single parenthood and the elderly population.

Models for Demographic Subgroups

It is certainly reasonable to consider the possibility that structural theory is most relevant to specific demographic subgroups. After all, research on structural theory in the United States has been particularly animated by a concern with young adults, single-mother families, and racial/ethnic minorities. In turn, it is worthwhile to explore how structural theory compares to liberal economic theory and institutionalized power relations theory for two key demographic subgroups: working-age adults and children.

Figure 7.10 displays the results for working-age adult headcount poverty. The results are generally similar to the results for overall headcount poverty. Structural variables continue to be more important than liberal economic variables. Compared to the results for overall poverty, however, there are some notable changes to the standardized effects and significance levels. Quite surprisingly, female labor force participation is insignificant, and the children in single-mother families variable is only near significant for working-age adult poverty. Individually, no structural variable is as consequential as welfare generosity, and the collective effect of the three significant or near significant structural variables is smaller than the collective effect of the two institutionalized power relations variables. Surprisingly, structural theory appears to be a weaker explanation of working-age adult poverty than overall poverty. Institutionalized power relations theory ends up as a slightly better explanation of working-age adult poverty.

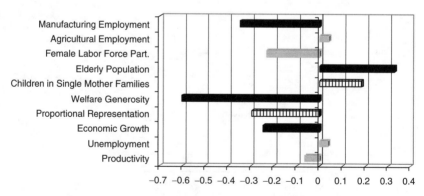

Figure 7.10.   Standardized Effects of Structural and Other Variables for Working-Age Adult Headcount Poverty. [The dark bars are significantly different from zero ($p < .05$). The hatched bars are nearly significant ($p < .10$). The shaded bars are not significantly different from zero. See appendix table A.21 for details.]

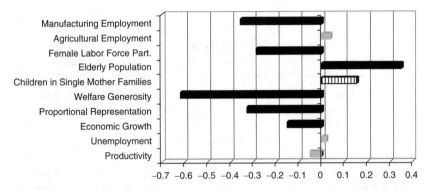

Figure 7.11. Standardized Effects of Structural and Other Variables for Children Headcount Poverty. [The dark bars are significantly different from zero ($p < .05$). The hatched bar is nearly significant ($p < .10$). The shaded bars are not significantly different from zero. See appendix table A.21 for details.]

Finally, figure 7.11 shows the results for children's headcount poverty. Even more than for working-age adult poverty, the results are broadly consistent with the results for overall poverty. Again, structural theory rivals institutionalized power relations theory but is far superior to liberal economics. Still, there are a few differences with overall poverty. For child poverty, only manufacturing employment has a larger effect, and the other three significant structural effects are slightly smaller. Again, welfare generosity has the largest effect of any one variable. Although there are good reasons to analyze demographic subgroups, the cross-national and historical patterns in and causes of overall poverty are very similar to the patterns in and causes of poverty among demographic groups like children.

Conclusion

Structural theory has been one of the most influential explanations of poverty in the social sciences, and probably the most popular explanation within sociology. This chapter evaluates structural theory by examining how five structural factors affect poverty in 18 affluent Western democracies, and compared structural theory with institutionalized power relations theory and liberal economics.

Manufacturing employment significantly reduces overall headcount poverty, overall poverty intensity, working-age adult headcount poverty, and children's headcount poverty. The deindustrialization of affluent democracies has clearly contributed to comparative historical variation in poverty. The lower levels of manufacturing employment in the United States partly account for the particularly high levels of poverty in the United States.

Bluestone and Harrison's concern with the distributional consequences of deindustrialization, one recognized by Wilson in his studies of inner-city poverty, warrants the continuing attention of poverty researchers.[58] The well-paid, secure, and stable jobs provided by manufacturing have declined, and as a result, poverty has been pushed upward in affluent democracies.

By contrast, agricultural employment does not significantly affect any of the measures of poverty. Even though agricultural employment has concerned inequality researchers since at least Kuznets, there is no evidence that poverty is shaped by levels of agricultural employment. This result shows how relative poverty is not simply the same phenomenon as income inequality. Although agricultural employment has been a key determinant of inequality in similar samples of affluent democracies, it simply has no effect on poverty.[59] Agricultural employment was a very small part of the labor force in all countries by the end of the period. Plausibly, it has become too marginal a sector to really influence variation in poverty any more.

Female labor force participation significantly reduces poverty. When controlling for the welfare generosity index and liberal economic variables, this variable has the largest impact of the structural variables on overall poverty. The rise in female labor force participation has partially offset the poverty augmenting consequences of other structural changes. In some ways, rising female labor force participation is encouraged by the rise in single motherhood and the decline in manufacturing employment. As a result, the United States probably would have much greater levels of poverty without its moderately high levels of female labor force participation.

The elderly as a percentage of the population is positively associated with poverty. The elderly are more vulnerable to being poor than are working-age adults in affluent Western democracies. As the elderly grow as a proportion of the population, poverty rises. Countries with larger elderly populations, holding all other variables constant, tend to have more poverty. The rising elderly populations, especially in Western Europe where their share of the population is much larger than in the United States, pose a challenge to the egalitarianism of those welfare states.

Finally, the percentage of children in single-mother families significantly increases poverty. Single-mother families are more likely to be poor than are two-parent families in most countries, and countries with more children in single-mother families tend to have more poverty. Of the significant structural factors, the effect of children in single-mother families is the smallest. This is noteworthy because single motherhood has gotten far more attention than probably any cause of poverty among scholars and commentators of U.S. poverty. Though single motherhood consistently has larger effects than economic growth, its smaller influence than female labor force participation, the elderly population, and even manufacturing employment demonstrates a misplaced overemphasis on this one structural factor. The conclusion that single motherhood is less relevant than other structural factors parallels others' conclusion that deindustrialization was more important than changes in family structure to the rise in family income inequality in the United States.[60] Single motherhood is important and the United States has greater poverty partly because of its high rates of single motherhood. However, this one structural factor cannot account for much of the cross-national differences in poverty, including why the United States is such an outlier in terms of poverty. To illustrate this point, consider the following thought experiment. In 2000, according to my estimates from the LIS, about 4.1% of the United States was poor and resided in a single-mother household. If we could magically make *all* of those poor single-mother families not poor, overall headcount poverty would decline by 4.1%. What would result? Well, the United States would still have an overall headcount poverty rate of 12.95%, which would put it below Spain and Ireland, and barely below Australia. By completely eradicating all single-mother poverty, the United States would still have the fourth highest rate of poverty among the 18 affluent democracies.

Despite the importance of structural factors, the ultimate conclusion is that structural theory is a useful but not quite as powerful explanation as institutionalized power relations theory. Both explanations are valuable, and both are far superior to liberal economics. Like the simulations in chapters 4 and 5, the difference between the United States and Sweden would be narrower with structural changes. Yet, an exclusive concentration on structural theory—as has often been the case in U.S. sociology—leads to an incomplete understanding of variation in poverty. Institutionalized power relations theory may be an even more effective explanation for cross-national and historical variation in poverty.

Structural theory emphasizes that as the percentage of people in vulnerable demographic or labor market circumstances increases, more poverty results. Sociologists tend to concentrate on these labor market and demographic factors as the main pressures on a nation's poverty levels. Yet, an exclusive concentration on structural factors is problematic. To truly understand poverty in affluent democracies, institutionalized power relations theory is indispensable. The welfare generosity index is always the single most important factor in terms of standardized effects. The effect of proportional representation systems is often comparable to the effects of the structural variables. How much welfare states institutionalize egalitarianism and protect citizens against economic insecurity—including insecurity resulting from vulnerable demographic and labor market circumstances—is more important than simply how many people are vulnerable. Hence, this chapter also illustrates the limitations of structural theory.

One final caveat is worth mentioning. In the event that data allow for valid and reliable cross-national comparisons, research should examine these sources of poverty for racial/ethnic minorities and immigrants. Historically, structural explanations have been concerned with the plight of inner-city African Americans, immigrants, and other ethnic minorities.[61] A complete evaluation of structural theory requires a serious consideration of ethnic

8

Politicizing Poverty

In his 1879 classic *Progress and Poverty*, Henry George wrote, "This association of poverty with progress is the great enigma of our times. It is the central fact from which spring industrial, social, and political difficulties that perplex the world, and with which statesmanship and philanthropy and education grapple in vain."[1] One hundred and thirty years later, affluent Western democracies experienced an unprecedented level of prosperity and a spectacular level of material well-being. Although not quite as strong as the decades following World War II, we live in an era of progressing consumption and living standards. Despite all this progress, poverty and inequality remained locked into the social landscape. Although no other country, perhaps in history, has ascended to the riches of the United States, this country also stands out for having the most poverty among the rich democracies. Just as in Henry George's classic text, poverty amidst progress continues to be one of the great enigmas of our times.

In the beginning of this book I called attention to the substantial cross-national and historical variation in poverty across affluent Western democracies. Many countries have been able to accomplish levels of poverty below 5% of the population, while others struggle with high poverty at around 15% of the population. These poverty levels have changed over time, with some countries experiencing growing poor populations from the 1970s to the 1990s, and a few experiencing declining poverty. Chapter 3 offered further detail and, in the process, sought to dispel some of the myths about patterns in poverty. Where overall poverty is high, poverty also tends to be high among women, men, the elderly, and children. Where poverty is high among women, it also is high among men, and where child poverty is high, it is also high among the elderly. Countries that are more egalitarian for one group also tend to be egalitarian for all other groups. Poverty varies dramatically across the affluent Western democracies and over the past few decades, but it reflects consistent patterns within the population. In every dimension, and for every demographic group, the United States stands out for its distinctively, even iconically, high poverty. Thus, the biggest question is why poverty varies so much across countries and over time.

This book proposes one explanation for the variation in poverty across affluent Western democracies. I argue that politics can account for why the United States consistently has about two to three times as much poverty as Western Europe and why poverty fluctuated over the past few decades. This theory places causal primacy in the welfare state in explaining such variation. The more generous a welfare state, the more people are protected from the economic insecurity and instability of markets. Welfare states manage against risk, organize the distribution of economic resources in an egalitarian direction, and institutionalize equality. There are many diverse features of the welfare state, but across all varieties of types of welfare states, there is a strong linear negative relationship between welfare generosity and poverty. The welfare state's influence is unmatched by any other cause. The effects of welfare generosity are always significantly negative regardless of what one controls for, regardless of the welfare regime, and regardless of the time period. The generosity of the welfare state is the dominant cause of how much poverty exists in affluent Western democracies.

Behind and embedded within the welfare state are latent coalitions for egalitarianism—the unanticipated and often accidental supporters of the welfare state. These latent coalitions are driven both by ideology and interest, and the principal manifestations of these latent coalitions are collective Leftist political actors. The relations among these collective political actors play out in the negotiation over the welfare state, and thus indirectly shape poverty. Where unions are strong, Leftist parties have historically ruled, women have been present in the legislature, voters are mobilized, and a proportional representation system exists, welfare states tend to be more generous. Because welfare states are such a powerful negative influence on poverty, Leftist politics has a fundamental indirect influence on poverty. Moreover, the presence of a proportional representation system appears to have a direct effect on poverty that supplements its indirect effect through the welfare state. Together, the welfare state and Leftist politics form a coherent and complementary set of social forces. By highlighting the crystallization of these two major causal influences, institutionalized power relations theory offers a distinctively political explanation of poverty. Rather than focusing on demography, labor markets, or economic performance, this book advocates for highlighting politics to explain poverty.

As the title of this chapter indicates, I am trying to "politicize" poverty. Thus, I place the inherently political choices over resources and the political organization of states, markets, and societies at the center of the study of poverty. I am explicitly trying to counter the view that poverty is the unavoidable by-product of demography or labor markets. Instead, this book contends that poverty is a political outcome. Equality is something institutionalized by latent coalitions for egalitarianism, Leftist politics, and welfare states. By contrast, where poverty is widespread, as epitomized by the United States, poverty is institutionalized.

It is worthwhile to articulate the obvious and non obvious ways in which poverty becomes institutionalized. When poverty is understood as an individual failing rather than a social or public or national problem, equality is not institutionalized. Where high levels of poverty are perceived by the public and policy makers as normal, unavoidable, or inevitable, equality is not institutionalized. In a political environment, where collective political actors never seek to challenge high levels of poverty and fear they lack support in pushing for generous social policies, poverty is institutionalized. To the extent that high poverty is not even questioned as a major social problem and is perceived as a natural feature of all economies, there has been a failure to politicize poverty. Where Leftist politics are too weak to push for a substantial reduction of poverty or where welfare programs are insufficient to address high poverty, inequality has been institutionalized. In sum, how societies collectively define and understand poverty and equality is an apt reflection of the process characterized by institutionalized power relations theory.

Theoretical Reorientation

Of course, there are other influences on poverty, and institutionalized power relations theory is not a deterministic explanation. Structural theory is a valuable explanation as well. Deindustrialization, growing elderly populations, and increasing single motherhood all contributed to poverty in the past few decades. These structural changes have been partially offset by rising female labor force participation, but structural demographic and labor market factors certainly play a role. Sociologists have favored structural theory because it unites demographic and labor market variables into one sociological model. The enthusiasm for structural theory is best represented by the sheer quantity of studies of single motherhood and U.S. poverty. Yet, there are two problematic qualities about sociology's present level of enthusiasm for structural theory.

First, it is problematic how rarely these structural factors are put in political context. It would be productive if sociologists asked why welfare states fail to ensure the economic security of single-mother families as much as they ask why single mothers do not get married or abstain from parenthood. Though chapter 7 demonstrated that single motherhood is not a dominating influence on poverty, it is striking how often sociological researchers center their explanations of poverty on the choices of poor mothers and their children.[2] Indeed, it is a strange irony that we spend so much time studying the choices of a group who have so few choices. If one is realistic about the limited choices these poor mothers and their children actually have, the constraints become more obvious, and more obviously the paramount question. Rather than studying the prevalence of single motherhood, and presuming that single motherhood necessarily must be linked with poverty, we should study why and how welfare states alleviate or fail to alleviate the economic insecurity of single-mother families.

Second, it is problematic that sociologists so disproportionately concentrate on demographic and labor market factors and neglect other causes. Partly, this is because so much of U.S. poverty research analyzes only the United States—an *outlier* among affluent Western democracies—and as a result, there is little variation in one's data by welfare generosity or Leftist politics. In turn, U.S. researchers have typically only studied the causes that do vary within the United States—for example, how single parenthood or deindustrialization has changed over time. This constrains our scholarly imagination by failing to place other societies' politics, economics, and demography into our scope of vision. What has been problematic about this focus on the United States and structural factors is how little attention other possible causes have received. Structural theory is a useful explanation, but it is incomplete. Unless the welfare state and Leftist politics gain more attention, research concentrating exclusively on structural factors will never provide a full understanding of poverty in affluent Western democracies.

In the United States, even more than the concentration on structural theory among sociologists, there has been an unbalanced devotion to liberal economics. Policy debates about poverty have been too loyal to liberal economic concerns with economic growth, free markets, unemployment, and productivity. As the historian Michael Katz explains, "The vocabulary of poverty impoverishes political imagination. For two centuries of American history, considerations of the productivity, cost, and eligibility have channeled discourse about need, entitlement, and justice within narrow limits bounded by the market."[3] Yet, despite being the dominant explanation in U.S. poverty debates, liberal economics is a far less effective explanation than either structural theory or institutionalized power relations theory. Chapters 6 and 7 demonstrate that only economic growth had a robust significant effect, while unemployment and productivity are sporadically influential. Also, there is absolutely no evidence that free markets are more effective to fighting poverty in the long run or that welfare generosity is counterproductive. It is fair to say that economic growth, productivity, and unemployment may have a modest influence on poverty levels. While it would be inappropriate for this book to advocate a total neglect of economic performance, there is, however, a striking disconnect between the devotion to liberal economics within U.S. poverty policy and debates, and the paucity of evidence for this approach. Liberal economics simply does not deserve the sort of paradigmatic centrality that it has received. As this book documents, institutionalized power relations is a far more effective explanation.

Further dedication to structural and liberal economic explanations is very unlikely to produce scholarly breakthroughs or novel insights into why poverty varies across time and place. Instead of continuing to study the relationship between economic growth and poverty or concentrating so much energy paying attention to single motherhood, poverty research is due for a theoretical reorientation. This book offers institutionalized power relations theory as a step in that direction. There are ample research questions to consider—from which social policies are most effective to how welfare states interact with structural change, to the changing strategies of Leftist politics. Compared to the mountain of research on structural theory and liberal economics, there is a great need for more research on the politics of poverty.

Locating Institutionalized Power Relations Theory in the Social Science of Poverty

To fully understand the theoretical reorientation advocated here, it is useful to locate institutionalized power relations theory within the broader social science of poverty. This literature is diverse and includes many disciplines and research programs. Chapter 1 claims that the prevailing view of poverty is anchored in individualism. But, to fully represent poverty research, it is fair to say that the social science of poverty varies across a continuum with individualism at one end. Realistically, the social science of poverty is not an exclusively individualist enterprise. Many poverty scholars—even some variants of individualists—focus more on context and relations and take a more critical stance than extreme individualism. Thus, one can frame the opposite end of the continuum as being more societal in explanation. To display this continuum, I deploy Andrew Abbott's heuristic of fractals.[4] Abbott explains that there is an inherent tendency for divisions to occur within scholarly communities, and these divisions tend to reappear at smaller and smaller levels within various explanations for a phenomenon. Figure 8.1 presents a "fractal map" of the social science of poverty. This fractal map is general and cannot possibly display every single explanation for poverty. Moreover, poverty is less like some other areas of inquiry in that it is not as clearly divided by established and well-recognized "theories." Still, this map tries to capture the major scholarly approaches that carried influence in the twentieth century.[5]

This fractal map posits that a major division in the social science of poverty is between individualistic and societal explanations. By societal, I mean relational, emergentist, contextual, and critical. By individualistic,

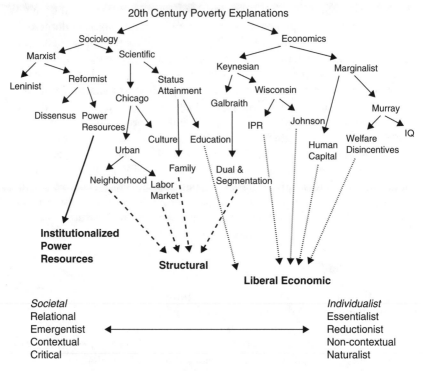

Figure 8.1.   Fractal Map of Poverty Literature

I mean essentialist, reductionist, universalist, and naturalist. Of course, the poverty literature could be represented in other ways. Nevertheless, this distinction is plausible for recounting the major explanations of poverty and for clarifying exactly where institutionalized power relations theory stands.

Perhaps not surprising to readers of the poverty literature, the division between societal and individualistic explanations maps onto the difference between the two main social sciences involved in poverty scholarship: economics and sociology. Both disciplines have made major contributions, but reflecting the paradigmatic assumptions of each, they are fairly different intellectual strands.

Within economics, the major division has been between more societalistic Keynesians and more individualistic marginalist explanations. Among the Keynesians, the societal–individualistic fractal repeats itself. Scholars like John Kenneth Galbraith, and dual labor market and segmented labor market descendents, like Bluestone and Harrison, and Gordon, Edwards, and Reich, have been much more societal and indeed shared a great deal with nearby sociologists. The University of Wisconsin economics department has played a huge role in poverty research partly because faculty like Robert Lampman were heavily involved in the Johnson administration's "war on poverty" and, of course, because for several decades the federally funded Institute for Poverty Research was housed there. Even emanating from the Wisconsin department, there were divisions between the more policy-oriented proposals coming from scholars like Lampman in the Johnson administration and how the Institute for Poverty Research came to be known under the leadership of Robert Haveman and others.

Among the marginalists, much poverty research has been done by scholars who emphasized the human capital deficits of the poor. But, more visible has been the radical individualism of scholars like Charles Murray. Murray has authored two major works that, despite their negative reception in the scientific community, have been tremendously influential in poverty debates. The works actually differ a great deal: his book on welfare disincentives, *Losing Ground*, is more societal, emphasizing how poor individuals respond to social policies (this work is closest to the behavioral account identified in chapter 1), whereas *The Bell Curve*, with Richard Hernstein, represents the biological account. Despite training as a political scientist, Murray is radically individualistic compared to even most economists. While his and others' welfare disincentives arguments have triggered a great deal of research, his biological IQ arguments have been linked with little subsequent scholarship.

Within sociology or scholarship inspired by sociology, one can discern a Marxist strand and a more scientific strand. Within scientific sociology, there have been recurring fractal divisions as well. The first division occurred between the Chicago school and the status attainment traditions. The Chicago school focused on the ecological study of neighborhoods and cities, and the immigrants and industrialization that were changing those cities. The Chicago school can be divided again into more societal urban accounts and what came to be known as the "culture of poverty" explanation. While the culture of poverty account has faded, the urban sociology tradition has flourished partly because of the tremendous influence of William Julius Wilson. Wilson's studies of disadvantaged inner-city African Americans shared a lot with scholars like Lee Rainwater and catalyzed the study of ghetto poverty. Even within the work inspired by Wilson, one can discern the fractal division between more societal research on neighborhoods and neighborhood effects, and labor market research focusing on racial discrimination, spatial mismatch, low-skilled workers, and unemployment.

The status attainment tradition (along with related mobility studies) really came after the Chicago school and sought to identify individual characteristics that enhanced one's chances of achieving a non poor socioeconomic status. At the next level, status attainment research that emphasized the choices and behaviors leading to individual mobility tended to focus on education. Status attainment research that emphasized the inheritance of status origins ended up highlighting the role of the family. Both status attainment traditions are very much alive in contemporary sociology. Family sociologists have identified the role of disadvantaged family backgrounds—like single motherhood—that increase one's chance of being poor. Education sociologists demonstrate that a college degree can reduce the chances of inheriting a disadvantaged family background.

Reflecting the intellectual politics of Marxism in the past 150 years, Marxist social scientists can be divided between Leninists and reformists.[6] Leninists have not really generated much useful social science for understanding poverty in affluent democracies, though they have offered some useful accounts of imperialism for explaining poverty in less developed countries. But, there is a community of scholars that views capitalism as so systematically impoverishing that they are radically societal in their account of poverty. The reformists, since the social democratic thinker Eduard Bernstein, tend to view capitalism as capable of modifications that allow for the sharing of resources and reduction of poverty. These reformists can be divided into more societal and individualistic fractals. The dissensus politics account manifests most visibly in the work of Frances Piven and Richard Cloward. The power resources account has been tremendously influential in the welfare state literature and, as discussed in chapter 5, extends to explain poverty and equality in affluent democracies. Still, the literature that emerged from this Marxist lineage has probably not generated as much scholarship as other lineages in this fractal map.

The bottom end points of the fractal map can be united in the three major possible explanations for poverty that this book considers for addressing this study's orienting question.[7] Across the individualistic–societal continuum, and through the intellectual genetics of poverty research, the social science of poverty results in liberal economic, structural, and institutionalized power relations theories. Some might disagree that these three really are "theories"—as opposed to paradigms or taken-for-granted frameworks. However, because these three can be articulated in terms of testable implications for macro-level patterns of poverty, they function as theories of poverty that justify the attention given in this book.

There have been a few notable attempts to unite much of this heterogeneous fractal map into one explanation of poverty. For example, in *One Nation, Underprivileged*, Mark Rank offers a structural vulnerability theory that bridges liberal economic, structural, and institutionalized power relations explanations.[8] Like liberal economists, Rank acknowledges the role of human capital. Yet, similar to status attainment scholars, Rank emphasizes the background characteristics that predict human capital attainment. Like structural theory, Rank focuses on demographic attributes and a lack of stable well-paid jobs. Also, like institutionalized power relations theory, Rank recognizes the crucial support provided by welfare programs. Pulling together these arguments, Rank compares poverty to a game of musical chairs:

Let us imagine eight chairs and ten players. The players begin to circle around the chairs until the music stops. Who fails to find a chair? If we focus on the winners and losers of the game, we will find that some combination of luck and skill will be involved. . . . In one sense, these are appropriately cited as the reasons for losing the game. However, if we focus on the game itself, then it is quite clear that, given only eight chairs, two players are bound to lose. Even if every player were suddenly to double his or her speed and agility, there would still be only two losers. From this broader context, it really does not matter what the loser's characteristics are, given that two are destined to lose.[9]

Institutionalized power relations theory shares this focus on the game itself, rather than the characteristics of the players. Quite similar to what I have written about structural theory, his structural vulnerability theory is a useful companion to institutionalized power relations theory. Yet, unlike Rank, who emphasizes the shortage of quality jobs, I would stress that the welfare state and Leftist politics are paramount. Whereas we both focus on the game, I would argue that the most important rules of the game are set in the political arena.

Finally, I would point out that I do not consider institutionalized power relations theory to be a radically societal account. It should be clear that I appreciate the value of a generalizable explanation across the contexts of affluent Western democracies. Institutionalized power relations theory is intended to be somewhat universal explanation within the contextual bounds of the affluent Western democracies since the 1960s.

But, Isn't the United States Different?

One of the limitations of U.S. research on poverty and welfare is that it has so often concentrated exclusively on studying the United States. Tim Smeeding and colleagues explain that much of the U.S. poverty literature "rests on an inherently parochial foundation, for it is based on the experiences of only one nation."[10] If that one nation was a typical or randomly selected draw from the affluent Western democracies, research on U.S. poverty could be generalized to other countries. But, as has been amply documented, the United States is extraordinary in many regards. No one quite matches its economic performance and wealth. More important, the United States has anomalously high inequality and poverty, anemic Leftist politics, and an unusually meager welfare state. Because the United States is an outlier in terms of the welfare state and poverty, this literature on U.S. welfare and poverty essentially samples on the dependent variable by selecting a case at the extreme end of the distribution. Even if one studies variation in poverty across the politics of U.S. states, the range of politics and welfare generosity is severely constrained relative to the variation between affluent Western democracies. Thus, there are good reasons to suspect that the research on U.S. welfare and poverty might not be generalizable to other affluent Western democracies.

Still, the uniqueness of the United States is actually an intriguing challenge for institutionalized power relations theory. No other affluent democracy has its particular legacy of slavery and history of racial division. The reasoning could be that the United States is distinct because of its ethnic heterogeneity and immigration, something that is supposedly absent from much of Europe. No other affluent democracy has been this loyal to free market ideology and liberal economics. One might argue that the United States is so different that one cannot extend institutionalized power relations theory across the Atlantic. To address this concern, one should consider two questions: whether the United States is actually unique in terms of ethnic heterogeneity, and whether the United States remains significantly different after considering institutionalized power relations theory.

As mentioned in chapter 5, one of the compelling criticisms of power resources theory was that it neglected racial divisions and racism. Perhaps collective action by labor was only possible and was only effective in triggering a generous welfare state because of the ethnic homogeneity of relatively small Northern European countries. After all, many have pointed out that ethnic homogeneity contributed to class solidarity and contributed to the broad appeal of protecting the entire citizenry with generous welfare programs.[11] This explanation has often functioned as an excuse for the meagerness of U.S. welfare. Yet, rarely does this view ever actually face empirical scrutiny.

Table 8.1 displays some basic patterns in ethnic and national diversity.[12] The first two columns display the amount of immigration in these countries, and the last column is a time-constant measure of ethnic diversity.[13] I qualitatively group the countries by high, medium, and low poverty levels. As table 8.1 shows, the United States is above average on two of the three measures of ethnic heterogeneity. The United States had the second highest levels of average net migration over the five-year period of 1996–2000, seventh highest percent foreign born, and fifth highest ethnic fractionalization. Five of the six highest countries in average net migration are among the high-poverty countries. The high-poverty countries also include some of the highest levels of percent foreign born and several of the countries that are high in terms of ethnic fractionalization.

Yet, what is also striking is how the patterns in ethnic and national diversity do not closely conform to patterns in poverty. Luxembourg, a country with one of the lowest levels of poverty, is actually the highest in terms of net migration and percent foreign born. Australia, Canada, Germany, and Switzerland all have higher levels of percent foreign born than the United States, and yet all of these countries have significantly less poverty than the United States. Even egalitarian Sweden had a slightly higher percent foreign born. Four of the five medium-poverty countries have percent foreign-born levels near those of the United States. A few of the high-poverty countries are quite ethnically and nationally homogeneous. Thus, upon close inspection of the actual empirical patterns, there does not appear to be any essential trade-off between immigration and low poverty.

Table 8.1.   Patterns in Ethnic and National Diversity Across Affluent Western
Democracies

	Net Migration, 1996–2000 Average (%)	Percent Foreign Born, 2000	Ethnic Fractionalization
High Poverty			
Australia	4.98	23.0	.09
Canada	4.29	18.1	.71
Ireland	5.31	8.7	.12
Italy	0.90	2.5	.12
Spain	3.85	5.3	.42
United Kingdom	2.37	7.9	.12
United States	5.31	11.0	.49
Medium Poverty			
Austria	1.00	10.5	.11
Belgium	1.18	10.3	.56
France	0.16	7.3	.10
Germany	2.27	12.5	.17
The Netherlands	2.32	10.1	.11
Low Poverty			
Denmark	2.66	5.8	.08
Finland	0.58	2.6	.13
Luxembourg	9.06	33.2	.53
Norway	2.58	6.8	.06
Sweden	1.09	11.3	.06
Switzerland	1.55	21.9	.53
Mean	2.86	11.6	.25

It is reasonable to acknowledge that the United States does have a distinct type of ethnic fractionalization in terms of historically entrenched racism and racial division. Yet, it is also important to point out that Belgium, Canada, Luxembourg, and Switzerland all have ethnic fractionalization levels higher than the United States and still maintain much lower poverty. Indeed, what is most apparent is that one can find ethnically and nationally diverse countries among each of the groups with high, medium, and low poverty. Even among the high-poverty countries, the United States is not substantially more diverse than the others. These patterns suggest there is no clear or strong relationship between ethnic heterogeneity and high poverty.

Table 8.2.   Bivariate Correlations between Immigration and Poverty and Welfare
Generosity in Affluent Western Democracies (*N* = 104)

	Overall Headcount	Overall Intensity	Welfare Generosity Index
Net Migration, Five-Year Average (%)	.019	.027	−.066
Welfare Generosity Index	−.731	−.711	

The only measure among these three that is available over time is the measure of average net migration. I calculated this measure as a five-year average to smooth unusual years, for all country-years for which poverty data are available. Table 8.2 displays the bivariate correlations between this measure of immigration and overall head count poverty, overall poverty intensity, and the index of welfare generosity. This table clearly shows that there is no association between net migration and poverty or welfare generosity. The correlations are very weak, especially relative to the correlations between welfare generosity and poverty. Thus, it seems quite unlikely that immigration or national diversity is a powerful cause of high poverty or a weak welfare state.

Even though there is no clear pattern between ethnic diversity and poverty, one can still reasonably question whether the United States still might be different. Although institutionalized power relations theory explains the broad sample of affluent Western democracies, there might be something distinctive about the United States. To assess this possibility, I estimated the final models from chapter 7, which included the institutionalized power relations, liberal economic, and structural theory variables. Then, I added a dummy variable to indicate the U.S. cases. If indeed the United States significantly stands out even after controlling for these variables, one could make the case that the United States is an outlier. This would suggest that institutionalized power relations theory cannot explain why the United States has such uniquely high poverty.

Figure 8.2 shows that, in fact, the dummy variables indicating U.S. cases are positively signed. Yet, these dummy variables are not statistically significantly different from zero. So, there is nothing significantly different about the United States once one controls for liberal economic, structural, and welfare state variables. Indeed, one can conclude that these variables explain away the U.S. distinctiveness. There is nothing significantly different about the U.S. cases relative to the rest of the sample once one models the variables featured in this book. Hence, it is reasonable to infer that institutionalized power relations theory and structural theory, the two explanations with the most support, can explain why the United States has such high poverty levels.[14]

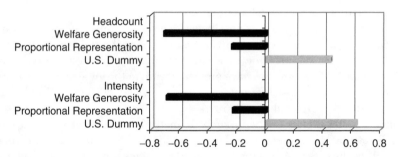

Figure 8.2.   Effects of Welfare Generosity and Proportional Representation (Standardized) and U.S. Dummy (Semi-Standardized) for Overall Poverty. [The dark bars are significantly different from zero ($p < .05$). The shaded bars are not significantly different from zero. See appendix table A.23 for details.]

Policy Implications

In chapter 1, I quoted from an essay by Isabel Sawhill as an example of individualism. It is instructive to revisit that essay when considering the policy implications of this book. Sawhill went on to remark, "No feasible amount of income redistristribution can make up for the fact that the rich are working and marrying as much or more than ever while the poor are doing just the reverse."[15] Like her individualistic behavioral theory of poverty, Sawhill argues that the best poverty policy is to change the behavior of poor people. At this point, the distance between institutionalized power relations theory and Sawhill's fatalistic behavioralism should be clear. The analyses presented in this book have shown that Sawhill is mistaken to infer that income redistribution is ineffective or even less effective than reducing single motherhood or unemployment. To elaborate on this point, let me suggest how institutionalized power relations theory can advance a wholly different set of policy implications.

Rather than worrying over the incentives and disincentives of welfare programs and how these might affect the behavior of poor individuals, anti-poverty policy should focus on broad-based social security programs. Following the three roles for the welfare state—managing risk, organizing the, distribution of economic resources, and institutionalizing equality—I would advocate for policies that emphasize these roles. The best strategy for fighting poverty is to establish generous policies and programs that manage the risks that tend to fall on the poor, organize the distribution of economic resources in a more egalitarian direction, and institutionalize commitments to economic security for all citizens. I offer a few examples of policies and programs that would accomplish these three roles in the United States. The point is to get antipoverty policy debates away from the infatuation with the disincentives for poor individuals and get them focused on broad-based programs that guarantee economic security for the entire citizenry.

Many times, authors feel a burden to come up with creative or original policy proposals. I would argue, instead, that the United States does not need novel proposals. What the U.S. poor need is the implementation of policies that we already know to be effective in many other affluent Western democracies. These policies have proven to work in the low-poverty affluent democracies that are so different from the United States. These policies have even worked comparably in countries with moderate levels of poverty. The United States stands out with such dramatically high poverty that even moderate steps toward a more generous welfare state would do something to reduce the extent of poverty. We need political wherewithal more than we need originality.

On the first role, several policies effectively manage against risk. One set of policies involves better unemployment compensation. In the United States, unemployment benefits normally are exhausted after 26 weeks. Many of those people remain unemployed for longer periods of time, and some even become so discouraged from looking for work that they drop out of the labor force altogether. The plight of the jobless is particularly acute among inner-city African Americans. The strategy of individualists is to reduce the generosity and length of unemployment benefits in order to provide an incentive to find work. Of course, this logic has always been disingenuous. The vast majority of unemployed need no additional incentive to work; the real problem is the absence of well-paid secure jobs. Instead of always expecting the U.S. economy to provide security for the unemployed, a more effective solution would extend unemployment benefits for a longer period of time and guarantee a modicum of economic security for family members when unemployment persists. A related component of social policy is health care and health insurance. In most affluent democracies, health care and health insurance are rights guaranteed for all citizens. In the United States, more than 45 million people are without health insurance. Many others are being crushed under the weight of health care bills. For the United States to have anything approaching a serious antipoverty policy, publicly funded health insurance must be guaranteed for all citizens. This one policy change would have profound consequences for alleviating the risks and economic insecurities of people that end up poor.

On the second role, more must be done to regulate the distribution of economic resources to enhance the standing of low-income households. The United States may be the best place to live if you are rich, but it may be the worst affluent democracy to live in if you are poor. This nation of extremes disproportionately facilitates the accumulation of wealth among the rich and does not do enough to facilitate the basic security of the poor. In one vivid example, Lisa Keister discusses the recent debate to repeal the estate tax (the tax on inherited wealth).[16] Keister shows that only the very rich (fewer than 2% of those who die) pay the estate tax. Yet, she explains that this tax can provide crucial revenue for a variety of generous welfare programs, and its repeal would benefit only the very wealthy. In order to alleviate poverty, the estate tax not only should be retained but should be augmented. It should be institutionalized that taxes are quite high for the rich who accumulate wealth that is exponentially higher than even those at the 90th percentile of households. The way in which U.S. taxation and government policy encourages the escalation and reproduction of wealth is deeply problematic to the poor. The expansion of the Earned Income Tax Credit has been a step in the right direction. However, a more aggressive and more encompassing negative income tax for the poor would be an even more effective policy to alleviate poverty. Also, it is imperative to organize taxation so as to ease the burden on working-class families who are vulnerable to fall into poverty. One policy change would involve making payroll taxes even more progressive. At present, these taxes do not go far enough to redistribute income from the rich to the poor. The United States should also emulate the practice of most affluent democracies and provide family assistance to all families with children. This could alleviate the added expenses from children, while providing a productive investment in the security of families and the development of the next generation.

On the third role, institutionalizing equality, the United States should make massive investments in public goods for transportation, communication, and education. Such public goods could enhance the economic standing of the broader population. Moreover, they would socialize many facets of life that have increasingly become privatized over the past few decades. There has been a recent push to target social policies at the poor, because targeted programs more efficiently concentrate on those in need. However, I would advocate for universal welfare programs that are guaranteed to all citizens. Such generalist programs garner far more political support and thus institutionalize collective expectations to protect everyone's economic security.[17] The privatization of social security should not be considered, and a greater share of the costs of health care, sickness, old age, and disability must be embraced by the public sector. One set of public goods that could be provided are public elder and child care. Such programs would greatly alleviate the costs of dependents and would assure that the care of the elderly and children is a socialized collective responsibility. It must be institutionalized that all citizens are guaranteed economic security and basic services for sustaining well-being. Certainly, such ambitious policies would be expensive. But, the most justified way to pay for these policies is to increase taxes on the rich. As observers of the winner-take-all market of the U.S. economy have noted, the United States is experiencing a rise at the top of the income distribution that is only matched by the Gilded Age of the 1920s. Certainly, these very rich households can contribute more to the well-being of the broader society.

More fundamental than policy interventions, the United States needs a more invigorated Leftist politics. The United States is the only affluent democracy where citizens lack a real right to organize a labor union. Sure, the law makes clear that workers have such rights, but the actual on-the-ground reality is one where workers have no protections and employers have all the power. At present, employers can coercively resist efforts to mobilize workers by illegal and legal tactics of intimidation and dismissal. Unfortunately, the nonenforcement of U.S. labor law has deeply eroded the basic right of association for workers. Labor unions are at historic low points in the U.S. workforce, and without labor unions, there is little pressure on the Democratic Party and no counterweight to the mounting influence of corporations and the rich on U.S. policy. Other political institutions could be reformed to enhance democratization, and this would indirectly alleviate poverty. For example, if the United States had higher voter turnout, the poor and working class would have greater influence in the electorate. Enfranchising the disenfranchised, and enabling all to vote—perhaps by making election day a holiday as it is in many affluent Western democracies—would realign U.S. politics in favor of the poor. Moreover, if the United States moved away from its undemocratic electoral college and single-member-district plurality system, and adopted a proportional representation system, poverty would certainly be lowered.

Ultimately, there are many paths the United States could take to reduce poverty. We know of several welfare programs and policies that would certainly alleviate poverty. We do not need novel ideas for tackling poverty. We need to follow the model set forth by the Western European countries that have all been more successful in alleviating poverty and institutionalizing equality.

Conclusion

This book attempts to reorient how we think about and study poverty. This study uses the cross-national and historical variation in poverty across affluent democracies as an empirical puzzle that any sound theory of poverty must explain. The first few chapters synthesize major advances in poverty measurement and argue for a relative measure of poverty conceptualized as social exclusion and capability deprivation. I also show that several of the commonly perceived patterns in poverty are myths. The real patterns in poverty show a pronounced symmetry where countries with high poverty for one group also tend to have high poverty for other groups and for the broader population. The fourth and fifth chapters demonstrate the capacity of institutionalized power relations theory to explain cross-national and historical variation in poverty. I propose that poverty is a political outcome, and that it is driven proximately by welfare state generosity and fundamentally by the power of Leftist collective political actors. Hence, this book aims to unite the progress made by political sociologists and political scientists who study the welfare state with the study of poverty. Moreover, the book extends the study of welfare state politics to the final distribution of economic resources. My aim is to draw a connection and contribute to a dialogue between poverty research and welfare state studies. For comparison, I also tested liberal economics and structural theory. While liberal economics is shown to be a weak explanation of poverty, structural theory is a useful companion to institutionalized power relations theory. Ultimately, I argue that institutionalized power relations theory is far superior to liberal economics and probably slightly more effective than structural theory.

In his 1964 Nobel Peace Prize Lecture, Martin Luther King, Jr., stated,

> There is nothing new about poverty. What is new, however, is that we have the resources to get rid of it. There is no deficit in human resources; the deficit is human will. The well-off and the secure have too often become indifferent and oblivious to the poverty and deprivation in their midst. The poor in our countries have been shut out of our minds, and driven from the mainstream of our societies, because we have allowed them to become invisible.

At the end of the day, poverty is the consequence of a society's failure to collectively take responsibility for ensuring the economic security of its citizens. To accomplish low poverty, it is essential that the welfare state manage risk, organize the distribution of economic resources in an egalitarian way, and institutionalize equality. It is far less important for governments to provide incentives for work, private savings, delayed parenthood, or marriage. The focus on individualism in poverty research has impoverished our understanding of this persistent social problem. As long as debates about poverty are more about the poor than about the state and society, poverty will continue to haunt the economic progress of affluent Western democracies. Poverty is truly a political problem.

Appendix

This appendix provides the methodological details and results for all of the analyses presented in the book. I organize this appendix in the order of analyses presented by chapter.

Details from Chapter 4

Estimation Technique

I use an unbalanced panel design where the unit of analysis is a country-year. Because of the limited availability of the Luxembourg Income Study (LIS 2008), cases are unevenly distributed across 18 countries (Ns) and 32 years (Ts). Due to unobserved time-invariant cross-national heterogeneity, ordinary least squares (OLS) regression is inappropriate (Hsiao 2003). Using Stata software, I analyzed models with several techniques (e.g., population-averaged, random effects with maximum likelihood estimation, fixed effects, and OLS with robust-clustered errors). The substantive conclusions were wholly consistent with these alternative techniques. For theoretical and methodological reasons, I present random effects (RE) models. First, RE models better facilitate estimating the effects of the independent variables on the dependent variables when *both* cross-national and historical variation are essential (Beck 2001; Beck and Katz 1996; Greene 1990: 495). Because the RE model is the matrix weighted average of the within-nations (fixed effects) and between-nations (between effects) estimators

(Greene 1990: 488; Hsiao 2003), the RE model is the best among imperfect strategies for estimating models to explain within- and between-nation variation. It is valuable to understand why some nations have more or less poverty, *and* why poverty increases or decreases over time. In fact, the standard deviations between nations are larger than within nations for most variables. Further, the number of Ns (18) exceeds the average number of Ts (5.8). As a result, the cross-national (between) variation is arguably more important than the historical (within) variation. Second, statistical tests accept RE models (i.e., the Bayesian information criterion prime [Beck and Katz 2001: 492; Raftery 1995; Teachmanet al. 2001] and Hausman's [1978] chi-square test). Third, according to the econometric literature, in small and unbalanced samples with more Ns than Ts, RE models may perform better than alternatives (Beck 2001; Bhargava and Sargan 1983; Greene 1990: 493, 495; Hsiao 2003). By contrast, the alternatives are often problematic in small and unbalanced samples, especially when the N far exceeds the Ts (e.g., fixed effects models are inefficient in this sample; Nickell [1981] shows that fixed effects models may produce biased estimates when N far exceeds T). Finally, I estimated all models with a variety of alternative techniques and the substantive conclusions are consistent (available upon request). Of course, it is important to acknowledge that RE models are far from perfect (e.g., RE models assume that omitted covariates and stable country characteristics are orthogonal to included covariates).

Table A.1.   Descriptive Statistics and Sources

	Mean (Standard Deviation)	N	Sources
Dependent Variables			
Overall Headcount	9.413(3.687)	104	Luxembourg Income Study (LIS), author's calculations
Overall Intensity	6.087(2.496)	104	LIS
Child Headcount	10.273(6.048)	104	LIS "Key Figures" (July 2007)
Elderly Headcount	14.493(7.610)	103	LIS "Key Figures" (July 2007)
Men's Headcount	7.750(2.745)	104	LIS
Women's Headcount	10.441(3.705)	104	LIS
Working-Age Adult Headcount	8.118(3.005)	101	LIS
Independent Variables			See also Huber et al. (2004)
Social Welfare Expenditures	22.455(5.347)	104	OECD(c)
Social Security Transfers	15.127(4.232)	104	OECD(c)
Decommodification	27.944(7.496)	95	Allan and Scruggs (2004)

(*continued*)

Table A.1.   (*continued*)

	Mean (Standard Deviation)	N	Sources
Government Expenditures	43.965(7.870)	104	OECD(c)
Public Health Spending	75.143(12.279)	104	OECD(a)
Public Employment	11.879(4.558)	104	Cusack (2004); Huber et al. (2004); OECD(b)
Welfare Generosity Index	.001(0.820)	104	See Social Welfare Expenditures, Social Security Transfers, Decommodification, Government Expenditures, and Public Health Spending
Socialist	.183(0.388)	104	Esping-Andersen (1990)
Liberal	.327(0.471)	104	Esping-Andersen (1990)
Post-1990	.577(0.496)	104	NA
Post-1990 Welfare Generosity Index	.231(0.547)	104	Esping-Andersen (1990)
Year	21.317(7.893)	104	NA
Year Welfare Generosity Index	8.001(15.321)	104	See Social Welfare Expenditures, Social Security Transfers, Decommodification, Government Expenditures, and Public Health Spending
Economic Growth	2.693(2.706)	104	OECD(a)
Unemployment	7.119(3.750)	104	OECD(a)
Productivity	48542.350(8319.369)	104	OECD(b)
Manufacturing Employment	27.284(5.537)	104	OECD(b)
Female Labor Force Participation	55.403(11.514)	104	OECD(a); OECD(b)
Elderly Population	14.030(2.105)	104	OECD(b)
Children in Single-Mother Families	2.122(1.007)	104	LIS "Key Figures" (July 2007); OECD(b)
Old-Age Pensions as % GDP	7.619(2.347)	91	OECD (2004)
Survivor's Benefits as % GDP	1.241(0.918)	91	OECD (2004)
Disability Benefits as % GDP	2.849(1.395)	91	OECD (2004)
Family Allowances as % GDP	2.036(1.121)	91	OECD (2004)
Unemployment Benefits as % GDP	1.516(1.057)	91	OECD (2004)

This table displays descriptive statistics with the maximum number of cases in common with the 104 LIS observations. Nevertheless, the standardized coefficients calculated in the figures are based on common numbers of observations as displayed in models below (casewise deletion).

Analyses for Chapter 4 Figures

For all models, I present figures in the text that display standardized coefficients or sometimes semi-standardized coefficients. Standardized coefficients are calculated by multiplying the coefficient times the standard deviation of the independent variable and dividing by the standard deviation of the dependent variable. Semi-standardized coefficients are calculated by dividing the coefficient by the standard deviation of the dependent variable. For each calculation, I used the appropriate sample to calculate model-specific standard deviations. For brevity, I do not report each variable's standard deviations for each model. The vast majority of models use the full sample of 104 cases, and those standard deviations are presented.

Table A.2. Results for Figure 4.3—Random Effects Models of Overall Headcount Poverty in Affluent Western Democracies, 1969–2002: Unstandardized Coefficients (z-scores)

	Model 1	Model 2	Model 3	Model 4	Model 5	Model 6
Social Welfare Expenditures	−0.485**(−6.18)					
Social Security Transfers		−0.414**(−5.17)				
Decommodification			−0.204**(−3.82)			
Government Expenditures				−0.257**(−6.11)		
Public Health Spending					−0.104*(−3.45)	
Public Employment					0.001(0.02)	
Welfare Generosity Index						−3.670**(−8.56)
Economic Growth	−0.255**(−3.64)	−0.268**(−3.56)	−0.235**(−2.72)	−0.280**(−3.95)	−0.266**(−3.96)	−0.295**(−4.52)
Unemployment	0.0001(0.00)	−0.056(−0.50)	−0.143(−1.10)	0.070(0.64)	−0.008(−0.08)	−0.021(−0.22)
Productivity	−2E−5(−0.77)	−1E−5(−0.43)	1E−5(0.59)	−2E−5(−0.79)	−2E−5(−0.92)	−4E−5*(−1.69)
Manufacturing Employment	−0.234**(−2.90)	−0.175**(−2.15)	−0.108(−1.32)	−0.089(−1.15)	−0.193*(−2.60)	−0.166*(−2.47)
Female Labor Force Participation	−0.070(−1.60)	−0.142**(−2.95)	−0.066(−1.36)	−0.072(−1.61)	−0.077(−1.76)	−0.105*(−2.75)
Elderly Population	0.673**(3.43)	0.463**(2.39)	0.024(0.13)	0.431**(2.39)	0.646**(3.64)	0.632**(3.88)
Children in Single-Mother Families	1.071**(3.02)	1.547**(4.24)	1.632**(4.36)	0.960**(2.68)	0.911**(2.77)	1.170**(3.79)
Constant	20.426**(3.95)	20.097**(3.15)	18.478**(3.36)	20.049**(3.86)	27.367(5.12)	11.347**(2.67)
R^2 Overall	.679	.642	.673	.584	.761	.766
N	104	104	95	104	104	104

*$p < .10$; **$p < .05$.

Table A.3. Results for Figure 4.4—Random Effects Models of Overall Poverty Intensity in Affluent Western Democracies, 1969–2002: Unstandardized Coefficients (z-scores).

	Model 1	Model 2	Model 3	Model 4	Model 5	Model 6
Social Welfare Expenditures	−0.328**(−5.86)				−0.291**(−5.86)	
Social Security Transfers		−0.268**(−4.67)				
Decommodification			−0.131**(−3.55)			
Government Expenditures				−0.176**(−5.90)		
Public Health Spending					−0.082**(−4.20)	
Public Employment					0.025(0.44)	
Welfare Generosity Index						−2.457**(−8.03)
Economic Growth	−0.182**(−3.62)	−0.189**(−3.50)	−0.175**(−2.83)	−0.201**(−3.96)	−0.192**(−4.07)	−0.211**(−4.49)
Unemployment	0.027(0.35)	−0.016(−0.20)	−0.091(−1.00)	0.077(0.99)	0.014(0.21)	0.003(0.05)
Productivity	−2E−5(−1.07)	−1E−5(−0.69)	1E−7(0.39)	−2E−5(−1.07)	−2E−5(−1.17)	−4E−5*(−1.93)
Manufacturing Employment	−0.147*(−2.56)	−0.107*(−1.83)	−0.072(−1.27)	−0.049(−0.89)	−0.116**(−2.36)	−0.105**(−2.18)
Female Labor Force Participation	−0.042(−1.34)	−0.089**(−2.57)	−0.048(−1.42)	−0.043(−1.37)	−0.054*(−1.84)	−0.067**(−2.44)
Elderly Population	0.433**(3.09)	0.284**(2.04)	−0.003(−0.02)	0.264**(2.08)	0.422**(3.53)	0.408**(3.50)
Children in Single-Mother Families	0.714**(2.82)	1.023**(3.90)	1.104**(4.22)	0.659**(2.60)	0.601**(2.71)	0.783**(3.54)
Constant	13.421**(3.64)	13.026**(3.35)	12.677**(3.29)	13.260**(3.61)	18.850**(5.32)	7.473**(2.46)
R² Overall	.662	.608	.653	.566	.772	.744
N	104	104	95	104	104	104

*p < .10; **p < .05

Table A.4.   Results for Figure 4.6—Random Effects Models of Poverty for Demographic Subgroups in Affluent Western Democracies, 1969–2002: Unstandardized Coefficients (z-scores)

	Headcount				
	Children	Elderly	Men	Women	Working-Age Adults
Welfare Generosity Index	$-5.459^{**}(-8.36)$	$-5.733^{**}(-4.71)$	$-2.560^{**}(-5.81)$	$-3.704^{**}(-7.53)$	$-2.515^{**}(-5.58)$
Economic Growth	$-0.397^{**}(-3.96)$	$-0.315(-1.40)$	$-0.264^{**}(-4.03)$	$-0.275^{**}(-3.50)$	$-0.294^{**}(-4.70)$
Unemployment	$0.124(0.86)$	$-0.507^{*}(-1.71)$	$-0.045(-0.47)$	$-0.116(-1.04)$	$0.073(0.79)$
Productivity	$-3E-5(-0.85)$	$-1E-4(-1.25)$	$-4E-5^{*}(-1.71)$	$-1E-4^{*}(-1.67)$	$-2E-5(-0.93)$
Manufacturing Employment	$-0.331^{**}(-3.23)$	$0.138(0.69)$	$-0.180^{**}(-2.63)$	$-0.104(-1.32)$	$-0.185^{**}(-2.73)$
Female Labor Force Participation	$-0.150^{**}(-2.57)$	$-0.204^{*}(-1.80)$	$-0.079^{**}(-2.03)$	$-0.125^{*}(-2.82)$	$-0.057(-1.47)$
Elderly Population	$0.963^{**}(3.87)$	$0.132(0.27)$	$0.444^{**}(2.67)$	$0.592^{**}(3.12)$	$0.451^{**}(2.74)$
Children in Single-Mother Families	$1.546^{**}(3.28)$	$1.667^{*}(1.81)$	$0.546^{*}(1.74)$	$1.353^{**}(3.76)$	$0.755(2.45)$
Constant	$12.368^{*}(1.90)$	$26.681^{**}(2.10)$	$12.811^{**}(2.95)$	$13.052^{**}(2.64)$	$9.632^{**}(2.25)$
R^2 Overall	.773	.477	.574	.689	.619
N	104	103	104	104	101

$^{*}p < .10$; $^{**}p < .05$.

Table A.5. Results for Figures 4.8 and 4.9—Random Effects Models of Overall Poverty in Affluent Western Democracies, 1969–2002: Unstandardized Coefficients (z-scores)

	Headcount			Intensity		
Welfare Generosity Index		−3.287**(−6.08)	−2.441**(−3.75)		−2.283**(−5.85)	−1.685**(3.61)
Liberal	4.864**(3.20)	2.253*(1.74)	0.761(0.56)	2.839**(2.54)	0.994(1.07)	−0.142(−0.15)
Socialist	−2.350(−1.52)	0.246(0.20)	−0.071(−0.05)	−1.719(−1.59)	0.041(0.05)	−0.306(−0.31)
Liberal × Welfare Generosity			−3.191**(−2.97)			−2.397**(−3.10)
Socialist × Welfare Generosity			−0.852(−0.80)			−0.456(−0.59)
Economic Growth	−0.185**(−2.51)	−0.290**(−4.43)	−0.307**(−4.79)	−0.134**(−2.51)	−0.207**(−4.33)	−0.218**(−4.70)
Unemployment	−0.148(−1.21)	−0.090(−0.87)	−0.039(−0.38)	−0.059(−0.67)	−0.025(−0.33)	0.014(0.19)
Productivity	1E−5(0.23)	−4E−5*(−1.70)	−1E−4**(−2.48)	−1E−6(−0.06)	−4E−5*(−1.96)	−5E−5**(−2.77)
Manufacturing Employment	−0.097(−1.10)	−0.186**(−2.51)	−0.196**(−2.72)	−0.048(−0.76)	−0.112**(−2.09)	−0.119**(−2.32)
Female Labor Force Participation	−0.062(−1.13)	−0.120**(−2.61)	−0.088*(−1.91)	−0.032(−0.81)	−0.072**(−2.14)	−0.048(−1.47)
Elderly Population	0.413*(1.90)	0.771**(4.05)	0.855**(4.57)	0.224(1.43)	0.470**(3.40)	0.535**(3.98)
Children in Single-Mother Families	0.751*(1.74)	0.823**(2.26)	0.600*(1.67)	0.553*(1.77)	0.617**(2.34)	0.440*(1.70)
Constant	8.244(1.51)	11.311**(2.51)	9.524**(2.15)	5.111(1.30)	7.340**(2.25)	6.030**(1.90)
R^2 Overall	.569	.768	.767	.543	.740	.749
N	104	104	104	104	104	104

$*p < .10$; $**p < .05$.

Table A.6. Results for Figures 4.10 and 4.11—Random Effects Models of Overall Poverty in Affluent Western Democracies, 1969–2002: Unstandardized Coefficients (z-scores).

	Headcount		Intensity	
Welfare Generosity Index	$-3.268**(-5.02)$	$-3.389**(-7.03)$	$-2.347**(-4.98)$	$-2.308**(-6.63)$
Year	$0.029(0.53)$		$0.016(0.41)$	
Year × Welfare Generosity	$-0.018(-0.73)$		$-0.005(-0.27)$	
Post-1990		$0.737(1.52)$		$0.470(1.33)$
Post-1990 × Welfare Generosity		$-0.438(-1.20)$		$-0.232(-0.88)$
Economic Growth	$-0.295**(-4.42)$	$-0.292**(-4.50)$	$-0.211**(-4.37)$	$-0.208**(-4.43)$
Unemployment	$-0.015(-0.16)$	$-0.014(-0.14)$	$-0.006(-0.09)$	$0.008(0.12)$
Productivity	$-5E-5*(-1.67)$	$-5E-5*(-1.93)$	$-4E-5*(-1.93)$	$-4E-5*(-2.15)$
Manufacturing Employment	$-0.125(-1.34)$	$-0.126*(-1.74)$	$-0.084(-1.25)$	$-0.079(-1.52)$
Female Labor Force Participation	$-0.108**(-2.75)$	$-0.106*(-2.75)$	$-0.067**(-2.35)$	$-0.067**(-2.40)$
Elderly Population	$0.549**(2.50)$	$0.504**(2.74)$	$0.368**(2.32)$	$0.329**(2.47)$
Children in Single-Mother Families	$1.147**(3.62)$	$1.058**(3.33)$	$0.756**(3.29)$	$0.707**(3.08)$
Constant	$11.160**(2.56)$	$12.276**(2.83)$	$7.332**(2.32)$	$8.026**(2.57)$
R^2 Overall	.769	.774	.742	.746
N	104	104	104	104

$*p < .10; **p < .05.$

Table A.7. Sensitivity Analysis: Random Effects Models of Overall Headcount Poverty on Precise Measures of Welfare Transfers in Affluent Western Democracies, 1980–2002: Unstandardized Coefficients (z-scores)

	Model 1	Model 2	Model 3	Model 4	Model 5	Model 6
Old Age Pensions	−0.545**(−2.40)					−0.238(−1.19)
Survivor's Benefits		−0.209(−0.43)				−0.146(−0.37)
Disability Benefits			−1.330**(−4.52)			−0.507(−1.53)
Family Allowances				−1.902**(−6.17)		−1.163**(−2.91)
Unemployment Benefits					−1.315**(−3.45)	−0.694*(−1.92)
Economic Growth	−0.257**(−3.25)	−0.234**(−2.86)	−0.279**(−3.68)	−0.239**(−3.35)	−0.222**(−3.01)	−0.268**(−3.70)
Unemployment	0.136(1.09)	0.119(0.92)	−0.004(−0.03)	0.207*(1.91)	0.277**(2.18)	0.194(1.57)
Productivity	1E−4**(2.34)	1E−4**(2.23)	4E−5(0.95)	1E−4**(2.30)	4E−5(1.08)	3E−5(0.79)
Manufacturing Employment	0.066(0.62)	0.115(1.05)	−0.074(−0.70)	0.108(1.20)	0.015(0.14)	−0.029(−0.29)
Female Labor Force Participation	0.019(0.35)	0.035(0.60)	−0.037(−0.73)	0.065(1.42)	0.024(0.46)	0.011(0.21)
Elderly Population	0.525**(2.00)	0.164(0.80)	0.281(1.52)	0.163(0.99)	0.091(0.49)	0.420*(1.81)
Children in Single-Mother Families	1.098**(2.64)	1.079**(2.51)	1.219**(3.18)	1.552**(4.40)	1.004**(2.50)	1.237**(3.44)
Constant	−3.608(−0.56)	−4.342(−0.64)	9.628(1.47)	−3.416(−0.63)	2.690(0.41)	5.674(0.86)
R^2 Overall	.351	.213	.666	.714	.448	.757

Notes: All welfare transfers measures are coded as percentage of GDP. Results for overall poverty intensity are substantively identical. * $p < .10$; ** $p < .05$.

Table A.8. Sensitivity Analysis: Random and Fixed Effects Models of Overall Headcount Poverty and Overall Poverty Intensity in Affluent Western Democracies, 1969–2002: Unstandardized Coefficients and (z-scores) ($N = 104$)

	Headcount		Intensity	
	Fixed Effects Model	Random Effects Model	Fixed Effects Model	Random Effects Model
Welfare Generosity Index	−3.246**(−4.37)	−3.670**(−8.56)	−2.356**(−4.31)	−2.457**(−8.03)
Economic Growth	−0.274**(−3.67)	−0.295**(−4.52)	−0.197**(−3.57)	−0.211**(−4.49)
Unemployment	−0.108(−0.87)	−0.021(−0.22)	−0.024(−0.26)	0.003(0.05
Productivity	−1E−4**(−2.10)	−4E−5*(−1.69)	−5E−5**(−2.32)	−4E−5*(−1.93)
Manufacturing Employment	−0.170(−1.69)	−0.166**(−2.47)	−0.102(−1.38)	−0.105**(−2.18)
Female Labor Force Participation	−0.088(−1.42)	−0.105**(−2.75)	−0.054(−1.19)	−0.067**(−2.44)
Elderly Population	0.767**(3.18)	0.632**(3.88)	0.494**(2.78)	0.408**(3.50)
Children in Single-Mother Families	0.735*(1.67)	1.170**(3.79)	0.488(1.51)	0.783**(3.54)
Constant	10.998*(1.76)	11.347**(2.67)	6.965(1.51)	7.473**(2.46)
R^2 OVERALL	.681	.766	.685	.744
Bayesian Information Criterion Prime	−81.574	−113.854	−83.083	−104.634
Hausman Test of Statistical Significance	.14 (not positive definite)		.45	

$*p < .10; **p < .05.$

192

Details from Chapter 5

Table A.9. Additional Descriptive Statistics for Chapter 5 (from Huber et al. 2004)

Independent Variables	Mean (Standard Deviation)	N
Union Density	36.947(18.913)	94
Current Left Government	0.383(0.383)	104
Cumulative Left Party Power	13.822(11.140)	104
Cumulative Women in the Legislature	7.616(5.317)	95
Voter Turnout	77.684(12.730)	104
Proportional Representation System	0.702(0.421)	104
Bargaining Centralization	2.978(1.430)	90

Analyses for Chapter 5 Figures

Table A.10. Results for Figure 5.7—Random Effects Models of Overall Poverty in Affluent Western Democracies, 1969–2002: Unstandardized Coefficients (z-scores).

	Headcount		Intensity	
Welfare Generosity Index	−0.087**(−3.64)	−3.499**(−6.56)	−0.060**(−3.70)	−2.331**(5.98)
Union Density	−0.224**(−2.74)	−0.012(−0.54)	−0.158**(−2.67)	−0.010(−0.62)
Economic Growth		−0.318**(−4.65)		−0.217**(−4.32)
Unemployment	−0.010(−0.08)	0.005(0.05)	0.028(0.32)	0.028(0.43)
Productivity	1E−5(0.29)	−1E−4**(−2.04)	3E−6(0.12)	−4E−5**(−2.18)
Manufacturing Employment	0.016(0.18)	−0.153*(−1.94)	0.024(0.38)	−0.090(−1.57)
Female Labor Force Participation	−0.028(−0.53)	−0.097**(−2.21)	−0.013(−0.36)	−0.060*(−1.86)
Elderly Population	0.110(0.59)	0.671**(3.82)	0.023(0.17)	0.415**(3.24)
Children in Single-Mother Families	1.318**(3.26)	1.005**(3.00)	0.934**(3.31)	0.691**(2.82)
Constant	9.422*(1.67)	11.201**(2.42)	−0.060**(−3.70)	7.361**(2.18)
R^2 Overall	.537	.751	.553	.720
N	94	94	94	94

*$p < .10$; **$p < .05$.

Table A.11. Results for Figure 5.8—Random Effects Models of Overall Poverty in Affluent Western Democracies, 1969–2002: Unstandardized Coefficients (z-scores)

	Headcount		Intensity	
Welfare Generosity Index		$-3.626**(-8.76)$		$-2.409**(-8.34)$
Current Left Government	$-0.446(-0.81)$	$-0.441(-0.99)$	$-0.261(-0.66)$	$-0.256(-0.79)$
Economic Growth	$-0.161*(-1.93)$	$-0.281**(-4.19)$	$-0.122*(-2.06)$	$-0.204**(-4.24)$
Unemployment	$-0.062(-0.49)$	$-0.007(-0.08)$	$-0.008(-0.09)$	$0.009(0.14)$
Productivity	$3E-5(1.00)$	$-4E-5(-1.48)$	$2E-5(0.78)$	$-3E-5*(-1.68)$
Manufacturing Employment	$-0.070(-0.77)$	$-0.153*(-2.31)$	$-0.036(-0.56)$	$-0.098**(-2.10)$
Female Labor Force Participation	$-0.054(-1.04)$	$-0.104**(-2.81)$	$-0.034(-0.93)$	$-0.068**(-2.61)$
Elderly Population	$0.068(0.34)$	$0.627**(3.94)$	$0.005(0.04)$	$0.400**(3.57)$
Children in Single-Mother Families	$1.309**(3.15)$	$1.213**(4.03)$	$0.914**(3.14)$	$0.832**(3.92)$
Constant	$9.958*(1.70)$	$10.757**(2.58)$	$6.438(1.57)$	$7.203**(2.45)$
R^2 Overall	.412	.777	.454	.755
N	104	104	104	104

$*p < .10; **p < .05.$

195

Table A.12. Results for Figure 5.9—Random Effects Models of Overall Poverty in Affluent Western Democracies, 1969–2002: Unstandardized Coefficients (z-scores)

	Headcount		Intensity	
Welfare Generosity Index	−0.145**(−3.09)	−3.400**(−7.31)	−0.097**(−3.02)	−2.283**(−6.92)
Cumulative Left Party Power	−0.141*(−1.80)	−0.058(−1.57)	−0.108*(−1.93)	−0.036(−1.35)
Economic Growth	−0.088(−0.73)	−0.273**(−4.12)	−0.025(−0.30)	−0.197**(−4.13)
Unemployment	2E−5(0.73)	−0.034(−0.36)	1E−5(0.47)	−0.003(−0.05)
Productivity	2E−5[0.73]	−4E−5*(−1.67)	1E−5[0.47]	−4E−5*(−1.88)
Manufacturing Employment	−0.105(−1.21)	−0.166*(−2.47)	−0.056(−0.92)	0.104**(−2.17)
Female Labor Force Participation	−0.042(−0.83)	−0.093*(−2.40)	−0.024(−0.68)	−0.060**(−2.16)
Elderly Population	0.298(1.45)	0.701**(4.17)	0.169(1.17)	0.448**(3.74)
Children in Single-Mother Families	1.418**(3.55)	1.224**(3.93)	0.990**(3.55)	0.827**(3.73)
Constant	9.304*(1.67)	10.492**(2.44)	5.730(1.47)	6.899**(2.26)
R^2 Overall	.601	.781	.617	.762
N	104	104	104	104

$*p < .10$; $**p < .05$.

Table A.13. Results for Figure 5.10—Random Effects Models of Overall Poverty in Affluent Western Democracies, 1969–2002: Unstandardized Coefficients (z-scores)

	Headcount		Intensity	
Welfare Generosity Index	$-0.331^{**}(-4.20)$	$-3.127^{**}(-5.39)$	$-0.211^{**}(-3.97)$	$-2.128^{**}(-5.13)$
Cumulative Women in the Legislature	$-0.185^{**}(-2.17)$	$-0.102(-1.23)$	$-0.142^{*}(-2.31)$	$-0.050(-0.85)$
Economic Growth	$-0.059(-0.46)$	$-0.296^{**}(-3.88)$	$-0.023(-0.26)$	$-0.217^{**}(-3.89)$
Unemployment	$1E-4^{*}(1.76)$	$-0.011(-0.10)$	$3E-5(1.46)$	$0.004(0.05)$
Productivity	$-0.088(-1.08)$	$-2E-5(-0.70)$	$-0.050(-0.90)$	$-2E-5(-0.98)$
Manufacturing Employment	$-0.017(-0.33)$	$-0.150^{**}(-2.05)$	$-0.014(-0.41)$	$-0.096^{*}(-1.86)$
Female Labor Force Participation	$0.024(0.13)$	$-0.078^{*}(-1.70)$	$-0.012(-0.09)$	$-0.057^{*}(-1.72)$
Elderly Population	$1.551^{**}(4.13)$	$0.521^{**}(2.77)$	$1.081^{**}(4.16)$	$0.333^{**}(2.50)$
Children in Single-Mother Families	$9.833^{*}(1.84)$	$1.215^{**}(3.61)$	$6.670^{*}(1.81)$	$0.832^{**}(3.48)$
Constant		$10.558^{**}(2.22)$		$7.343^{**}(2.18)$
R^2 Overall	.624	.753	.618	.732
N	95	95	95	95

$^{*}p < .10;\ ^{**}p < .05.$

Table A.14. Results for Figure 5.11. Random Effects Models of Overall Poverty in Affluent Western Democracies, 1969–2002: Unstandardized Coefficients (z-scores)

	Headcount		Intensity	
Welfare Generosity Index		$-3.620**(-7.84)$		$-2.383**(-7.30)$
Voter Turnout	$-0.075**(-2.20)$	$-0.009(-0.37)$	$-0.057**(-2.54)$	$-0.012(-0.68)$
Economic Growth	$-0.191**(-2.37)$	$-0.295**(-4.50)$	$-0.146**(-2.55)$	$-0.211**(-4.47)$
Unemployment	$-0.085(-0.68)$	$-0.029(-0.30)$	$-0.029(-0.34)$	$-0.004(-0.06)$
Productivity	$2E-5(0.64)$	$-4E-5*(-1.74)$	$-1E-5(0.45)$	$-4E-5*(-1.96)$
Manufacturing Employment	$-0.080(-0.91)$	$-0.166**(-2.44)$	$-0.043(-0.71)$	$-0.104**(-2.16)$
Female Labor Force Participation	$-0.083(-1.60)$	$-0.107**(-2.71)$	$-0.058(-1.63)$	$-0.070**(-2.52)$
Elderly Population	$0.087(0.45)$	$0.638**(3.86)$	$0.031(0.23)$	$0.409**(3.49)$
Children in Single-Mother Families	$1.307**(3.22)$	$1.148**(3.67)$	$0.921**(3.30)$	$0.776**(3.49)$
Constant	$17.902**(2.72)$	$12.353**(2.44)$	$12.499**(2.78)$	$8.728**(2.44)$
R^2 Overall	.498	.765	.538	.747
N	104	104	104	104

$*p < .10; **p < .05.$

Table A.15. Results for Figure 5.12—Random Effects Models of Overall Poverty in Affluent Western Democracies, 1969–2002: Unstandardized Coefficients (z-scores)

	Headcount		Intensity	
Welfare Generosity Index	−5.024**(−3.93)	−3.330**(−7.06)	−3.539***(−4.00)	−2.201**(−6.52)
Proportional Representation		−1.960*(−1.93)		−1.499*(−2.07)
Economic Growth	−0.169**(−2.28)	−0.278**(−4.29)	−0.123**(−2.34)	−0.197**(−4.22)
Unemployment	−0.179(−1.51)	−0.071(−0.73)	−0.093(−1.10)	−0.032(−0.46)
Productivity	1E−5(0.18)	−4E−5*(−1.86)	−3E−6(−0.14)	−4E−5*(−2.12)
Manufacturing Employment	−0.164*(−1.87)	−0.193**(−2.80)	−0.102*(−1.65)	−0.124*(−2.52)
Female Labor Force Participation	−0.076(−1.54)	−0.111**(−2.86)	−0.048(−1.39)	−0.071**(−2.56)
Elderly Population	0.160(0.85)	0.640**(3.90)	0.086(0.65)	0.414**(3.52)
Children in Single-Mother Families	0.733*(1.78)	0.901**(2.71)	0.469(1.62)	0.575***(2.41)
Constant	19.338**(3.27)	14.803**(3.20)	12.978**(3.13)	10.063**(3.04)
R^2 Overall	.463	.766	.482	.747
N	104	104	104	104

$*p < .10; **p < .05.$

Table A.16. Sensitivity Analysis—Random Effects Models of Overall Headcount Poverty in Affluent Western Democracies, 1969–2002: Unstandardized Coefficients (z-scores) (N = 90)

	Model 1	Model 2	Model 3	Model 4
Welfare Generosity Index		-3.319**(-6.24)		-3.274**(-5.49)
Bargaining Centralization	-0.821*(-3.39)	-0.279(-1.27)	-0.495*(-1.82)	-0.240(-1.02)
Union Density			-0.059**(-2.27)	-0.010(-0.39)
Economic Growth	-0.309*(-3.43)	-0.351**(-4.75)	-0.294**(-3.37)	-0.345**(-4.62)
Unemployment	-0.104(-0.76)	0.025(0.21)	-0.053(-0.39)	0.028(0.23)
Productivity	1E-4**(2.15)	-3E-5(-1.09)	5E-5(1.39)	-4E-5(-1.23)
Manufacturing Employment	-0.061(-0.73)	-0.149**(-2.02)	-0.003(-0.03)	-0.141*(-1.69)
Female Labor Force Participation	-0.070(-1.41)	-0.097**(-2.25)	-0.034(-0.65)	-0.092*(-1.94)
Elderly Population	-0.064(-0.34)	0.568**(3.01)	-0.048(-0.25)	0.571**(2.87)
Children in Single-Mother Families	1.203**(2.95)	0.907**(2.59)	1.259**(3.09)	0.866**(2.37)
Constant	13.642**(2.47)	12.060**(2.53)	11.710**(2.09)	12.001**(2.40)
R^2 Overall	.638	.776	.631	.766

Results for poverty intensity are substantively identical except bargaining centralization would not be statistically significant in model 3 as well (but union density would be significant). * $p < .10$; ** $p < .05$

Details from Chapter 6

Table A.17. Additional Descriptive Statistics (from Huber et al. 2004; LIS)

Variable	Mean (Standard Deviation)	N
Dependent Variable: Absolute Poverty	16.922(12.280)	18
Independent Variable: Welfare Generosity Index Squared	4.667(3.311)	104

Analyses for Chapter 6 Figures

Table A.18. Results for Figures 6.4, 6.5, and 6.7—Random Effects Models of Poverty in Affluent Western Democracies, 1969–2002: Unstandardized Coefficients (z-scores)

	Overall Headcount	Overall Intensity	Working-Age Adult Headcount
Economic Growth	−0.158**(−2.17)	−0.118**(−2.33)	−0.178**(−2.53)
Unemployment	0.207**(3.21)	0.148**(3.32)	0.266**(4.21)
Productivity	1E−5(0.31)	−1E−6(−0.07)	3E−5(0.95)
Welfare Generosity Index	−2.252**(−4.99)	−1.517**(−4.91)	−1.213**(−2.78)
Welfare Generosity Index Squared	0.304(1.03)	0.289(1.41)	0.161(0.57)
Proportional Representation	−2.841**(−2.73)	−1.985**(−2.80)	−2.425**(−2.44)
Constant	9.733**(5.60)	6.611**(5.52)	6.884**(3.80)
R^2 Overall	.700	.688	.567
N	104	104	101

$*p < .10; **p < .05.$

Table A.19.   Results for Figure 6.8—Ordinary Least Squares Models of Absolute Poverty in 18 Affluent Western Democracies circa 2000: Unstandardized Coefficients (z-scores).

	Model 1	Model 2
Economic Growth	−1.687(−1.02)	−0.943(−0.51)
Unemployment	0.294(0.25)	0.413(0.32)
Productivity	−0.0002(−0.36)	−0.0003(−0.54)
Welfare Generosity Index	−4.111(−0.92)	−0.347(−0.06)
Welfare Generosity Index Squared		4.824(0.78)
Proportional Representation		−7.608(−0.78)
Constant	31.931(1.17)	37.832(1.25)
R^2	.195	.278

$*p < .10; **p < .05.$

Details from Chapter 7

Table A.20.   Additional Descriptive Statistics (from Huber et al. 2004; OECD(b))

Independent Variable	Mean (Standard Deviation)	N
Agricultural Employment	4.987(2.570)	104

Analyses for Chapter 7 Figures

Table A.21.   Results for Figures 7.6, 7.7, 7.9, and 7.10—Random Effects Models of Poverty in Affluent Western Democracies, 1969–2002: Unstandardized Coefficients (z-scores)

	Overall Headcount	Overall Intensity	Working-Age Adult Headcount	Child Headcount
Manufacturing Employment	−0.197**(−2.82)	−0.125**(−2.48)	−0.212**(−3.02)	−0.390**(−3.77)
Agricultural Employment	0.067(0.50)	0.004(0.04)	0.046(0.35)	0.092(0.47)
Female Labor Force Participation	−0.108**(−2.75)	−0.070*(−2.48)	−0.060(−1.50)	−0.152**(−2.61)
Elderly Population	0.674**(3.79)	0.416**(3.25)	0.465**(2.57)	1.004**(3.80)
Children in Single-Mother Families	0.897**(2.68)	0.567**(2.35)	0.548*(1.67)	0.929*(1.87)
Welfare Generosity Index	−3.278**(−6.74)	−2.200**(−6.27)	−2.182**(−4.33)	−4.570**(−6.34)
Proportional Representation	−2.227*(−1.95)	−1.541*(−1.87)	−2.089*(−1.77)	−4.738**(−2.81)
Economic Growth	−0.266**(−3.84)	−0.196**(−3.92)	−0.273**(−4.09)	−0.340**(−3.28)
Unemployment	−0.072(−0.74)	−0.033(−0.47)	0.029(0.30)	0.032(0.22)
Productivity	−4E−5*(−1.72)	−4E−5*(−2.09)	−3E5(−0.95)	−4E−5(−0.99)
Constant	14.002**(2.83)	10.057**(2.82)	12.402**(2.45)	18.578**(2.54)
R^2 Overall	.773	.747	.629	.789
N	104	104	101	104

*$p < .10$; **$p < .05$.

Details from Chapter 8

Table A.22.   Additional Descriptive Statistics (from Huber et al. 2004; OECD(a))

Independent Variables	Mean (Standard Deviation)	N
Net Migration, Five-Year Average	2.928(6.333)	104
U.S. Dummy	0.067(0.252)	104

Analyses for Chapter 8 Figures

Table A.23.   Results for Figure 8.2—Random Effects Models of Poverty in Affluent Western Democracies, 1969–2002: Unstandardized Coefficients (z-scores)

	Overall Headcount	Overall Intensity
U.S. Dummy	1.663(0.84)	1.573(1.15)
Welfare Generosity Index	−3.202**(−6.33)	−2.116**(−5.93)
Proportional Representation	−2.102*(−1.78)	−1.408*(−1.70)
Economic Growth	−0.263**(−3.76)	−0.190**(−3.78)
Unemployment	−0.082(−0.83)	−0.037(−0.53)
Productivity	$-5\text{E}-5$*(−1.81)	$-4\text{E}-5$**(−2.13)
Manufacturing Employment	−0.204**(−2.87)	−0.131**(−2.60)
Agricultural Employment	0.066(0.49)	0.016(0.16)
Female Labor Force Participation	−0.108**(−2.70)	−0.071**(−2.51)
Elderly Population	0.689**(3.79)	0.432**(3.36)
Children in Single-Mother Families	0.767**(2.12)	0.458*(1.77)
Constant	14.273**(2.83)	10.064**(2.83)
R^2 Overall	.779	.768
N	104	104

*$p < .10$; **$p < .05$.

Notes

Chapter 1

1. See, for example, McLeod and Shanahan (1993); Pampel and Williamson (2001); Rank (2005); Wilensky (2002).

2. Gans (1995: 127). This is an abridged quote, the full quote is: "The principal subject of poverty research, although not its sole subject, ought to be the forces, processes, agents, institutions, and so on that 'decide' that a proportion of the population will end up poor."

3. Hicks (1999); Huber and Stephens (2001); Korpi (1983).

4. Fligstein (2001). Kerckhoff (1995: 342–343) makes a similar point in emphasizing how institutions shape attainment and mobility by serving as the "sorting machines" of stratification.

5. North (1990: 112). Bourdieu (2005: 12) also writes: "The economic field is, more than any other, inhabited by the state, which contributes at every moment to its existence and persistence, and also to the structure of the relations of force that characterize it."

6. Brooks and Manza (2007); Skocpol (1992).

7. Fligstein (2001); see also Bourdieu's (2005) discussion of how the state constructs the market and demand.

8. As Mann (1983) explained, "Power does not principally concern the relations of sovereign individuals under the shelter of sovereign states. Instead it arises from the relations, complex and interpenetrating, between enduring organizations and authorities like classes, states, churches, communities, and bureaucracies." See also Lukes (1988); Wrong (1988).

9. Knoke et al. (1996).

10. Link and Phelan (1995); Lieberson's (1985) concept of "basic" causes is quite similar.

11. Manza and Brooks (1999).

12. As Pierson (2004: 14–15) remarks, "Thus the long-term effects of institutional choices, which are frequently the most profound and interesting ones, should often be seen as the *by-products* of social processes rather than embodying the goals of social actors" (emphasis original).

13. Pierson (2004). This book's definition of institution is broadly consistent with Campbell's (2004: 1):

> [Institutions] consist of formal and informal rules, monitoring and enforcement mechanisms, and systems of meaning that define the context within which individuals, corporations, labor unions, nation-states, and other organizations operate and interact with each other. Institutions are settlements born from struggle and bargaining. They reflect the resources and power of those who made them and, in turn, affect the distribution of resources and power in society. Once created, institutions are powerful external forces that help determine how people make sense of their world and act in it. They channel and regulate conflict and thus ensure stability in society.

14. Piven and Cloward (1997).

15. Knoke et al. (1996).

16. Weber, Gerth and Mills (1958: 128).

17. Campbell (2004); Hacker (2002); Pierson (2004).

18. A great deal has been written on this episode; my account draws especially on Daschle et al. (2008), Hacker (2002), Quadagno (2005), Skocpol (1996), and Starr (1995).

19. Daschle et al. (2008: 78–79).

20. Daschle et al. (2008: 93).

21. Starr (1995).

22. Hacker (2002); Quadagno (2005).

23. Daschle, Greenberger and Lambrew (2008: 100).

24. Tilly (1998: 21, 29) writes: "Since the fading of systems theories a generation ago, methodological individualism and phenomenological individualism have dominated analyses of inequality.... Since the late nineteenth century, individualistic models of inequality have crowded out categorical models.... When they adopted status attainment models of mobility and inequality, sociologists accentuated the shift from collective to individual effects."

25. For my purposes, "individualist perspectives" are synonymous with "individualism," "individualist," and "individualistic approaches."

26. As Gans (1995: 126) writes, "Most of the research on the poor concerns their personal characteristics, as if the neighborhood in which the poor are currently residing or how long they are on or off welfare were really major causes or even significant correlates of poverty."

27. As Rank (2005: 49, 50, 52) explains:

> Within the United States, the dominant perspective has been that of poverty as an individual failing.... The emphasis on individual attributes as the primary

cause of poverty has been reinforced by social scientists engaged in poverty research.... The unit of analysis in these studies is by definition the individual, rather than the wider social or economic structures, resulting in statistical models of individual characteristics that predict individual behavior.... To summarize, the current research approach to understanding U.S. poverty has examined the impact that individual and family characteristics exert upon the likelihood that Americans will experience poverty and/or welfare use.

28. See Iceland (2003: ch. 4).

29. Blau and Duncan (1967).

30. Jencks and colleagues (1979).

31. Sawhill (2003: 83).

32. See, for example, Harris (1996).

33. Gans (1995: 126) points out, "When the research paradigm is framed around characteristics, some researchers will inevitably blame the losers and the squeezed, in the way that poverty researchers and their predecessors have done since the inception of poverty research."

34. Hernstein and Murray (1994).

35. Hernstein and Murray (1994: 127, 135).

36. For a devastating critique of their methods and analyses, see Fischer et al. (1996).

37. See, for example, Hills (2004); Hunt (1996); G. Wilson (1996).

38. Referring to "social types" as supraindividual entities, Wright et al. (1992: 127) offer a sound articulation of this epistemological point:

To ban social types as objects of investigation is to impoverish the explanatory objectives of social science, and to contravene reasonable practices in the social sciences. Micro-foundations are important for macro-social theory because of the ways they help focus our questions and because of the way they enrich our answers. But there is more to science than elaboration. If social types, as we suspect, are multiply realized, then micro-foundational accounts, important though they may be, cannot suffice to capture the explanatory power of macro-level theories.

39. Relatedly, it is worth noting that individualism relies upon the seductive but false imagery that individuals—as a unit of analysis—are indivisible. Alternatively, appreciating the role of collective and macro-level causes, one embraces the reality that many of the most important "social" causes are complex combinations of constituent parts (Searle 2003). It might be comforting if social science could realistically boil everything down to a unitary cause—the way molecular biologists isolate a gene. However, the state, market, and society generally are simply more complex than an individual or aggregation of individuals. Embracing this realistic position necessitates that the social sciences continue to study macro-level causes the way the biological sciences still need ecologists and not just molecular biologists.

40. Lieberson (1985: 108) explains, "If the conceptual level or theoretical issue is on a given level of analysis, then the empirical evidence obtained at a *lower* level will not be relevant for determining the merit or validity of the theory" (emphasis original).

41. Hawley (1992). Hawley (1992: 5) notes:

A reductionist fallacy identifies an object with its elements. Such instances, say Cohen and Nagel (1934: 383), are found in an argument that sees "scientific books as nothing but words, animate or inanimate nature as nothing but atoms, lines as nothing but points, and society as nothing but individuals, instead of holding books, nature, lines and society to be constituted by words, atoms, points and individuals, respectively, connected in certain ways."

42. Mills (1959: 9).

43. This is not to say that all individualist social science neglects relational dynamics. Of course, there are distinguished traditions within social psychology and Marxism, as but two examples, of using an explicitly relational approach while adhering to methodological individualism. However, extant individualist perspectives on poverty have mostly neglected relational dynamics.

44. Gans (1995: 126) also writes, "Studies ignore the fact that if the economy and society create and tolerate poverty, some groups and individuals have to be selected to suffer it."

45. Tilly (1998: 34). Tilly (1998: 35) elaborates, "[E]xtension of relational analyses within the study of social inequality does not deny the existence of individuals or individual-level effects. It does, however, place individualistic processes in their organizational context. It does, finally, challenge any ontology that reduces all social processes to the sentient actions of individual persons."

46. Christopher et al. (2002).

47. Fischer et al. (1996: 1539–1540) write:

Explaining who gets ahead and who falls behind in the race for success explains nothing about systems of inequality. For example, the income gap between corporate CEOs and workers is far wider in the United States than in Europe, and that gap has widened greatly in the last few decades. Individual traits cannot explain such cross-cultural or historical variations in inequality. Nor does knowing that an individual trait has a statistically significant effect on individual success explain the degree of inequality in the system. To understand variations in systems of inequality, we have to turn to social factors, and...to concrete social policies....[Our] unique contribution to the *Bell Curve* controversy is...addressing the larger, and for sociologists, more important question of how we explain levels of social inequality. *The Bell Curve*'s reductionism is useless here.

48. Gans (1995).

49. I do not mean to imply an affinity for postindustrial theory, but rather use the label for an era beginning in the late 1960s or early 1970s—as in Wilensky's (2002) "rich democracies."

50. At the end of chapter 4's appendix materials, I present a sensitivity analysis where I use fixed effects models. The results are consistent.

51. See Brady (2003a, 2003b, 2003c, 2004, 2005, 2006) and Brady and Kall (2008).

52. Wilson (1987).

53. Anderson (1990); Duneier (1999); Edin and Lein (1997); Newman (1999); Venkatesh (2000). Of course, these constitute only a small sample of the vast and excellent ethnographic literature on poverty.

Chapter 2

1. See Grusky and Kanbur (2006).

2. Hagenaars (1991: 134).

3. Betson and Warlick (1998); Hill and Michael (2001); Uchitelle (1999).

4. In another study (Brady 2003a), I showed that about two-thirds of sociological studies published between 1990 and 2000 used the official measure. Though a similar content analysis for economic and public policy journals has not been done, the proportion is probably comparable or even higher.

5. Betson and Warlick (1998: 351).

6. Wilson (1991: 3, 2).

7. The report was edited by Citro and Michael (1995: xvi).

8. Katz (1989: 115–117); O'Connor (2001); Wilson (1991).

9. Orshansky (1965).

10. Stone (2002).

11. As early as 1970, Orshansky (see Orshansky 1976: 236) wrote in a "Memorandum for Daniel P. Moynihan on the 'History of the Poverty Line'" that "This meant, of course, that the food-income relationship which was the basis for the original poverty measure no longer was the current rationale." She also wrote: "By the end of 1967, there was increasing awareness that the poverty line was lagging behind the general rise in standard of living enjoyed by the majority . . . [and] did not measure accurately the total price rise facing the poor."

12. Katz (1989: 115–117); O'Connor (2001); see also Betson and Warlick (1998).

13. See Orshansky (1976); Stone (2002).

14. Orshansky wrote this in a 1969 *Social Security Bulletin* article (see Orshansky 1976: 245).

15. Betson and Warlick (1998); Blank (1997); Citro and Michael (1995).

16. As mentioned above, Orshansky (1976) identified most of the problems in this paragraph as early as the late 1960s. See also Ruggles (1990); Foster (1998); Citro and Michael (1995).

17. Sen (1976) would call this a violation of the "transfer axiom."

18. Ruggles (1990); Smeeding et al. (2001).

19. Betson and Warlick (1998); Citro and Michael (1995); Lichter (1997).

20. Blank (1997).

21. Smeeding et al. (1993: 247).

22. Atkinson (1998a); Cantillion (1997).

23. Atkinson (1990, 1998a); Hagenaars (1991).

24. Betson and Warlick (1998); Jorgenson (1998).

25. Hills (2004); Ormerod (1998); Paugam (1998); Procacci (1998); Wacquant (1995).

26. Silver (1994, 1995).

27. Cantillion (1997: 130).

28. Schuyt and Tan (1998: 14).

29. Dahrendorf (1990: 151).

30. Engbersen (1991).

31. Gore (1995).

32. Harrington (1981: 11).

33. Rankin and Quane (2000); Wilson (1991).

34. Galbraith (1998: 235).

35. Despite his influence on poverty and inequality debates (see Sen 1992), Rawls (1999) made very few overt references to poverty. Atkinson (1987: 760) notes that the word "poverty" does not even appear in Rawls's (1999) extensive index. He discusses poverty a bit more later (e.g., Rawls 2001), but mainly one needs to rely on his discussion of economic inequality.

36. Rawls (2001: 130).

37. Rawls (2001: 129).

38. Atkinson (1987).

39. Nussbaum (2006); Sen (1992, 1999).

40. Nussbaum (2006: 49).

41. Rawls (1999); see also Atkinson (1987).

42. Barry (1973, 1998).

43. Rainwater and Smeeding (2004: 10).

44. Atkinson (1998a: 27).

45. Barry (1998: 22).

46. Cantillion (1997: 131).

47. Atkinson (1998b: 20).

48. Gore (1995); Rodgers (1995); Sen (1992).

49. Madden (2000); Sen (1983); Shanahan and Tuma (1994).

50. Atkinson (1998a); Hagenaars (1991); Madden (2000); Sen (1992).

51. Sen (1992, 1999).

52. Smeeding et al. (1993: 246).

53. Hagenaars (1991: 146).

54. Rainwater and Smeeding (2004: 9).

55. Jorgenson (1998).

56. Cox and Alm (1999).

57. For specific methodological critiques, see Hagenaars (1991), Lichter (1997), and Triest (1998).

58. Harrington (1981: 188).

59. Ruggles (1990).

60. Ravallion (1998: 21).

61. Hagenaars (1991: 141).

62. President's Commission on Income Maintenance Programs (1969).

63. Townsend (1980: 300).

64. Sen (1992: 110).

65. Stewart (2006).

66. Shanahan and Tuma (1994).

67. Barry (1998); Gore (1995).

68. Atkinson (1998a: 2).

69. Rainwater and Smeeding (2004); Silver (1994).

70. Rawls (1999: 84).

71. Rawls (2001: 132).

72. Rawls (2001: 132; emphasis added).

73. One could use Rawls's maximin criterion to argue that he endorsed absolute measures of poverty. But Rawls (e.g., 1999: 68) wrote much about

how justice depends on democratic equality and that this was compromised by large differences between classes. For example, Rawls (2001: 131) wrote,

Significant political and economic inequalities are often associated with inequalities of social status that encourage those of lower status to be viewed both by themselves and by others as inferior....It is close to being wrong or unjust in itself that in a status system, not everyone can have the highest rank. Status is a positional good, as is sometimes said. High status assumes other positions beneath it; so if we seek a higher status for ourselves, we in effect support a scheme that entails others' having a lower status.

74. Sen (1999: 89; emphasis original).

75. Atkinson (1998b).

76. Townsend (1980); Sen (1976).

77. Orshansky (1976: 234, 233; emphasis added).

78. Harrington (1981: 18, 187–188).

79. An odd irony is that U.S. sociologists, who should have a commitment to relational measures like relative poverty, have actually been slower to take up relative measures and abandon the official U.S. measure (compared to international poverty research generally).

80. Townsend (1962: 219).

81. Hills (2004); Rainwater and Smeeding (2004).

82. Hills (2004).

83. Hill and Michael (2001); Betson and Warlick (1998); Triest (1998).

84. See, for example, Stewart (2006). Lichter (1997: 130) explains,

Absolute increases in child poverty are arguably less important than several other dimensions of the current poverty problem....Today's poverty among children must be judged against the living conditions and consumption levels of society as a whole and other advantaged groups—current and past. It is with regard to this relative dimension that implies increasing social and cultural differentiation in the future as the current generation of poor children enters adulthood.

85. Marmot (2004).

86. Lichter (1997).

87. Sen (1976: 219).

88. Smeeding et al. (1993).

89. See, for example, Beramendi and Anderson (2008); Bradley et al. (2003); Iversen and Soskice (2006); Korpi and Palme (2003); Mahler et al. (1999).

90. Esping-Andersen (1990; 2003: 65); Fligstein (2001).

91. Wright (2004: 3–4).

92. Fligstein (2001).

93. Bergh (2005).

94. In other research (Brady 2003a), I have shown that there is much more empirical variation in post-fisc than in pre-fisc poverty, and it is this crucial societal variation that needs explanation. Further, societal patterns in pre-fisc and post-fisc poverty are simply not empirically associated in a way that suggests the relevance of pre-fisc poverty. If pre-fisc poverty is a real problem, it should be very positively associated with what we know is a real problem: post-fisc poverty. Yet, the correlation is quite weak and is often negative.

95. Sen (1976).

96. Hagenaars (1991).

97. Atkinson (1987).

98. Sen (1976: 219).

99. Blank (1997: 139).

100. Osberg and Xu (2000). Because it treats poverty as continuous, unlike the dichotomous headcount, I have previously called poverty intensity the "interval measure" (to differentiate it from Sen's "ordinal measure"). However, it is easier to simply use the prevailing label.

101. Foster et al. (1984); Sen (1976).

102. In the ordinal measure, the Gini index is often used instead of the coefficient of variation. However, research on inequality demonstrates that the Gini index can be replaced with the simpler coefficient of variation (CV), which is substantively identical and easier to compute (Allison 1978). While more mathematically complicated formulas exist, several scholars have demonstrated that the ordinal measure can be reduced this way (Myles and Picot 2000; Osberg and Xu 2000).

103. Foster et al. (1984). In Brady (2003a), I discussed the *sum of ordinals measure* of poverty (SO). SO is simply the sum of headcounts for various descending thresholds, and thus builds on relational distribution measures of inequality (Handcock and Morris 1999). For example, I calculated the headcounts for 60%, 50%, 40%, 30%, 20%, 10%, and 5% of the median income and summed the values. This SO measure mimics the properties of poverty intensity and can be easily converted to something similar to the ordinal measure by weighting the lower thresholds (5%, 10%, and 20%) more heavily. While useful for graphically displaying the patterns in poverty, SO probably offers little beyond the intensity and ordinal measures. Thus, I do not discuss SO further in this book.

104. Brady (2003a).

105. Atkinson (1987); Hagenaars (1991); Myles and Picot (2000); Osberg and Xu (2000).

Chapter 3

1. For details on the LIS, a good place to start is its Web page (www.lisproject.org).

2. I use the LIS variable DPI (disposable income). All estimates are weighted by HWEIGHT*D4.

3. Because the expenses caused by additional members do not linearly increase, and because there is pooling of resources among household members, this scale has been found appropriate (Rainwater and Smeeding 2004). While there is debate over equivalence scales (Triest 1998), the LIS staff examined the statistical behavior of more than 30 different scales and concluded that most are consistent (see Buhmann et al. 1988).

4. Indeed, the LIS has recently developed a Luxembourg Wealth Study as a complement.

5. Hagenaars (1991); Ruggles (1990); Sen (1992).

6. Estimates vary, but probably the bottom 40% of the U.S. wealth distribution has zero wealth (see, e.g., Keister 2000). Because less than 20% of the United States is poor, it is unlikely that a substantial share of these poor is holding significant wealth (of course, one might worry about elderly pensions, but this obscures that this elderly wealth is drawn down as income).

7. Even the poor elderly had a median net worth of 38–41% of the median net worth of all elderly. Of course, the poor elderly have a much higher net worth than the nonelderly poor, but the elderly's net worth is a function of pension savings that function as income. The analyses used the LIS version of the 2001 U.S. Survey of Consumer Finances standardized within the Luxembourg Wealth Study (LWS, which is a part of the LIS). Poor people are defined as those with less than half the median income (using the LWS measure "DPIW"), standardized by the square root of household members. The analyses were conducted in December 2007.

8. Rainwater and Smeeding (2004) also point out that survey respondents mainly focus on income when defining what it means to be poor.

9. These numbers are based on 2000 median household income statistics from the U.S. census Web page (Census Bureau, www.census.gov). This is not the same median as in the LIS, and these numbers have not been adjusted for household size.

10. See, for example, Rainwater and Smeeding (2004); Smeeding et al. (2001).

11. Pontusson (2005).

12. Esping-Andersen (1990, 1999); Huber and Stephens (2001); Korpi and Palme (1998); see also chapter 4.

13. Official U.S. poverty figures (1974–2000) are available on the Census Bureau Web page (Census Bureau, www.census.gov).

14. Hill and Michael (2001); Uchitelle (1999).

15. One criticism of relative measures is that one is basically measuring inequality. While poverty is a component of patterns at the bottom of the income distribution and is associated with inequality, there are important differences between inequality and these poverty measures. In analyses with the LIS data, I found that the Gini coefficient of income inequality has a correlation of .86 with the headcount measure and .85 with the intensity measure. But, the overall headcount and intensity measures correlate .99. As Osberg and Xu (2000: 68) point out, "Although there is a positive correlation between income inequality and poverty intensity, the relationship is far from perfect." Given that inequality and poverty indices measure different phenomena, poverty and inequality are better understood as complementary but theoretically distinct concepts and measures.

16. Kenworthy (2004: 94, 101) writes,

An absolute measure uses the same poverty line (in converted currency units) across all nations . . . . I set the poverty line at $12,763, which is 50 percent of the 2000 median posttax-posttransfer household income per equivalent person in the United States . . . . The choice of $12,763 per equivalent person is an arbitrary one, of course. But any other number would be equally arbitrary.

17. The sources for PPP conversion are the Penn World tables 6.2 for non-Euro countries and the Penn World table 6.1 for Euro countries (Heston et al. 2006; Heston et al. 2002).

18. Irish currency before 2000 is standardized to 2000 real Irish pounds.

19. These poverty lines assume that U.S. standards of living in 2000 are appropriate for evaluating poverty in other countries and earlier years, for Ireland especially, as Kenworthy (2004: 187) writes, "This poverty line is absolute not only across countries but also over time, which strikes me as sensible given that the period covered is only twenty-five years."

20. Casper et al. (1994); Christopher et al. (2002); Pearce (1978).

21. McLanahan and Kelly (1999).

22. Sassoon (1996).

23. Blau and Kahn (1992).

24. Christopher et al. (2002).

25. Wright (1995).

26. Misra (2002); Sainsbury (1999).

27. McCall (2001).

28. Orloff (1993).

29. Meyers and Gornick (2001).

30. Working-age women's poverty correlates with adult women's poverty for both the headcount ($r = .88$) and intensity ($r = .90$) measures. Working-age men's poverty correlates with adult men's poverty for both the headcount ($r = .94$) and intensity ($r = .95$) measures. See Brady and Kall (2008).

31. In addition, Australia is AUL, Austria is AUT, Belgium is BEL, Denmark is DEN, Finland is FIN, France is FRA, Ireland is IRE, Italy is ITA, Luxembourg is LUX, the Netherlands is NET, Norway is NOR, Spain is SPA, Sweden is SWE, Switzerland is SWZ, and the United Kingdom is UKM.

32. This pattern is even stronger for the correlation between working-age women and all working-age adults (headcount and intensity $r = .98$).

33. The correlation is even stronger among working-age adults (headcount and intensity $r = .91$).

34. Brady and Kall (2008).

35. Preston (1984). Preston also asserts that growing elderly populations undermine political support for children's programs, and that elderly programs subtract from the resources available to children. This argument never had support in the literature and has subsequently been refuted by political sociologists and political scientists. Even though the welfare state has been a vibrant topic of research for decades in sociology and political science, oddly, Preston failed to cite any of that research. The size of the elderly population has a positive, not negative, effect on a variety of measures of welfare generosity, including programs for the nonelderly (Brady et al. 2005). Had Preston referenced this work, perhaps he would not have come to this conclusion.

36. Bianchi (1999); Lichter (1997).

37. Blank (1997: 20).

38. Page and Simmons (2000: 21–22).

39. In the comparisons of child and elderly poverty, only the headcount measure is available, primarily because there are occasionally too few elderly or children in the LIS data set to estimate a reliable measure of the income gap.

40. Unfortunately, an estimate of elderly poverty for France in 1981 is not available because of a limited number of elderly in the sample.

41. Rowntree (1906); see also Rank (2005).

42. Smeeding et al. (1990) have shown that while a minority of U.S. retirees have a high income, a large percentage have an income just above the official U.S. poverty line. Smeeding et al. (2001) show that with a threshold of 40% of the median income—which is closer to the official U.S. threshold—the rate of elderly poverty would be much lower in the United States and several other countries. This sensitivity to the chosen threshold accounts for why the elderly are less likely to be officially poor than relatively poor. A headcount measure does not have to be very much higher to get a different result, particularly for the United States and the elderly.

Chapter 4

1. Freeman et al. (1997).

2. Cantillion (1997); Epstein (2003); Freeman (1999); Mayer (1997); Murray (1984).

3. Katz (1989: 113).

4. Epstein (2003: 63).

5. Prasad (2005).

6. Bernstein (1999); Hernandez (1999); Pear (1999).

7. For a definitive treatment of scholarship of the welfare state, see Wilensky (2002).

8. For examples of this extensive literature on the welfare state's effects on poverty, see Bradley et al. (2003), Cantillion (1997), Danziger and Weinberg (1994), DeFina and Thanawala (2001), Hanratty and Blank (1992), Hills (2004), Jantti and Danziger (2000), Kelly (2005), McFate et al. (1995), Moller et al. (2003), Nolan et al. (2000), Page and Simmons (2000), Smeeding et al. (2001), Tomaskovic-Devey (1991), and Zuberi (2006).

9. Esping-Andersen (1999).

10. Gangl (2006).

11. Zuberi (2006).

12. Fligstein (2001).

13. Bergh (2005); Esping-Andersen (2003); Wright (2004).

14. Korpi (1983: 188).

15. See especially Fligstein (2001).

16. Brooks and Manza (2007).

17. See, for example, Brady et al. (2005); Huber and Stephens (2001); Hicks (1999); Lindert (2004).

18. Wilensky (1975).

19. Esping-Andersen (1990: 2, 19, 58); see also Esping-Andersen (1999).

20. Korpi and Palme (1998).

21. Korpi and Palme (1998); unfortunately, this measure has never been publicly available, so scholars have been unable to replicate their findings and conclusions.

22. Esping-Andersen (1990); Freeman (1999).

23. Allan and Scruggs (2004).

24. Huber and Stephens (2000: 323).

25. See Brady (2005).

26. Bergman (1996); Currie and Yelowitz (2000); Huber and Stephens (2001); Wolfe (1994).

27. Blank (1997).

28. Blank (1997); Huber and Stephens (2001); Korpi and Palme (1998).

29. Huber and Stephens (2000: 324).

30. Esping-Andersen (1990); Korpi and Palme (1998).

31. Huber and Stephens (2001).

32. Blank (1997); Volscho and Fullerton (2005).

33. Blank (1994); Ellwood and Welty (2000); Gans (1995); Gornick and Jacobs (1998); Hout (1984); Newman (1999).

34. Freeman (1995); Hall and Soskice (2001); Huber and Stephens (2001); Korpi and Palme (1998); Marshall (1963); Titmus (1974).

35. Esping-Andersen (1990).

36. Esping-Andersen (1990: 2).

37. Esping-Andersen (1990: 2).

38. Hall and Soskice (2001).

39. Hicks and Esping-Andersen (2005: 511–512); also, "Overall spending levels may prove to be ambiguous measures of a welfare state" (2005: 516).

40. Korpi and Palme (1998).

41. Esping-Andersen (1990: 76–77).

42. Esping-Andersen (1999: 16–17, 32).

43. Esping-Andersen (1999); Korpi and Palme (1998).

44. Clayton and Pontusson (1998); Esping-Andersen (1999); Gilbert (2002); Huber and Stephens (2001); Sassoon (1996). Of course, not all agree that there has been a crisis of welfare state retrenchment (Brady et al. 2005; Wilensky 2002).

45. Western (1997); Western and Healy (1999).

46. Stephens et al. (1999: 191).

47. Huber and Stephens (2001: 123).

48. Esping-Andersen (1999); see also Bonoli (2007).

49. Okun (1975).

50. Blyth (2002); Freeman et al. (1997).

51. All measures are in the present year, because lagged values and moving averages produce identical results. In Brady (2005), I also considered military spending as a percentage of gross domestic product as a welfare state measure. However, this variable never had a significant effect, so I exclude it here.

52. Allan and Scruggs (2004); Esping-Andersen (1990).

53. My analyses are intended to represent the welfare state as an integrated complex of different social policies. The implication is that the welfare state matters most as a combination of a variety of different programs, services, taxes, and transfers (Zuberi 2006). A reasonable alternative would be to decompose at least welfare transfers into its precise components. In appendix table A.7, I present sensitivity analyses that examine the five

largest components of welfare transfers: old-age pensions, survivor benefits, disability benefits, family allowances, and unemployment benefits. These data are available only for 1980 and afterward and have some missing observations ($N = 91$). Nevertheless, the results are consistent with the main conclusions for this chapter. Interestingly, family allowances and unemployment benefits appear to be the most salient precise transfer programs, followed by old-age pensions and disability benefits (survivor benefits do not appear to matter).

54. Cusack (2004). For Spain and Luxembourg, Cusack's measure was unavailable. So, I substituted data on general government services as a percentage of civilian employment from the Organization for Economic Cooperation and Development (OECD(a)). The two measures are highly correlated. Dropping those cases does not change the results.

55. The alpha for this scale is .88. This variable is constructed to approximate a mean of 0 and standard deviation of 1 for each indicator, but the average z-score of these indicators that forms the scale does not exactly have a mean of 0 and standard deviation of 1. Using Stata software's "alpha" command, the scale is generated regardless of missing values. A score is created by dividing the number of items over which the sum is calculated.

56. See Wilensky (1997, 2002); Zuberi (2006).

57. I use Esping-Andersen's (1990) original coding of countries.

58. In appendix table A.8, I also present a sensitivity analysis of fixed versus random effects models. As discussed elsewhere in the appendix, available statistical tests suggest that random effects models are acceptable and may be preferred.

59. This simulation uses the standardized coefficients as displayed in figure 4.3.

60. See Moller et al. (2003) for a discussion of this issue.

61. While I do not statistically test the differences between coefficients, we can certainly reject the hypothesis that the effects are smaller for children than for the elderly, smaller for adult women than for adult men, and smaller for working-age adults than for children or the elderly.

62. Also, the Bayesian information criterion prime (Raftery 1995) prefers the models without welfare state regimes and only with the welfare generosity index.

63. Esping-Andersen (1990); Korpi and Palme (1998).

64. Blank (1997: 291).

65. Unlike the public health spending measure, the poverty measures do not incorporate in-kind benefits. Hence, it is possible that the public health spending × welfare regime interactions may be less appropriate for testing Esping-Andersen's arguments. However, this concern does not apply to social security transfers.

Chapter 5

1. Sassoon (1996: 692).

2. Ipsen (1991); see also Blyth (2002); Sassoon (1996); Schmidt (1992).

3. Ipsen (1991, 1994); Hoge (1998).

4. See, for example, Alt (1985).

5. Leicht (1989: 1043).

6. Wallerstein (1999: 668).

7. Rubin (1988); Rueda (2005).

8. Harrington (1981: 6).

9. Korpi (1983).

10. Piven and Cloward (1979, 1993, 1997).

11. See also Fording (2001). Schram (2002) offers a slightly different view of Piven and Cloward called "radical incrementalism," focusing on their joint roles as scholar-activists.

12. Hicks (1999); Huber and Stephens (2001); Korpi (1983).

13. Beramendi and Anderson (2008).

14. Burris (2001); Domhoff (1998).

15. Huber and Stephens (2001: 17).

16. Huber and Stephens (2001: 17).

17. As Korpi (1983: 187) explains:

The variations in the differences between these two basic types of power resources—control over the means of production and the organization of wage-earners into unions and political parties—are thus assumed to be of major importance for the distributive processes in capitalist democracies and for their final result; the extent of inequality.

18. See, for example, Korpi (1985).

19. Steensland (2006).

20. Brooks and Manza (2007).

21. The evidence is far more ambiguous for white working-class women; see Brady et al. (2009).

22. Manza and Brooks (1999). Even when the affluent vote Rightist, this is driven by ideology as much as by interest (see Brooks and Brady 1999).

23. Brooks and Brady (1999).

24. Korpi (1989: 313) writes that power resources theory offers "a game theoretical perspective on the analysis of interdependent actors." See also Korpi (1985); van den Berg and Janoski (2005).

25. Korpi (2003); Korpi and Palme (2003).

26. See Brady et al. (2005) for evidence against welfare state "crisis" or retrenchment.

27. Pierson (2004); Hacker (2002).

28. Pierson (2001). On balance, power resources theory often considers institutions, but such institutions were always very secondary to the manifest class conflict that primarily drives welfare politics. Korpi (1985: 38) wrote, "The power resources approach, leads us to view societal institutions largely as the residues of previous activations of power resources, often in the context of manifest conflicts which for the time being have been settled through various types of compromises."

29. Brady et al. (2005).

30. Hacker (2002); Myles and Pierson (2001).

31. Rosenfeld (2006). A somewhat contrary position should be noted, however: Dixon and Martin (2007) explain that labor militancy contributes

to unionization. If unionization is effective, one could argue that strikes might indirectly benefit the poor.

32. Orloff (1993); Quadagno (1994).

33. Bolzendahl and Brooks (2007).

34. Quadagno (1994).

35. Gilens (1999). In a similar vein, G. Wilson (1996) shows that attitudes about what causes poverty often depend on people's impressions of the racial composition of the particular group of poor. For example, people tend to be more individualistic in explaining welfare dependency (perceived as minority coded) and more structural in explaining homelessness. See also Misra et al. (2003); Schram et al. (2003).

36. Huber and Stephens (2001).

37. Huber and Stephens (2001: 17).

38. Huber and Stephens (2001: 18–19).

39. This point echoes Przeworski's (1986) classic demonstration that the working class never was a majority of the electorate and so could not have triggered socialism electorally.

40. Hall and Soskice (2001); see also Mares (2003); Swank and Martin (2001); Swenson (2002).

41. On power resources theory's commitment to this sort of two-class model, see van den Berg and Janoski (2005).

42. Swenson (2002).

43. This is a clear point where my account builds on the power constellations approach—for example, their "ratchet effect" and focus on cumulative political party effects (Huber and Stephens 2001)—as well as new politics of the welfare state scholars (e.g., Myles and Pierson 2001).

44. Campbell (2004).

45. Brooks and Manza (2007).

46. Manza and Brooks (1999) show that skilled/unskilled workers have moved in a Republican direction in the past few decades. Brady et al. (2009) demonstrate that white working-class men moved dramatically toward the Republicans beginning in the 1996 presidential election.

47. These causal pathways also build upon power resources theory; see Korpi (1983: 187, figure 9.1).

48. Brady et al. (2005); Hicks (1999); Huber and Stephens (2001).

49. Amenta (1998); Pontusson (2005).

50. Huber and Stephens (2001).

51. Burstein (1998).

52. Andrews (2001).

53. Huber and Stephens (2001).

54. Freeman and Medoff (1984); Leicht (1989); Leicht et al. (1993); Volscho and Fullerton (2005); Wallace et al. (1989. 1999).

55. Western and Healy (1999).

56. Gustafsson and Johansson (1999).

57. Wallerstein (1999); but see Golden and Londregan (2006) for a challenge to his results.

58. Bachrach and Baratz (1970); DiFazio (1998).

59. Freeman (1999).

60. Western (1997).

61. In appendix table A.16, I compare a measure of corporatism against this measure as an alternative measure of Leftist politics. I use Golden et al.'s (2007) second measure of bargaining centralization (because it is more strongly correlated with poverty than their first measure and more weakly correlated with union density [although the two still correlate at .58]). Bargaining centralization has a significant effect on poverty that is fully mediated by welfare generosity. Also, if one includes both union density and bargaining centralization in the same model, union density is more significant and appears to capture most of the effects of bargaining centralization. Therefore, the results are consistent if one substitutes measures of corporatism for measure of union density (see Brady 2003c).

62. Importantly, Huber et al. (2004) code only true Leftist parties as Leftist and do not consider centrist or some Left-center parties as Leftist parties. As a result, the Canadian Liberal Party and the U.S. Democratic Party are coded as centrist rather than Leftist parties. In analyses available upon request, I found the substantive conclusions were consistent if I recoded the Canadian Liberals and/or the U.S. Democrats as Leftist parties. For example, cumulative Left government has a significant negative effect that is channeled through welfare generosity (although this effect is moderately smaller and less significant than if those two parties are coded centrist).

63. Of course, poverty could cause lower voter turnout. It could be that egalitarianism encourages civic participation. But, because the measure of voter turnout often is based on an election that occurred several years before the poverty estimate, this is less likely.

64. There is some debate about how to code Ireland. I follow Huber et al. (2004) and code Ireland as a 1.0. Although Dail, the lower house of Parliament, is elected for five-year terms by proportional representation (single transferable vote), the Senand is indirectly elected and partly nominated (Woldendorp et al. 2000). Although the prime minister heads the cabinet, the president is elected for seven-year terms (although she or he has mainly formal and symbolic functions). If Ireland is recoded as .5 for the proportional representation variable, all of the results and conclusions are robust. Indeed, the results are actually slightly stronger for the combined explanation.

65. Iversen and Soskice (2006); Alesina and Glaeser (2004). Iversen and Soskice (2006) demonstrate that this political calculus ends up not benefiting the Right nearly as much.

66. Some readers might be curious about possible interaction effects between welfare generosity and Leftist politics. In analyses not shown, I tried interactions of welfare generosity and each of the six measures of Leftist politics. None of the interaction terms was significant.

67. As is well known, France illustrates the limitations of union density as a measure. Union coverage rates (the extent to which employees are covered by union agreements) are much higher in France, but unfortunately union coverage data are simply not available for the majority of country-years in my sample.

68. In the 95 cases in common for which poverty data exist, the cumulative women in the legislature and cumulative left government variables correlate .72.

69. Alesina and Glaeser (2004).

70. Baron and Kenny (1986) explain that, for a mediating relationship, one also needs to show that the Leftist politics variable significantly influences welfare generosity. Although an extensive literature documents the effects of these Leftist politics variables for welfare generosity, it is worthwhile to validate this empirically. In models with no other independent variables and based on the 104 observations in the sample, cumulative left party power ($z = 2.91$), women's cumulative presence in the legislature ($z = 3.66$), and PR systems ($z = 2.29$) all have significant positive effects. With appropriate controls, union density and voter turnout can be shown to have significant effects while the effect of current left cabinet is more tenuous.

71. Wilson (1999); Wright (2000).

Chapter 6

1. Associated Press (1997); Broder (1999a, 1999b).

2. Purdum (1999).

3. Edelman (1999).

4. DeParle (1999).

5. Edelman (1999).

6. Kilborn (1999a, 1999b).

7. Broder (1999b).

8. Kilborn (1999a).

9. Before the end of his term, Clinton agreed to merge poverty initiatives with House Speaker Dennis Hastert. The end package was committed to liberal economics with the expansion of the number of empowerment zones, tax credits, capital gains relief, and the establishment of 40 renewal communities that would have no capital gains tax. The program essentially involved a number of incentives to lure private investors to poor areas. It is important to note, however, Clinton had earlier successfully pushed for a large expansion in the Earned Income Tax Credit.

10. O'Connor (2001).

11. Murray (1984); see also, for example, Gilder (1981).

12. One exception is Goodin et al. (1999).

13. My discussion of liberal economics is influenced by Gordon's (1972) classic critique of orthodox economics in *Theories of Poverty and Underemployment*, where he articulated the paradigm of orthodox economics as differentiated from dual labor market and radical perspectives in terms of their disciplinary matrices. My treatment of liberal economics has been especially influenced by O'Connor (2001; see also Esping-Andersen 1990; Goodin et al. 1999; Silver 1994). Oddly, the article behind this chapter (Brady 2003b) has been one of the few to update the debate in 30 years

since Gordon. Following the evolution of economics since Gordon, the label "liberal economics" is meant to be roughly synonymous with free-market fundamentalism or neoliberalism. Obviously, the title of this chapter is also a tribute to Marx's *The Poverty of Philosophy*.

14. Gordon (1972: 34, 39); Marshall (1964).

15. Aaron (1967); Gordon (1972: 32); Hayek (1960).

16. Osterman (1991).

17. Heilbroner (1980); Mill (1963: 216).

18. Hayek (1994: 20).

19. Though they don't really belong in this group of "liberal" economists, Bluestone and Harrison (2000) make a forceful argument that economic growth reduces inequality and poverty.

20. Friedman (1982: 169–170).

21. Balke and Slottje (1993); Bluestone and Harrison (2000); Freeman (2001); Gordon (1972: 98); Jorgenson (1998); Sawhill (1988: 1088).

22. Ellwood and Summers (1986: 79; emphasis added).

23. Haveman and Schwabish (1999: 18; emphasis added); see also Cain (1998).

24. Uchitelle (1999); see also Ziliak et al. (2000).

25. Gundersen and Ziliak (2004: 78, 83).

26. Blank (1997: 221–222).

27. Blank (2000: 6, 10).

28. Blank et al. (2006: 1).

29. Blank (1997: 138, 291) wrote, "All of this evidence supports the view that cash transfers generally improve the economic well-being of their recipients." And, "Many of our antipoverty efforts have accomplished exactly what they set out to accomplish." At the same time, there is a lot of ambiguity because Blank is skeptical that the United States will ever have a more generous welfare state. As a result, she proposes a three-tiered system of narrow, means-tested, targeted programs that almost exclusively rely on the market. Blank (1997: 291) "propose[s] a reconfigured system of public assistance that moves us away from large-scale cash support and toward a more work-focused system." Although Blank (1994: 204) noted, "At best, employment programs can serve as one piece of a larger overall strategy to fight poverty," her policy recommendations emphasize a strong macroeconomy, improving the human capital of children, job training, work incentives for welfare beneficiaries, tax relief, employment services, and targeting youth in high unemployment neighborhoods (Blank 1994, 1997).

30. O'Connor (2001: 143).

31. Mill (1963: 142) wrote, "I conceive that, even in the present state of society and industry, every restriction of it [competition] is an evil, and every extension of it, even if for the time injuriously affecting some class of labourers, is always an ultimate good."

32. Friedman (1982: 199–200).

33. Friedman (1982: 169).

34. Katz (1989); Lindert (2004); O'Connor (2001); Piven and Cloward (1997).

35. Ricardo (1931: 96).

36. Banfield (1970); Gilbert (2002); Gilder (1981); Lindbeck (1995); Mead (1992); Murray (1984); Okun (1975).

37. Galbraith (2000).

38. Bane and Ellwood (1994); Darity and Myers (1987); Leisering and Leibfried (1999).

39. Danziger et al. (1981).

40. Freeman et al. (1997); Lindbeck (1998).

41. DeParle (1997a, 1997b).

42. Hernandez (1999).

43. Pear (1999).

44. Bernstein (1999).

45. Freeman et al. (1997: 11, 25, 27).

46. Krugman (1994a: 27–28; see also 1994b).

47. Krugman (1994a: 27–28; see also 1994b).

48. Krugman (2000). To be fair, some have noted that Krugman's writings on these sorts of issues have evolved and reflect an appropriately changed position in recent years (Tomasky 2007).

49. Galbraith (2000); O'Connor (2001).

50. Ricardo (1931).

51. Gordon (1972: 29).

52. Becker (1976).

53. Karoly (2001); Murnane (1994); O'Connor (2001: 141).

54. Smith (1937 [1776]: book I, chapter X, part I).

55. Marshall (1964: 634, 635).

56. Davis and Moore (1994 [1953]).

57. Blau and Duncan (1967: 402–403).

58. Featherman and Hauser (1976); Jencks et al. (1972).

59. Corcoran (1995); Hout (1988).

60. Karoly (2001); O'Connor (2001).

61. Jencks et al. (1972: 7).

62. Katz (1989: 50).

63. Moynihan (1965).

64. Weinstein (1999).

65. Bluestone and Harrison (2000); Levy (1998).

66. Gordon (1998: 550).

67. Sawhill (1988).

68. Gordon (1972: 30).

69. Ricardo (1931: 81–82).

70. Gordon (1972: 32).

71. O'Connor (2001: 143).

72. Freeman (1991, 2001); Tobin (1994).

73. Gundersen and Ziliak (2004: 73).

74. Sawhill (1988: 1089).

75. Williams (1991).

76. Hauser and Nolan (2000).

77. W.J. Wilson (1987, 1996).

78. Jencks and Peterson (1991); Marks (1991).

79. Korpi (2003).

80. Cohn and Fossett (1996); Eggers and Massey (1991); Lichter (1988); Massey et al. (1994); Mouw (2000).

81. Smith (1937 [1776]: 821–822).

82. Gilbert (1997: 274; emphasis added).

83. Gilbert (1997: 275).

84. Hayek (1960: 44–45; emphasis added).

85. For example, Blank (1997).

86. Hanratty and Blank (1992). It is interesting that Blank also was a member of the National Research Council panel (see chapter 2) that proposed abandoning the official measure and replacing it with a relative measure (Citro and Michael 1995). Indeed, Blank has been a rather vocal critic of the official measure. This stands in stark contrast to her routine use of the official U.S. measure in empirical analyses—especially those designed to show the effectiveness of economic growth (e.g., Blank 2000). Given her occasional use of relative measures and her critiques of the official measure and support for abandoning it in favor of a relative measures, it would be an awfully slippery argument to claim that she only meant for economic growth to be effective against absolute poverty.

87. Freeman (2001: 480).

88. Betson and Warlick (1998); Citro and Michael (1995); DeFina and Thanawala (2001).

89. O'Connor (2001); see also Katz (1989).

90. O'Connor (2001: 154).

91. O'Connor (2001: 154; see also 183).

92. Kenworthy (2004).

93. Brady (2003b, 2006).

94. See, for example, Hanratty and Blank (1992); Zuberi (2006). For this comparison, I use the operationalizations of economic growth (three-year moving average), unemployment $(t - 1)$, and productivity (t) that are used in the subsequent analyses and all figures.

95. In ordinary least squares models including only one of each of the variables (economic growth, unemployment, productivity, welfare generosity, welfare generosity squared, and PR system), none of the variables has a significant effect. The closest is actually PR $(t = -1.67)$, and the signs of the others are consistent.

96. See Lindert (2004) for a convincing challenge to the claim that welfare states undermine economic growth.

97. Gottschalk and Moffitt (1994); Moffitt (1992).

98. Lichter and Jayakody (2002); O'Connor (2001).

99. Blank (1997: 65).

100. Hout (1988).

101. Blank (1997: 31): while 20% of poor families contain one adult who works full time year-round, the majority receive some income from employment, and 63% contain at least one worker.

102. Brady et al. (2008).

103. Blank (1997: 32).

104. Blank (1997: 32); see also Edin and Lein (1997).

105. Blank (1997: 57).

Chapter 7

1. Wilson (1993).

2. FBI (various years).

3. Of course, there is not any *one* structural theory of poverty. Structural theories have always been a diverse set of claims with a shared orientation to demographics and labor markets (O'Connor 2001). I appreciate that some regard this structural theory as less of a "theory" and more an explanation collecting the variables that most sociologists regard as important for poverty. To be clear, I am referring to the mainstream sociological structural theory of poverty, and have no intention of encompassing all "structural" explanations in sociology or even of poverty. For example, as I discuss in chapter 8, Rank's (2005) "structural vulnerability" theory is sort of a hybrid between structural theory in sociology, liberal economics, and some of the arguments in my institutionalized power relations theory. Rank emphasizes the roles of background characteristics in predicting human capital and other demographic attributes that correlate with poverty, as well as structural failings that produce a societal lack of opportunities and supports. For Rank (2005: 176), structure refers most to "[t]he most obvious example of this is the mismatch between the number of decent-paying jobs and the pool of labor in search of such jobs." Unfortunately, I am not aware of international data that could really test his explanation (especially in a way that would not make his theory true by definition).

4. W.J. Wilson (1987, 1996).

5. Clark (1965); Myrdal (1965); O'Connor (2001); Rainwater (1969).

6. Harrington (1981).

7. Galbraith (1998).

8. Gordon (1972); Gordon et al. (1982).

9. Sugrue (1996).

10. See, for example, Anderson (1990); Newman (1999).

11. Harrison and Bluestone (1988); McCall (2001); Nielsen and Alderson (1997).

12. Eggers and Massey (1991); O'Connor (2001); Small and Newman (2001); Tomaskovic-Devey (1991).

13. Jencks and Peterson (1991); McFate et al. (1995); Wilson (1993).

14. Esping-Andersen (1999).

15. Obviously, I am neglecting at least one important structural factor: *immigration*. Unfortunately, valid and reliable data on immigration are not consistently available over time. The Organization for Economic Cooperation and Development and the World Bank provide data on the percentage of the population foreign born, but these data are not available before the 1980s and are spotty for many nations. Alderson and Nielsen (2002) and Moller et al. (2003) analyze "net migration"—the difference of population, birth, and death estimates in the current and past year. However, this would only track the "flow" of migrants and would not be a measure of the "stock" of migrants. Thus, it might not be directly comparable with the other structural variables in this chapter. Also, Moller et al. (2003) found that net migration does not significantly affect poverty before taxes and transfers. Ultimately, it is simply

beyond the bounds of this study to analyze immigration thoroughly. That said, I return briefly to the issue of immigration in chapter 8.

16. Alderson and Nielsen (2002).

17. Bluestone and Harrison (1982).

18. Brady and Denniston (2006).

19. Alderson and Nielsen (2002); Bluestone and Harrison (2000); Gustafsson and Johansson (1999); Harrison and Bluestone (1988); Nielsen and Alderson (1997).

20. Chevan and Stokes (2000).

21. McCall (2001); Morris and Western (1999: 637).

22. Bluestone and Harrison (1982: 76).

23. W.J. Wilson (1996: 26, 31).

24. Brady and Wallace (2001); Eggers and Massey (1991); Kasarda (1993); Tomaskovic-Devey (1991).

25. Jargowsky (1997: 122).

26. Kuznets (1953).

27. Nielsen and Alderson (1997).

28. Nielsen and Alderson (1997); Robinson (1984).

29. Alderson and Nielsen (2002).

30. Harrington (1981: 41).

31. Billings and Blee (2000); Lobao and Meyer (2001); Lobao and Schulman (1991); Tickmayer and Duncan (1990).

32. Duncan (1999).

33. Notably, these findings are typically based on analyses that do not control for single motherhood; see Alderson and Nielsen (2002); Gustafsson and Johansson (1999).

34. Cancian et al. (1993).

35. Nielsen and Alderson (1997).

36. Morris and Western (1999: 630).

37. Bianchi (1999); Blank (1997); Christopher et al. (2002).

38. Eggebeen and Lichter (1991); Harris (1996).

39. Gornick et al. (1998).

40. Hedstrom and Ringen (1990); Nielsen and Alderson (1997); O'Rand and Henretta (1999).

41. Gustafsson and Johansson (1999).

42. Harrington (1981); Newman (2003).

43. Bianchi (1999); Blank (1997); Preston (1984).

44. Brady (2004); Burtless and Smeeding (2001); Citro and Michael (1995); Jencks and Torrey (1988); Smeeding et al. (2001).

45. Esping-Andersen (1999); O'Rand and Henretta (1999).

46. Lichter and Eggebeen (1993); Nielsen and Alderson (1997).

47. Bianchi (1999); Blank (1997); Cancian and Reed (2001); Eggebeen and Lichter (1993); Lichter et al. (2003); Thomas and Sawhill (2002); Wu and Wolfe (2001).

48. Anderson (1990); Eggers and Massey (1991); Newman (1999); Small and Newman (2001); W.J. Wilson (1987, 1993, 1996).

49. Eggers and Massey (1991); Tomaskovic-Devey (1991).

50. Casper et al. (1994); Kamerman (1995); McFate et al. (1995); Rose (1995).

51. Christopher et al. (2002: 219).

52. Heuveline and Weinshenker (2008); Kiernan (2001); Lichter (1997); Moller et al. (2003); Sorensen (1999).

53. Christopher et al. (2002); Esping-Andersen (1999); Kamerman (1995); McLanahan and Garfinkel (1995).

54. First, as I showed in Brady (2006), my measure is very highly associated with the original LIS estimates ($r = .95$ in present study). Second, as I also showed in that article, my measure ($r = .45$) is more strongly correlated with poverty than are the LIS estimates ($r = .33$). Third, using the LIS estimates may create greater collinearity problems in the models, because the LIS estimates are more correlated with female labor force participation than my measure. To verify that this decision was not producing inaccurate results, I estimated all models with the LIS estimates instead. The conclusions would be consistent, and my measure has larger and more significant coefficients than do the LIS measure in all models. Thus, I chose to proceed with my measure.

55. Brady and Denniston (2006).

56. Heuveline and Weinshenker (2008).

57. In results available upon request, I analyzed each structural variable individually (with and without the other variables), and the conclusions are consistent.

58. Bluestone and Harrison (1982); W.J. Wilson (1987, 1996).

59. Alderson and Nielsen (2002).

60. Chevan and Stokes (2000).

61. O'Connor (2001).

Chapter 8

1. George (1960 [1879]).

2. See, for example, Harris (1996).

3. Katz (1989: 1).

4. Abbott (2001).

5. My diagnosis of the twentieth-century poverty literature builds from O'Connor (2001) and Katz (1989), among others.

6. See Korpi (1983) for an articulate account of this distinction.

7. Certainly, this uniting of end points obscures some of the fine-grained differences between scholars. For example, I doubt most economists would be comfortable being lumped in with Charles Murray. Education-focused status attainment sociologists would have even more problems with this characterization. But, at the end of the day, if one follows these end points to their logical conclusion, one finds that there is actually a discernible cohesion among these diverse scholars.

8. Rank (2005).

9. Rank (2005: 75).

10. Smeeding et al. (2001: 162).

11. Alesina and Glaeser (2004).

12. OECD (2007). Italy and Spain values are for 2001; France are for 1999.

13. Alesina et al. (2003). This measure is available for only one time point, typically in the mid to late 1990s, although for a few countries the estimates are from the 1980s.

14. In analyses not shown, I estimated a model including an interaction of welfare generosity and the U.S. dummy as well as the main effects of those variables. The U.S. dummy continued to be insignificant, as did the interactions.

15. Sawhill (2003: 79).

16. Keister (2003).

17. Korpi and Palme (1998).

References

Aaron, Henry. 1967. "The Foundations of the 'War on Poverty' Reexamined." *American Economic Review* 57: 1229–1240.

Abbott, Andrew. 2001. *Chaos of Disciplines*. Chicago: University of Chicago Press.

Alderson, Arthur S., and Francois Nielsen. 2002. "Globalization and the Great U-Turn." *American Journal of Sociology* 107: 1244–1299.

Alesina, Alberto, Arnaud Devleeschauwer, William Easterly, Sergio Kurlat, and Romain Wacziarg. 2003. "Fractionalization." *Journal of Economic Growth* 8: 155–194.

Alesina, Alberto, and Edward L. Glaeser. 2004. *Fighting Poverty in the U.S. and Europe*. New York: Oxford University Press.

Allan, James B., and Lyle Scruggs. 2004. "Political Partisanship and Welfare State Reform in Advanced Industrial Societies." *American Journal of Political Science* 48(3): 496–512.

Allison, Paul D. 1978. "Measures of Inequality." *American Sociological Review* 43: 865–880.

Alt, James E. 1985. "Political Parties, World Demand, and Unemployment: Domestic and International Sources of Economic Activity." *American Political Science Review* 79: 1016–1040.

Amenta, Edwin. 1998. *Bold Relief*. Princeton: Princeton University Press.

Anderson, Elijah. 1990. *Streetwise*. Chicago: University of Chicago Press.

Andrews, Kenneth T. 2001. "Social Movements and Policy Implementation." *American Sociological Review* 66: 71–95.

Associated Press. 1997. "Senator Re-enacts RFK's Tour on Poverty." *Chicago Tribune* May 30: 5.

Atkinson, Anthony B. 1998a. *Poverty in Europe.* Malden, MA: Blackwell.

———.1998b, January. "Chapter One: Social Exclusion, Poverty and Unemployment." CASE Paper No. 4. London: Centre for Analysis of Social Exclusion.

———.1990. "Introduction." Pp. xvii–xxv in T. Smeeding, M. O'Higgins, and L. Rainwater (eds.), *Poverty, Inequality, and Income Distribution in Comparative Perspective.* Washington, DC: Urban Institute Press.

———.1987. "On the Measurement of Poverty." *Econometrica* 55: 749–764.

Bachrach, Peter, and Morton S. Baratz. 1970. *Power and Poverty: Theory and Practice.* New York: Oxford University Press.

Balke, Nathan S., and Daniel J. Slottje. 1993. "Poverty and Change in the Macroeconomy: A Dynamic Macroeconomic Model."*Review of Economics and Statistics* 75: 117–122.

Bane, Mary Jo, and David T. Ellwood. 1994. *Welfare Realities: From Rhetoric to Reform.* Cambridge, MA: Harvard University Press.

Banfield, Edward C. 1970. *The Unheavenly City: The Nature and Future of Our Urban Crisis.* Boston, MA: Little, Brown.

Baron, Reuben M., and David A. Kenny. 1986. "The Moderator-Mediator Variable Distinction in Social Psychological Research: Conceptual, Strategic and Statistical Considerations." *Journal of Personality and Social Psychology* 51: 1173–1182.

Barry, Brian. 1998. "Social Exclusion, Social Isolation and the Distribution of Income." CASE Paper No. 12. London: Centre for Analysis of Social Exclusion, London School of Economics.

———.1973. *The Liberal Theory of Justice.* Oxford: Clarendon Press.

Beck, Nathaniel. 2001. "Time Series-Cross Section Data: What Have We Learned in the Past Few Years." *Annual Review of Political Science* 4: 271–293.

Beck, Nathaniel, and Jonathan N. Katz. 2001. "Throwing Out the Baby with the Bath Water." *International Organization* 55: 487–495.

———.1996. "Nuisance over Substance." *Political Analysis* 6: 1–36.

Becker, Gary. 1976. *The Economic Approach to Human Behavior.* Chicago: University of Chicago Press.

Beramendi, Pablo, and Christopher Anderson. 2008. *Democracy, Inequality and Representation.* New York: Russell Sage Foundation.

Bergh, Andreas. 2005. "On the Counterfactual Problem of Welfare State Research: How Can We Measure Redistribution?" *European Sociological Review* 21: 345–357.

Bergmann, Barbara R. 1996. *Saving Our Children from Poverty: What the United States Can Learn from France.* New York: Russell Sage Foundation.

Bernstein, Nina. 1999. "Giuliani Proclaims Success on Pledge to Curb Welfare." *New York Times* December 12: A1, A22.

Betson, David M., and Jennifer L. Warlick. 1998. "Alternative Historical Trends in Poverty." *American Economic Review* 88: 348–351.

Bhargava, Alok and J.D. Sargan. 1983. "Estimating Dynamic Random Effects Models from Panel Data Covering Short Time Periods." *Econometrica* 51: 1635–1660.

Bianchi, Suzanne M. 1999. "Feminization and Juvenilization of Poverty: Trends, Relative Risks, Causes, and Consequences." *Annual Review of Sociology* 25: 307–333.

Billings, Dwight B., and Kathleen Blee. 2000. *The Road to Poverty.* New York: Cambridge University Press.

Blank, Rebecca M. 2000. "Fighting Poverty: Lessons from Recent U.S. History" *Journal of Economic Perspectives* 14: 3–19.

——. 1997. *It Takes a Nation.* Princeton, NJ: Princeton University Press.

——. 1994. "The Employment Strategy: Public Policies to Increase Work and Earnings." Pp. 168–204 in S. H. Danziger, G. D. Sandefur, and D. H. Weinberg (eds.), *Confronting Poverty: Prescriptions for Change.* Cambridge, MA: Harvard University Press.

Blank, Rebecca M., Sheldon H. Danziger, and Robert F. Schoeni. 2006. "Introduction: Work and Poverty during the Past Quarter Century." Pp. 1–20 in *Working and Poor.* New York: Russell Sage Foundation.

Blau, Francine D., and Lawrence M. Kahn. 1992. "The Gender Earnings Gap: Learning from International Comparisons." *American Economic Review* 82: 533–538.

Blau, Peter M., and Otis Dudley Duncan. 1967. *The American Occupational Structure.* New York: Free Press.

Bluestone, Barry, and Bennett Harrison. 1982. *The Deindustrialization of America.* New York: Basic Books.

——. 2000. *Growing Prosperity: The Battle for Growth with Equity in the 21st Century.* New York: Houghton Mifflin.

Blyth, Mark. 2002. *Great Transformations.* New York: Cambridge University Press.

Bolzendahl, Catherine, and Clem Brooks. 2007. "Women's Political Resources and Welfare State Spending in 12 Capitalist Democracies." *Social Forces* 85: 1509–1534.

Bonoli, Giuliano. 2007. "Time Matters: Postindustrialization, New Social Risks, and Welfare State Adaptation in Advanced Industrial Democracies." *Comparative Political Studies* 40: 495–520.

Bourdieu, Pierre. 2005. *The Social Structures of the Economy.* Malden, MA: Polity Press.

Bradley, David, Evelyne Huber, Stephanie Moller, Francois Nielsen, and John D. Stephens. 2003. "Distribution and Redistribution in Postindustrial Democracies." *World Politics* 55: 193–228.

Brady, David. 2006. "Structural Theory and Relative Poverty in Rich Western Democracies, 1969–2000." *Research in Social Stratification and Mobility* 24: 153–175.

——. 2005. "The Welfare State and Relative Poverty in Rich Western Democracies, 1967–1997." *Social Forces* 83: 1329–1364.

——. 2004. "Reconsidering the Divergence between Elderly, Child, and Overall Poverty." *Research on Aging* 26: 487–510.

——. 2003a. "Rethinking the Sociological Measurement of Poverty." *Social Forces* 81: 715–752.

——. 2003b. "The Poverty of Liberal Economics." *Socio-Economic Review* 1: 369–409.

Brady, David. 2003c. "The Politics of Poverty: Left Political Institutions, the Welfare State and Poverty." *Social Forces* 82: 557–588.

Brady, David, Jason Beckfield, and Martin Seeleib-Kaiser. 2005. "Economic Globalization and the Welfare State in Affluent Democracies, 1975–2001." *American Sociological Review* 70: 921–948.

Brady, David, and Ryan Denniston. 2006. "Economic Globalization, Industrialization, and Deindustrialization in Affluent Democracies." *Social Forces* 85: 297–329.

Brady, David, Andrew S. Fullerton, and Jennifer Moren Cross. 2008. "More Than Just Nickels and Dimes: A Multi-level Analysis of Working Poverty in 18 Affluent Democracies." Unpublished Manuscript, Duke University.

Brady, David, and Denise Kall. 2008. "Nearly Universal, but Somewhat Distinct: The Feminization of Poverty in Affluent Western Democracies, 1969–2000." *Social Science Research* 37: 976–1007.

Brady, David, Benjamin Sosnaud, and Steven Frenk. 2009. "The Shifting White Working Class Voting in U.S. Presidential Elections, 1972–2004." *Social Science Research* 38: 118–133.

Brady, David, and Michael Wallace. 2001. "Deindustrialization and Poverty: Manufacturing Decline and AFDC Recipiency in Lake County, Indiana, 1964–1993." *Sociological Forum* 21: 321–358.

Broder, John M. 1999a. "A Pledge of Federal Help for the Economic Byways: Clinton Seeks and Investment in Appalachia." *New York Times* July 6: A10.

——. 1999b. "Clinton, in Poverty Tour, Focuses on Profits." *New York Times* July 7: A12.

Brooks, Clem, and David Brady. 1999. "Income, Economic Voting and Long Term Political Change, 1952–1996." *Social Forces* 77: 1339–1375.

Brooks, Clem, and Jeff Manza. 1999. *Why Welfare States Persist*. Chicago: University of Chicago Press.

Buhmann, Brigitte, Lee Rainwater, Guenther Schmaus, and Timothy M. Smeeding. 1988. "Equivalence Scales, Well-Being, Inequality, and Poverty: Sensitivity Estimates across Ten Countries Using the Luxembourg Income Study (LIS) Database." *Review of Income and Wealth* 34: 115–142.

Burris, Val. 2001. "The Two Faces of Capital: Corporations and Individual Capitalists as Political Actors." *American Sociological Review* 66: 361: 381.

Burstein, Paul. 1998. "Bringing the Public Back In: Should Sociologists Consider the Impact of Public Opinion on Public Policy?" *Social Forces* 77: 27–62.

Burtless, Gary, and Timothy M. Smeeding. 2001. "The Level, Trend, and Composition of Poverty." Pp. 27–68 in *Understanding Poverty*, edited by S. Danziger and R. Haveman. New York and Cambridge, MA: Russell Sage Foundation and Harvard University Press.

Cain, Glen G. 1998. "The State of the Economy and the Problem of Poverty: Implications for the Success or Failure of Welfare Reform." Discussion Paper 1183-98. Madison: Institute for Research on Poverty, University of Wisconsin, Madison.

Campbell, John L. 2004. *Institutional Change and Globalization*. Princeton, NJ: Princeton University Press.

Cancian, Maria, Sheldon Danziger, and Peter Gottschalk. 1993. "Working Wives and Family Income Inequality among Married Couples." Pp. 195–221 in *Uneven Tides*, edited by S. Danziger and P. Gottschalk. New York: Russell Sage Foundation.

Cancian, Maria, and Deborah Reed. 2001. "Changes in Family Structure." Pp. 69–96 in *Understanding Poverty*, edited by S. Danziger and R. Haveman. New York and Cambridge, MA: Russell Sage Foundation and Harvard University Press.

Cantillion, Bea. 1997. "The Challenge of Poverty and Exclusion." Pp. 115–166 in *Social Policy Studies* No. 21: "Family, Market, and Community: Equity and Efficiency in Social Policy." Paris, France: Organisation for Economic Co-operation.

Casper, Lynne M., Sara S. McLanahan, and Irwin Garfinkel. 1994. "The Gender-Poverty Gap: What We Can Learn from Other Countries." *American Sociological Review* 59: 594–605.

Census Bureau. U.S. Department of Commerce. www.census.gov.

Chevan, Albert, and Randall Stokes. 2000. "Growth in Family Income Inequality, 1970–1990: Industrial Restructuring and Demographic Change." *Demography* 37: 365–380.

Christopher, Karen, Paula England, Katherin Ross, Tim Smeeding, and Sara McLanahan. 2002. "The Sex Gap in Poverty in Modern Nations: Single-Motherhood, the Market and the State." *Sociological Perspectives* 45: 219–242.

Citro, Constance, and Robert T. Michael (eds.). 1995. *Measuring Poverty: A New Approach*. Washington, DC: National Academy Press.

Clark, Kenneth B. 1965. *Dark Ghetto: Dilemmas of Social Power*. New York: Harper and Row.

Clayton, Richard, and Jonus Pontusson. 1998. "Welfare State Retrenchment Revisited: Entitlement Cuts, Public Sector Restructuring, and Inegalitarian Trends in Advanced Capitalist Societies." *World Politics* 51:67–98.

Cohn, Samuel, and Mark Fossett. 1996. "What Spatial Mismatch? The Proximity of Blacks to Employment in Boston and Houston." *Social Forces* 75(2): 557–572.

Corcoran, Mary. 1995. "Rags to Rags: Poverty and Mobility in the United States." *Annual Review of Sociology* 21: 237–267.

Cox, W. Michael, and Richard Alm. 1999. *Myths of Rich and Poor: Why We're Better Off Than We Think*. New York: Basic Books.

Currie, Janet, and Aaron Yelowitz. 2000. "Health Insurance and Less Skilled Workers." Pp. 233–261 in *Finding Jobs: Work and Welfare Reform*, edited by D. E. Card and R. M. Blank. New York: Russell Sage Foundation.

Cusack, Thomas R. 2004 (May). Data on Public Employment and Wages for 21 OECD Countries. Berlin: SPECTRUM Science Center.

Dahrendorf, Ralf. 1990. *The Modern Social Conflict—an Essay on the Politics of Liberty*. Berkeley, CA: University of California Press.

Danziger, Sheldon D., Robert H. Haveman, and Robert Plotnik. 1981. "How Income Transfers Affect Work, Savings and Income Distribution." *Journal of Economic Literature* 19: 975–1028.

Danziger, Sheldon H., and Daniel H. Weinberg. 1994. "The Historical Record: Trends in Family Income, Inequality, and Poverty." Pp. 18–50 in *Confronting Poverty: Prescriptions for Change*, edited by S. H. Danziger, G. D. Sandefur, and D. H. Weinberg. New York: Russell Sage Foundation.

Darity, William A., Jr., and Samuel L. Myers, Jr. 1987. "Do Transfer Payments Keep the Poor in Poverty?" *American Economic Review* 77: 216–222.

Daschle, Tom, Scott S. Greenberger, and Jeanne M. Lambrew. 2008. *Critical*. New York: St. Martins Press.

Davis, Kingsley, and Wilbert E. Moore. 1953. "Some Principles of Stratification: A Critical Analysis." *American Sociological Review* 18: 387–394.

DeFina, Robert H., and Kishor Thanawala. 2004. "International Evidence on the Impact of Transfers and Taxes on Alternative Poverty Indexes." *Social Science Research* 33: 322–338.

———. 2001. "The Impact of Taxes and Transfers on Alternative Poverty Indexes." *Review of Social Economy* 59: 395–416.

DeParle, Jason. 1999. "Making a Belated Pilgrimage: Clinton's Poverty Tour Draws Skepticism and Indifference." *New York Times* July 9: A10.

———. 1997a. "U.S. Welfare System Dies as State Programs Emerge." *New York Times* June 30: A1, A10.

———. 1997b. "With the Economy Humming, Welfare Has Its Image Polished." *New York Times* September 11: A1, A11.

DiFazio, William. 1998. "Why There Is No Movement of the Poor." Pp. 141–166 in *Post-Work*, edited by S. Aronowitz and J. Cutler. New York: Routledge.

Dixon, Marc, and Andrew Martin. 2007. "Can the Labor Movement Succeed without the Strike?" *Contexts* 6(2): 36–39.

Domhoff, G. William. 1998. *Who Rules America? Power and Politics in the Year 2000*, 3rd ed. Mountain View, CA: Mayfield.

Duncan, Cynthia M. 1999. *Worlds Apart: Why Poverty Persists in Rural America*. New Haven: Yale University Press.

Duneier, Mitchell. 1999. *Sidewalk*. New York: Farrar, Strauss and Giroux.

Edelman, Peter. 1999. "Clinton's Cosmetic Poverty Tour." *New York Times* July 8: A25.

Edin, Kathryn, and Laura Lein. 1997. *Making Ends Meet*. New York: Russell Sage Foundation.

Eggebeen, David J., and Daniel T. Lichter. 1991. "Race, Family Structure, and Changing Poverty among American Children." *American Sociological Review* 56: 801–817.

Eggers, Mitchell L., and Douglas S. Massey. 1991. "The Structural Determinants of Urban Poverty: A Comparison of Whites, Blacks, and Hispanics." *Social Science Research* 20: 217–255.

Ellwood, David T., and Lawrence Summers. 1986. "Poverty in America: Is Welfare the Answer or the Problem." Pp. 78–105 in *Fighting Poverty: What Works and What Doesn't*, edited by Sheldon Danziger and Daniel Weinberg. Cambridge, MA: Harvard University Press.

Ellwood, David T., and Elisabeth D. Welty. 2000. "Public Service Employment and Mandatory Work: A Policy Whose Time Has Come and Gone and Come Again?" Pp. 299–372 in *Finding Jobs: Work and Welfare Reform*, edited by D. E. Card and R. M. Blank. New York: .

Engbersen, G. 1991. "Moderne Armoede: Feit En Fictie." *Sociologische Gids* 37: 7–23.

Epstein, Richard A. 2003. *Skepticism and Freedom: A Modern Case for Classical Liberalism.* Chicago: University of Chicago Press.

Esping-Andersen, Gøsta. 2003. "Why No Socialism Anywhere? A Reply to Alex Hicks and Lane Kenworthy." *Socio-Economic Review* 1: 63–70.

——.1999. *Social Foundations of Postindustrial Economies.* New York: Oxford University Press.

——.1990. *The Three Worlds of Welfare Capitalism.* Princeton, NJ: Princeton University Press.

FBI (Federal Bureau of Investigation). Various Years. *Uniform Crime Reports* Washington, DC: Department of Justice.

Featherman, David L., and Robert M. Hauser. 1976. "Sexual Inequalities and Socioeconomic Achievement in the U.S., 1962–1973." *American Sociological Review* 41: 462–483.

Fischer, Claude S., Michael Hout, Martin Sanchez Jankowski, Samuel R. Lucas, Ann Swidler, and Kim Voss. 1996. *Inequality by Design: Cracking the Bell Curve Myth.* Princeton, NJ: Princeton University Press.

Fligstein, Neil. 2001. *The Architecture of Markets.* Princeton, NJ: Princeton University Press.

Fording, Richard C. 2001. "The Political Response to Black Insurgency: A Critical Test of Competing Theories of the State." *American Political Science Review* 95: 115–130.

Foster, James E. 1998. "What Is Poverty and Who Are the Poor? Redefinition for the United States in the 1990s: Absolute versus Relative Poverty." *American Economic Review* 88: 335–341.

Foster, James, Joel Greer, and Erik Thorbecke. 1984. "A Class of Decomposable Poverty Measures." *Econometrica* 52: 761–766.

Freeman, Richard B. 2001. "The Rising Tide Lifts . . . " Pp. 97–126 in *Understanding Poverty*, edited by S. Danziger and R. Haveman. New York and Cambridge, MA: Russell Sage Foundation and Harvard University Press.

——.1999. *The New Inequality.* Boston: Beacon Press.

——.1995. "The Large Welfare State as a System." *American Economic Review* 85: 16–21.

——.1991. "Employment and Earnings of Disadvantaged Young Men in a Labor Shortage Economy." Pp. 103–121 in *The Urban Underclass*, edited by C. Jencks and P. E. Peterson. Washington, DC: Brookings Institution.

Freeman, Richard B., and James L. Medoff. 1984. *What Do Unions Do?* New York: Basic Books.

Freeman, Richard B., Robert Topel, and Birgitta Swedenborg. 1997. *The Welfare State in Transition: Reforming the Swedish Model.* Chicago: University of Chicago Press.

Friedman, Milton. 1982 [1962]. *Capitalism and Freedom.* Chicago: University of Chicago Press.

Galbraith, James K. 2000. "How the Economists Got It Wrong." *American Prospect* February 14: 18–20.

Galbraith, John Kenneth. 1998 [1958]. *The Affluent Society.* New York: Mariner Books.

Gangl, Markus. 2006. "Scar Effects of Unemployment: An Assessment of Institutional Complementarities." *American Sociological Review* 71: 986–1013.

Gans, Herbert J. 1995. *The War against the Poor: The Underclass and Anti-poverty Policy.* New York: Basic Books.

George, Henry. 1960 [1879]. *Progress and Poverty.* New York: Robert Schalkenbach Foundation.

Gilbert, Geoffrey. 1997. "Adam Smith on the Nature and Causes of Poverty." *Review of Social Economy* 55: 273–291.

Gilbert, Neil. 2002. *Transformation of the Welfare State.* New York: Oxford University Press.

Gilder, George. 1981. *Wealth and Poverty.* New York: Basic Books.

Gilens, Martin. 1999. *Why Americans Hate Welfare.* Chicago: The University of Chicago Press.

Golden, Miriam, and John B. Londregan. 2006. "Centralization of Bargaining and Wage Inequality: A Correction of Wallerstein." *American Journal of Political Science* 50: 208–213.

Golden, Miriam, Michael Wallerstein, and Peter Lange. 2007. "Unions, Employers, Collective Bargaining and Industrial Relations in 16 OECD Countries between 1950 and 1992: Union Centralization among Advanced Industrial Societies—An Empirical Study." hdl:1902.1/10193 UNF:3:8OOmkFNF4DKwSZw0NSqYyw Miriam Golden [Distributor].

Goodin, Robert E., Bruce Heady, Ruud Muffels, and Henk-Jan Dirven. 1999. *The Real Worlds of Welfare Capitalism.* New York: Cambridge University Press.

Gordon, David M. 1998 [1994]. "'Twixt the Cup and the Lip: Mainstream Economics and the Formation of Economic Policy." Pp. 544–576 in *Economics and Social Justice,* edited by S. Bowles and T. E. Weisskopf. Northampton, MA: Elgar.

——. 1972. *Theories of Poverty and Underemployment: Orthodox, Radical, and Dual Labor Market Perspectives.* Lexington, MA: Lexington Books.

Gordon, David M., Richard Edwards, and Michael Reich. 1982. *Segmented Work, Divided Workers: The Historical Transformation of Labor in the United States.* New York: Cambridge University Press.

Gore, Charles. 1995. "Chapter 1 Introduction: Markets, Citizenship and Social Exclusion." Pp. 1–40 in *Social Exclusion: Rhetoric Reality Responses,* edited by Gerry Rodgers, Charles Gore, and Jose B. Figueiredo. Geneva: International Labour Organization.

Gornick, Janet C., and Jerry A. Jacobs. 1998. "Gender, the Welfare State, and Public Employment: A Comparative Study of Seven Industrialized Countries." *American Sociological Review* 63: 688–710.

Gornick, Janet C., Marcia K. Meyers, and Katherin E. Ross. 1998. "Public Policies and the Employment of Mothers: A Cross-National Study." *Social Science Quarterly* 79: 35–54.

Gottschalk, Peter, and Robert A. Moffitt. 1994. "Welfare Dependence: Concepts, Measures, and Trends." *American Economic Review* 84: 38–42.

Greene, William H. 1990. *Econometric Analysis.* New York: Macmillan.

Grusky, David B., and Ravi Kanbur. 2006. *Poverty and Inequality.* Stanford: Stanford University Press.

Gundersen, Craig, and James P. Ziliak. 2004. "Poverty and Macroeconomic Performance across Space, Race, and Family Structure." *Demography* 41: 61–86.

Gustafsson, Bjorn, and Mats Johansson. 1999. "In Search of Smoking Guns: What Makes Income Inequality Vary over Time in Different Countries." *American Sociological Review* 64: 585–605.

Hacker, Jacob. 2002. *The Divided Welfare State*. New York: Cambridge University Press.

Hagenaars, Aldi J. M. 1991. "The Definition and Measurement of Poverty." Pp. 134–156 in *Economic Inequality and Poverty: International Perspectives*. Armonk, NY: M. E. Sharpe.

Hall, Peter A., and David Soskice. 2001. *Varieties of Capitalism: The Institutional Foundations of Comparative Advantage*. New York: Oxford University Press.

Handcock, Mark S., and Martina Morris. 1999. *Relative Distribution Methods in the Social Sciences*. New York: Springer-Verlag.

Hanratty, Maria J., and Rebecca M. Blank. 1992. "Down and Out in North America: Recent Trends in Poverty Rates in the United States and Canada." *Quarterly Journal of Economics* 107: 233–254.

Harrington, Michael. 1981 [1962]. *The Other America: Poverty in the United States*. New York: Penguin.

Harris, Kathleen Mullan. 1996. "Life after Welfare: Women, Work and Repeat Dependency." *American Sociological Review* 61: 407–426.

Harrison, Bennett, and Barry Bluestone. 1988. *The Great U-Turn: Corporate Restructuring and the Polarizing of America*. New York: Basic Books.

Hauser, Richard, and Brian Nolan. 2000. "Unemployment and Poverty: Change over Time." Pp. 25–46 in *Welfare Regimes and the Experience of Unemployment in Europe*, edited by D. Gallie and S. Paugam. New York: Oxford University Press.

Hausman, J.A. 1978. "Specification Tests in Econometrics." *Econometrica* 46: 1251–1271.

Haveman, Robert, and Jonathan Schwabish. 1999. "Macroeconomic Performance and the Poverty Rate: A Return to Normalcy." Discussion Paper No. 1187–99. Madison: Institute for Research on Poverty, University of Wisconsin, Madison.

Hawley, Amos H. 1992. "The Logic of Macrosociology." *Annual Review of Sociology* 18: 1–15.

Hayek, Friedrich A. 1994 [1944]. *The Road to Serfdom*. Chicago: University of Chicago Press.

——. 1960. *The Constitution of Liberty*. Chicago: University of Chicago Press.

Hedstrom, Peter, and Stein Ringen. 1990. "Age and Income in Contemporary Society." Pp. 77–104 in *Poverty, Inequality and Income Distribution in Comparative Perspective*, edited by T. M. Smeeding, M. O'Higgins, and L. Rainwater. Washington, DC: Urban Institute Press.

Heilbroner, Robert. 1980. *The Worldly Philosophers*. New York: Touchstone.

Hernandez, Raymond. 1999. "More Who Leave Welfare Rolls in New York Are Found to Get Jobs." *New York Times* August 5: A19.

Hernstein, Richard J., and Charles Murray. 1994. *The Bell Curve*. New York: Free Press.

Heston, Alan, Robert Summers and Bettina Aten, Penn World Table Version 6.2, Center for International Comparisons of Production, Income and Prices at the University of Pennsylvania, September 2006.

Heston, Alan, Robert Summers and Bettina Aten, Penn World Table Version 6.1, Center for International Comparisons at the University of Pennsylvania (CICUP), October 2002.

Heuveline, Patrick, and Matthew Weinshenker. 2008. "The International Child Poverty Gap: Does Demography Matter?" *Demography* 45: 173–191.

Hicks, Alexander. 1999. *Social Democracy and Welfare Capitalism: A Century of Income Security Politics.* Ithaca, NY: Cornell University Press.

Hicks, Alexander, and Gosta Esping-Andersen. 2005. "Comparative Historical Studies of Public Policy and the Welfare State." Pp. 509–525 in *The Handbook of Political Sociology*, edited by T. Janoski, R. Alford, A. M. Hicks, and M. A. Schwartz. New York: Cambridge University Press.

Hill, Carolyn J., and Robert T. Michael. 2001. "Measuring Poverty in the NLSY97." *Journal of Human Resources* 36: 727–761.

Hills, John. 2004. *Inequality and the State.* New York: Oxford University Press.

Hoge, Warren. 1998. "Swedish Party Pledging Expanded Welfare Gains Slim Victory." *New York Times* September 21.

Hout, Michael. 1988. "More Universalism, Less Structural Mobility: The American Occupational Structure in the 1980s." *American Journal of Sociology* 93: 1358–1400.

——. 1984. "Occupational Mobility of Black Men: 1962 to 1973." *American Sociological Review* 49: 308–322.

Hsiao, Cheng. 2003. *Analysis of Panel Data*, 2nd ed. New York: Cambridge University Press.

Huber, Evelyne, and John D. Stephens. 2001. *Development and Crisis of the Welfare State.* Chicago: University of Chicago Press.

——. 2000. "Partisan Governance, Women's Employment, and the Social Democratic Service State." *American Sociological Review* 65: 323–342.

Huber, Evelyne, John D. Stephens, Charles Ragin, David Brady, and Jason Beckfield. 2004. Comparative Welfare States Data Set. Northwestern University, University of North Carolina, Chapel Hill, Indiana University, and Duke University. Available at www.lisproject.org.

Hunt, Matthew O. 1996. "The Individual, Society, or Both? A Comparison of Black, Latino, and White Beliefs about the Causes of Poverty." *Social Forces* 75: 293–322.

Iceland, John. 2003. *Poverty in America.* Berkeley, CA: University of California Press.

Ipsen, Erik. 1994. "Sweden's Record Short Honeymoon." *International Herald Tribune* October 4. http://www.iht.com/articles/1994/10/04/swede.php

——. 1991. "Bildt Takes European View of Sweden." *International Herald Tribune* November 19. http://www.iht.com/articles/1991/11/19/bild.php.

Iversen, Torben, and David Soskice. 2006. "Electoral Institutions and the Politics of Coalitions: Why Some Democracies Redistribute More Than Others." *American Political Science Review* 100: 165–181.

Jantti, Marcus, and Sheldon Danziger. 2000. "Income Poverty in Advanced Countries." Pp. 309–378 in *Handbook of Income Distribution*, edited by A. B. Atkinson and F. Bourguignon. New York: Elsevier.

Jargowsky, Paul A. 1997. *Poverty and Place: Ghettos, Barrios, and the American City*. New York: Russell Sage Foundation.

Jencks, Christopher, Susan Bartlett, Mary Corcoran, James Crouse, David Eaglesfield, Gregory Jackson, Kent McClelland, Peter Mueser, Michael Olneck, Joseph Schwartz, Sherry Ward, and Jill Williams. 1979. *Who Gets Ahead? The Determinants of Economic Success in America*. New York: Basic Books.

Jencks, Christopher, and Paul E. Peterson. 1991. *The Urban Underclass*. Washington, DC: Brookings Institution.

Jencks, Christopher, Marshall Smith, Henry Acland, Mary Jo Bane, David Cohen, Herbert Gintis, Barbara Heyns, and Stephen Michelson. 1972. *Inequality: A Reassessment of the Effect of Family and Schooling in America*. New York: Basic Books.

Jencks, Christopher, and Barbara Boyle Torrey. 1988. "Beyond Income and Poverty: Trends in Social Welfare among Children and the Elderly since 1960." Pp. 229–273 in *The Vulnerable*, edited by J. L. Palmer, T. Smeeding, and B. B. Torrey. Washington, DC: Urban Institute Press.

Jorgenson, Dale W. 1998. "Did We Lose the War on Poverty?" *Journal of Economic Perspectives* 12: 79–96.

Kamerman, Sheila B. 1995. "Gender Role and Family Structure Changes in the Advanced Industrialized West: Implications for Social Policy." Pp. 231–256 in *Poverty, Inequality and the Future of Social Policy*, edited by K. McFate, R. Lawson, and W. J. Wilson. New York: Russell Sage Foundation.

Karoly, Lynn A. 2001. "Investing in the Future: Reducing Poverty through Human Capital Investments." Pp. 314–356 in *Understanding Poverty*, edited by S. Danziger and R. Haveman. New York and Cambridge, MA: Russell Sage Foundation and Harvard University Press.

Kasarda, John D. 1993. "Urban Industrial Transition and the Underclass." Pp. 43–64 in *The Ghetto Underclass*, edited by W. J. Wilson. Newbury Park, CA: Sage.

Katz, Michael B. 1989. *The Undeserving Poor*. New York: Pantheon.

Kelly, Nathan J. 2005. "Political Choice, Public Policy, and Distributional Outcomes." *American Journal of Political Science* 49: 865–880.

Keister, Lisa A. 2003. "Repealing the Estate Tax: A Recipe for More Inequality." *Contexts* 2: 42–49.

———. 2000. Wealth in America. New York: Cambridge University Press.

Kenworthy, Lane. 2004. *Egalitarian Capitalism*. New York: Russell Sage Foundation.

Kerckhoff, Alan C. 1995. "Institutional Arrangements and Stratification Processes in Industrialized Societies." *Annual Review of Sociology* 15: 323–347.

Kiernan, Kathleen. 2001. "European Perspectives on Nonmarital Childbearing." Pp. 77–108 in *Out of Wedlock*, edited by L. Wu and B. L. Wolfe. New York: Russell Sage Foundation.

Kilborn, Peter L. 1999a. "Clinton, Amid the Squalor on a Reservation, again Pledges Help." *New York Times* July 8: A12.

———. 1999b. "Memphis Blacks Find Cycle of Poverty Difficult to Break." *New York Times* October 5: A1.

Knoke, David, Franz Urban Pappi, Jeffrey Broadbent, and Yutaka Tsujinaka. 1996. *Comparing Policy Networks.* New York: Cambridge University Press.

Korpi, Walter. 2003. "Welfare State Regress in Western Europe: Politics, Institutions, Globalization, and Europeanization." *Annual Review of Sociology* 29: 589–609.

——.1989. "Power, Politics and State Autonomy in the Development of Social Citizenship." *American Sociological Review* 54: 309–328.

——. 1985. "Power Resources Approach vs. Action and Conflict: On Causal and Intentional Explanations in the Study of Power." *Sociological Theory* 3(2): 31–45.

——.1983. *The Democratic Class Struggle.* Boston: Routledge.

Korpi, Walter, and Joakim Palme. 2003. "New Politics and Class Politics in the Context of Austerity and Globalization: Welfare State Regress in 18 Countries, 1975–1995." *American Political Science Review* 97: 425–446.

——.1998. "The Paradox of Redistribution and Strategies of Equality: Welfare State Institutions, Inequality, and Poverty in the Western Countries." *American Sociological Review* 63: 661–687.

Krugman, Paul. 2000. "Blessed Are the Weak." *The New York Times* May 3: A31.

——.1994a. *The Age of Diminished Expectations.* Cambridge, MA: MIT Press.

——.1994b. *Peddling Prosperity.* Cambridge, MA: MIT Press.

Kuznets, Simon. 1953. "Economic Growth and Income Inequality." *American Economic Review* 45: 1–28.

Leicht, Kevin T. 1989. "On the Estimation of Union Threat Effects." *American Sociological Review* 54:1035–1047.

Leicht, Kevin T., Michael Wallace, and Don Sherman Grant II. 1993. "Union Presence, Class, and Individual Earnings Inequality." *Work and Occupations* 20: 429–451.

Leisering, Lutz, and Stephan Leibfried. 1999. *Time and Poverty in Western Welfare States: United Germany in Perspective.* New York: Cambridge University Press.

Levy, Frank. 1998. *The New Dollars and Dreams: American Incomes and Economic Change.* New York: Russell Sage Foundation.

Lichter, Daniel T. 1997. "Poverty and Inequality among Children." *Annual Review of Sociology* 23:121–145.

——.1988. "Racial Differences in Underemployment in American Cities." *American Journal of Sociology* 93: 771–792.

Lichter, Daniel T., and David J. Eggebeen. 1993. "Rich Kids, Poor Kids: Changing Income Inequality among American Children." *Social Forces* 71: 761–780.

Lichter, Daniel T., Deborah Roempke Graefe, and J. Brian Brown. 2003. "Is Marriage a Panacea? Union Formation among Economically Disadvantaged Unwed Mothers." *Social Problems* 50: 60–86.

Lichter, Daniel T, and Rukamalie Jayakody. 2002. "Welfare Reform: How Do We Measure Success?" *Annual Review of Sociology* 28: 117–141.

Lieberson, Stanley. 1985. *Making It Count: The Improvement of Social Research and Theory* Berkeley: University of California Press.

Lindbeck, Assar. 1998. "The Welfare State and the Employment Problem." *American Economic Review* 84: 71–75.

——. 1995. "Hazardous Welfare-State Dynamics." *American Economic Review* 85: 9–15.

Lindert, Peter H. 2004. *Growing Public*, Vol. 1. New York: Cambridge University Press.

Link, Bruce G., and Jo Phelan. 1995. "Social Conditions as Fundamental Causes of Disease." *Journal of Health and Social Behavior* Extra Issue: 80–94.

Lobao, Linda, and Katherine Meyer. 2001. "The Great Agricultural Transition: Crisis, Change and Social Consequences of Twentieth Century U.S. Farming." *Annual Review of Sociology* 27: 103–124.

Lobao, Linda M., and Michael D. Schulman. 1991. "Farming Patterns, Rural Restructuring, and Poverty: A Comparative Regional Analysis." *Rural Sociology* 56: 565–602.

Lukes, Steven. 1988. *Power: A Radical View*. London: Macmillan.

Luxembourg Income Study (LIS) Database, http://www.lisproject.org/techdoc.htm (multiple countries; 2008).

Madden, David. 2000. "Relative or Absolute Poverty Lines: A New Approach." *Review of Income and Wealth* 46: 181–199.

Mahler, Vincent A., David K. Jesuit, and Douglas D. Roscoe. 1999. "Exploring the Impact of Trade and Investment on Income Inequality." *Comparative Political Studies* 32: 363–395.

Mann, Michael. 1983. "Review of *Power*, by Eric Wrong." *American Journal of Sociology* 88(5): 1030–1032.

Manza, Jeff, and Clem Brooks. 1999. *Social Cleavages and Political Change: Voter Alignments and U.S. Party Coalitions*. New York: Oxford University Press.

Mares, Isabel. 2003. "The Sources of Business Interest in Social Insurance: Sectoral versus National Differences." *World Politics* 55: 229–258.

Marks, Carole. 1991. "The Urban Underclass" *Annual Review of Sociology* 17: 445–466.

Marmot, Michael. 2004. *The Status Syndrome*. New York: Owl Books.

Marshall, Alfred. 1964 [1890]. *Principles of Economics*. Pp. 567–637 in *Classics of Economic Theory*, edited by G. W. Wilson. Bloomington, IN: Indiana University Press.

Marshall, T. H. 1963. *Class, Citizenship, and Social Development*. Chicago: University of Chicago Press.

Massey, Douglas S., Andrew B. Gross, and Kumiko Shibuya. 1994. "Migration, Segregation, and the Geographic Concentration of Poverty." *American Sociological Review* 59: 425–445.

Mayer, Susan E. 1997. *What Money Can't Buy: Family Income and Children's Life Chances*. Cambridge, MA: Harvard University Press.

McCall, Leslie. 2001. *Complex Inequality*. New York: Routledge.

McFate, Katherine, Roger Lawson, and William Julius Wilson. 1995. *Poverty, Inequality and the Future of Social Policy*. New York: Russell Sage Foundation.

McLanahan, Sara, and Irwin Garfinkel. 1995. "Single Mother Families and Social Policy." Pp. 367–383 in *Poverty, Inequality and the Future of*

Social Policy, edited by K. McFate, R. Lawson, and W. J. Wilson. New York: Russell Sage Foundation.

McLanahan, Sara, and Erin L. Kelly. 1999. "The Feminization of Poverty: Past and Future." In *Handbook o f the Sociology of Gender*, edited by J. S. Chafetz. New York: Kluwer.

McLeod, Jane D., and Michael Shanahan. 1993. "Poverty, Parenting, and Children's Mental Health." *American Sociological Review* 58: 351–366.

Mead, Lawrence. 1992. *The New Politics of Poverty*. New York: Basic Books.

Meyers, Marcia K., and Janet Gornick. 2001. "Gendering Welfare State Variation: Income Transfers, Employment Supports, and Family Poverty." Pp. 215–243 in *Women and Welfare: Theory and Practice in the United States and Europe*, edited by N. Hirschmann and U. Liebert. Rutgers, NJ: Rutgers University Press.

Mill, John Stuart. 1963 [1861]. *Utilitarianism*. Toronto: University of Toronto Press.

Mills, C. Wright. 1959. *The Sociological Imagination*. New York: Oxford University Press.

Misra, Joya. 2002. "Class, Race, and Gender and Theorizing Welfare States." *Research in Political Sociology* 11: 19–52.

Misra, Joya, Stephanie Moller, and Marina Karides. 2003. "Envisioning Dependency: Changing Media Depictions of Welfare in the Twentieth Century." *Social Problems* 50: 482–504.

Moffitt, Robert. 1992. "Incentive Effects of the U.S. Welfare System: A Review." *Journal of Economic Literature* 30: 1–61.

Moller, Stephanie, David Bradley, Evelyne Huber, Francois Nielsen, and John D. Stephens. 2003. "Determinants of Relative Poverty in Advanced Capitalist Democracies." *American Sociological Review* 68: 22–51.

Morris, Martina, and Bruce Western. 1999. "Inequality in Earnings at the Close of the 20th Century." *Annual Review of Sociology* 25: 623–657.

Mouw, Ted. 2000. "Job Relocation and the Racial Gap in Unemployment in Detroit and. Chicago, 1980 to 1990." *American Sociological Review* 65: 730–753.

Moynihan, Daniel P. 1965. *The Negro Family: The Case for National Action*. Washington, DC: Office of Policy Planning and Research, U.S. Department of Labor.

Murnane, Richard J. 1994. "Education and the Well-Being of the Next Generation." Pp. 289–307 in *Confronting Poverty: Prescriptions for Change*, edited by S. H. Danziger, G. D. Sandefur, and D. H. Weinberg. Cambridge, MA: Harvard University Press.

Murray, Charles. 1984. *Losing Ground: American Social Policy, 1950–1980*. New York: Basic Books.

Myles, John, and Garnett Picot. 2000. "Poverty Indices and Policy Analysis." *Review of Income and Wealth* 46: 161–179.

Myles, John, and Paul Pierson. 2001. "The Comparative Political Economy of Pension Reform." Pp. 305–333 in *The New Politics of the Welfare State*, edited by P. Pierson. New York: Oxford University Press.

Myrdal, Gunnar. 1965. *Challenge to Affluence*. New York: Vintage Books.

Newman, Katherine S. 2003. *A Different Shade of Gray*. New York: New Press.

——. 1999. *No Shame in My Game*. New York: Alfred A. Knopf.

Nickell, Stephen. 1981. "Biases in Dynamic Models with Fixed Effects." *Econometrica* 49: 1417–1426.

Nielsen, Francois, and Arthur S. Alderson. 1997. "The Kuznets Curve and the Great U-Turn: Income Inequality in U.S. Counties." *American Sociological Review* 62: 12–33.

Nolan, Brian, Richard Hauser, and Jean-Paul Zoyem. 2000. "The Changing Effects of Social Protection on Poverty." Pp. 87–106 in *Welfare Regimes and the Experience of Unemployment in Europe*, edited by D. Gallie and S. Paugam. New York: Oxford University Press.

North, Douglas C. 1990. *Institutions, Institutional Change and Economic Performance*. New York: Cambridge University Press.

Nussbaum, Martha C. 2006. "Poverty and Human Functioning: Capabilities as Fundamental Entitlements." Pp. 47–75 in *Poverty and Inequality*, edited by D. B. Grusky and R. Kanbur. Stanford: Stanford University Press.

O'Connor, Alice. 2001. *Poverty Knowledge*. Princeton, NJ: Princeton University Press.

OECD(a). Various Years. *Health Data CD-ROM*. Paris: Organization for Economic Cooperation and Development.

——(b). Various Years. *Labor Force Statistics*. Paris: Organization for Economic Cooperation and Development.

——(c). Various Years. *Historical Statistics*. Paris: Organization for Economic Cooperation and Development.

——. 2004. *Social Expenditures Database*. Paris: Organization for Economic Cooperation and Development.

——. 2007. *International Migration Outlook*. Paris: Organization for Economic Cooperation and Development.

Okun, Arthur M. 1975. *Equality and Efficiency: The Big Tradeoff*. Washington, DC: Brookings Institution.

O'Rand, Angela, and John C. Henretta. 1999. *Age and Inequality*. Boulder, CO: Westview Press.

Orloff, Ann Shola. 1993. "Gender and the Social Rights of Citizenship: The Comparative Analysis of Gender Relations and Welfare States." *American Sociological Review* 58: 303–328.

Ormerod, Paul. 1998. "Unemployment and Social Exclusion: An Economic View." Pp. 23–40 in *The Future of European Welfare*, edited by M. Rhodes and Yves Meny. New York: St. Martin's Press.

Orshansky, Mollie. 1976. *The Measure of Poverty: Technical Paper I: Documentation of Background Information and Rationale for Current Poverty Matrix*. Washington, DC: U.S. Department of Health, Education and Welfare.

——. 1965. "Counting the Poor: Another Look at the Poverty Profile." *Social Security Bulletin* 28: 3–29.

Osberg, Lars, and Kuan Xu. 2000. "International Comparisons of Poverty Intensity: Index Decomposition and Bootstrap Inference." *Journal of Human Resources* 35: 51–81.

Osterman, Paul. 1991. "Gains from Growth? The Impact of Full Employment on Poverty in Boston." Pp. 122–134 in *The Urban Underclass*, edited by C. Jencks and P. E. Peterson. Washington, DC: Brookings Institution.

Page, Benjamin I., and James R. Simmons. 2000. *What Government Can Do: Dealing with Poverty and Inequality*. Chicago: University of Chicago Press.

Pampel, Fred C., and John B. Williamson. 2001. "Age Patterns of Suicide and Homicide Mortality Rates in High-Income Nations." *Social Forces* 80: 251–282.

Paugam, Serge. 1998. "Poverty and Social Exclusion: A Sociological View." Pp. 41–62 in *The Future of European Welfare*, edited by M. Rhodes and Yves Meny. New York: St. Martin's Press.

Pear, Robert. 1999. "Clinton Hears Success Stories of Ex-Welfare Recipients." *New York Times* August 4: A10.

Pearce, Diane. 1978. "The Feminization of Poverty: Women, Work, and Welfare." *Urban and Social Change Review* 11: 28–36.

Pierson, Paul. 2004. *Politics in Time: History, Institutions and Social Analysis*. Princeton: Princeton University Press.

——. 2001. *The New Politics of the Welfare State*. New York: Oxford University Press.

Piven, Frances Fox, and Richard A. Cloward. 1997. *The Breaking of the American Social Compact*. New York: New Press.

——. 1993. *Regulating the Poor: The Functions of Public Welfare*. New York: Vintage Books.

——. 1979 [1977]. *Poor People's Movements: Why They Succeed, How They Fail*. New York: Vintage.

Pontusson, Jonas. 2005. *Inequality and Prosperity: Social Europe vs. Liberal America*. Ithaca, NY: Cornell University Press.

Prasad, Monica. 2005. "Once Again, It's the Economy, Stupide!" *Chicago Tribune* November 11. http://www.chicagotribune.com/news/opinion/chi-0511110349nov11,0,7350164.story?coll=chi-newsopinioncommentary-hed

President's Commission on Income Maintenance Programs. 1969. *Poverty amid Plenty*. Washington, DC: U.S. Government Printing Office.

Preston, Samuel H. 1984. "Children and the Elderly: Divergent Paths for America's Dependents." *Demography* 21: 435–457.

Procacci, Giovanna. 1998. "Against Exclusion: The Poor and the Social Sciences." Pp. 63–78 in *The Future of European Welfare*, edited by M. Rhodes and Yves Meny. New York: St. Martin's Press.

Przeworski, Adam. 1986. *Capitalism and Social Democracy*. Cambridge: Cambridge University Press.

Purdum, Todd S. 1999. "Clinton Ends Visit to Poor with an Appeal for Support." *New York Times* July 9: A10.

Quadagno, Jill. 2005. *One Nation Uninsured*. New York: Oxford University Press.

——. 1994. *The Color of Welfare*. New York: Oxford University Press.

Raftery, Adrian. 1995. "Bayesian Model Selection in Social Research." *Sociological Methodology* 25: 111–163.

Rainwater, Lee. 1969. *Behind Ghetto Walls*. Chicago: Aldine.

Rainwater, Lee, and Timothy M. Smeeding. 2004. *Poor Kids in a Rich Country: America's Children in Comparative Perspective*. New York: Russell Sage Foundation.

Rank, Mark Robert. 2005. *One Nation, Underprivileged*. New York: Oxford University Press.

Rankin, Bruce H., and James M. Quane. 2000. "Neighborhood Poverty and the Social Isolation of Inner-City African-American Families." *Social Forces* 79: 139–164.

Ravallion, Martin. 1998. *Poverty Lines in Theory and Practice*. Living Standards Measurement Study Working Paper Number 133. Washington, DC: World Bank.

Rawls, John. 2001. *Justice as Fairness: A Restatement*. Cambridge, MA: Harvard University Press.

———.1999 [1971]. *A Theory of Justice*, rev. ed. Cambridge, MA: Harvard University Press.

Ricardo, David. 1931 [1817]. *The Principles of Political Economy*. New York: Macmillan.

Robinson, Robert V. 1984. "Structural Change and Class Mobility in Capitalist Societies." *Social Forces* 63: 51–71.

Rodgers, Gerry. 1995. "What Is Special about a 'Social Exclusion' Approach?" Pp. 43–55 in *Social Exclusion: Rhetoric Reality Responses*, edited by Gerry Rodgers, Charles Gore, and Jose B. Figueiredo. Geneva: International Labour Organization.

Rosenfeld, Jake. 2006. "Desperate Measures: Strikes and Wages in Post-Accord America." *Social Forces* 85: 235–265.

Rowntree, Benjamin Seebohm. 1906. *Poverty: A Study in Town Life*. London: Macmillan.

Rubin, Beth A. 1988. "Inequality in the Working Class: The Unanticipated Consequences of Union Organization and Strikes." *Industrial and Labor Relations Review* 41: 553–566.

Rueda, David. 2005. "Insider-Outsider Politics in Industrialized Democracies: The Challenge to Social Democratic Parties." *American Political Science Review* 99: 61–74.

Ruggles, Patricia. 1990. *Drawing the Line: Alternative Poverty Measures and Their Implications for Public Policy*. Washington, DC: Urban Institute Press.

Sainsbury, Diane. 1999. *Gender and Welfare State Regimes*. New York: Oxford University Press.

Sassoon, Donald. 1996. *One Hundred Years of Socialism: The West European Left in the Twentieth Century*. London: Fontana Press.

Sawhill, Isabel V. 2003. "The Behavioral Aspects of Poverty." *The Public Interest* 153 (Fall): 79–93.

———.1988. "Poverty in the U.S.: Why Is It So Persistent?" *Journal of Economic Literature* 26: 1073–1119.

Schmidt, William E. 1992. "In a Post-Cold War Era, Scandinavia Rethinks Itself." *New York Times* February 23.

Schram, Sanford F. 2002. *Praxis for the Poor*. New York: New York University Press.

Schram Sanford F., Joe Soss, and Richard C. Fording. 2003. *Race and the Politics of Welfare Reform*. Ann Arbor, MI: University of Michigan Press.

Schuyt, C., and A. Tan. 1998. "De Maatschappelijke Betekenis Van Armoede. Deel II." Pp. 34–54 in *Op Zoek Naar Armoede En Bestaansonzekerheid*

Langs Twee Sporen, edited by J. A. M. Berghman. Rijswijk: Nationale Raad Voor Maatschappelijk Welzijn.

Searle, John. 2003. "Social Ontology and Political Power." Pp. 195–210 in *Socializing Metaphysics: The Nature of Social Reality*, edited by F. F. Schmidt. Lanham, MD: Rowman and Littlefield.

Sen, Amartya. 1999. *Development as Freedom*. New York: Anchor Books.

——.1992. *Inequality Reexamined*. Cambridge, MA: Harvard University Press.

——.1983. "Poor, Relatively Speaking." *Oxford Economic Papers* 35: 153–169.

——.1976. "Poverty: An Ordinal Approach to Measurement." *Econometrica* 44: 219–231.

Shanahan, Suzanne Elise, and Nancy Brandon Tuma. 1994. "The Sociology of Distribution and Redistribution." Pp. 733–765 in *The Handbook of Economic Sociology*, edited by N. J. Smelser and R. Swedberg. Princeton, NJ: Princeton University Press.

Silver, Hilary. 1995. "Reconceptualizing Social Disadvantage: Three Paradigms of Social Exlcusion." In *Social Exclusion: Rhetoric, Reality, Responses*, edited by G. Rodgers, C. Gore, and J. B. Figueiredo. Geneva: International Labour Organisation.

——.1994. "Social Exclusion and Social Solidarity: Three Paradigms." *International Labour Review* 133: 531–578.

Skocpol, Theda. 1996. *Boomerang*. New York: Norton.

——.1992. *Protecting Soldiers and Mothers*. Cambridge, MA: Harvard University Press.

Small, Mario Luis and Katherine Newman. 2001. "Urban Poverty after *The Truly Disadvantaged*: The Rediscovery of the Family, the Neighborhood, and Culture." *Annual Review of Sociology* 27: 23–45.

Smeeding, Timothy M., Lee Rainwater, and Gary Burtless. 2001. "U.S. Poverty in Cross-National Context." Pp. 162–189 in *Understanding Poverty*, edited by S. Danziger and R. Haveman. New York and Cambridge, MA: Russell Sage Foundation and Harvard University Press.

Smeeding, Timothy M., Lee Rainwater, Martin Rein, Richard Hauser, and Gaston Schaber. 1990. "Income Poverty in Seven Countries: Initial Estimates from the LIS Database." Pp. 57–76 in *Poverty, Inequality and Income Distribution in Comparative Perspective*, edited by T. M. Smeeding, M. O'Higgins, and L. Rainwater. Washington, DC: Urban Institute Press.

Smeeding, Timothy M., Peter Saunders, John Coder, Stephen Jenkins, Johan Fritzell, Aldi J. M. Hagenaars, Richard Hauser, and Michael Wolfson. 1993. "Poverty, Inequality, and Family Living Standards Impacts across Seven Nations: The Effect of Noncash Subsidies for Health, Education and Housing." *Review of Income and Wealth* 39: 229–256.

Smith, Adam. 1937 [1776]. *An Inquiry into the Nature and Causes of the Wealth of Nations*. New York: Modern Library, Random House.

Sorensen, Annemette. 1999. "Family Decline, Poverty, and Social Exclusion: The Mediating Effects of Family Policy." *Comparative Social Research* 18: 57–78.

Starr, Paul. 1995. "What Happened to Health Care Reform?" *The American Prospect* 20 (Winter): 20–31.

Steensland, Brian. 2006. "Cultural Categories and the American Welfare State: The Case of Guaranteed Income Policy." *American Journal of Sociology* 111: 1273–1326.

Stephens, John D., Evelyne Huber, and Leonard Ray. 1999. "The Welfare State in Hard Times." Pp. 164–193 in *Continuity and Change in Contemporary Capitalism*, edited by H. Kitschelt, P. Lange, G. Marks, and J. D. Stephens. New York: Cambridge University Press.

Stewart, Qunicy T. 2006. "Reinvigorating Relative Deprivation: A New Measure for a Classic Concept." *Social Science Research* 35: 779–802.

Stone, Deborah. 2002. "Making the Poor Count." *American Prospect* November 30. http://www.prospect.org/cs/articles?article=making_the_poor_count.

Sugrue, Thomas J. 1996. *The Origins of the Urban Crisis: Race and Inequality in Postwar Detroit*. Princeton, NJ: Princeton University Press.

Swank, Duane, and Cathie Jo Martin. 2001. "Employers and the Welfare State: The Political Economic Organization of Firms and Social Policy in Contemporary Capitalist Democracies." *Comparative Political Studies* 34: 889–923.

Swenson, Peter A. 2002. *Capitalists against Markets*. New York: Oxford University Press.

Teachman, Jay, Greg J. Duncan, W. Jean Yeung, and Dan Levy. 2001. "Covariance Structure Models for Fixed and Random Effects." *Sociological Methods and Research* 30: 271–288.

Thomas, Adam, and Isabel Sawhill. 2002. "For Richer or for Poorer: Marriage as an Anti-poverty Strategy." *Journal of Policy Analysis and Management* 21: 587–599.

Tickmayer, Ann R., and Cynthia M. Duncan. 1990. "Poverty and Opportunity Structure in Rural America." *Annual Review of Sociology* 16: 67–86.

Tilly, Charles. 1998. *Durable Inequality*. Berkeley, CA: University of California Press.

Titmus, Richard D. 1974. *Social Policy: An Introduction*. London: Allen and Unwin.

Tobin, James. 1994. "Poverty in Relation to Macroeconomic Trends, Cycles, and Policies." Pp. 147–167 in *Confronting Poverty: Prescriptions for Change*, edited by S. H. Danziger, G. D. Sandefur, and D. H. Weinberg. Cambridge, MA: Harvard University Press.

Tomaskovic-Devey, Donald. 1991. "A Structural Model of Poverty Creation and Change: Political Economy, Local Opportunity, and U.S. Poverty, 1959–1979." *Research in Social Stratification and Mobility* 10:289–322.

Tomasky, Michael. 2007. "The Partisan." *New York Review of Books* 54(18): November 22.

Townsend, Peter. 1980. "Research on Poverty." Pp. 299–306 in *Wealth, Income and Inequality*, edited by A. B. Atkinson. New York: Oxford University Press.

——. 1962. "The Meaning of Poverty." *British Journal of Sociology* 13: 210–227.

Triest, Robert K. 1998. "Has Poverty Gotten Worse?" *Journal of Economic Perspectives* 12: 97–114.

Uchitelle, Louis. 1999. "Devising New Math to Define Poverty: Millions More Would Be Poor in Fresher Census Formula." *New York Times* October 18: A1, A14.

van den Berg, Axel, and Thomas Janoski. 2005. "Conflict Theories in Political Sociology." Pp. 72–95 in *The Handbook of Political Sociology*, edited by T. Janoski, R. Alford, A. M. Hicks, and M. A. Schwartz. New York: Cambridge University Press.

Venkatesh, Sudhir. 2000. *American Project: The Rise and Fall of a Modern Ghetto*. Cambridge, MA: Harvard University Press.

Volscho, Thomas W., and Andrew S. Fullerton. 2005. "Metropolitan Earnings Inequality: Unions and Government Sector Effects." *Social Science Quarterly* 86: 1324–1337.

Wacquant, Loic J. D. 1995. "The Comparative Structure and Experience of Urban Exclusion: 'Race,' Class, and Space in Chicago and Paris." Pp. 543–570 in *Poverty, Inequality and the Future of Social Policy: Western States in the New World Order*, edited by K. McFate, R. Lawson, and W. J. Wilson. New York: Russell Sage Foundation.

Wallace, Michael, Larry J. Griffin, and Beth A. Rubin. 1989. "The Positional Power of American Labor, 1963–1977." *American Sociological Review* 54:197–214.

Wallace, Michael, Kevin T. Leicht, and Lawrence E. Raffalovich. 1999. "Unions, Strikes, and Labor's Share of Income: A Quarterly Analysis of the United States." *Social Science Research* 28: 265–288.

Wallerstein, Michael. 1999. "Wage-Setting Institutions and Pay Inequality in Advanced Industrial Societies." *American Journal of Political Science* 43: 649–680.

Weber, Max, H.H. Gerth and C. Wright Mills. 1958. *From Max Weber: Essays in Sociology* New York: Oxford University Press.

Weinstein, Michael M. 1999. "When Work Is Not Enough." *New York Times* August 26: C1, C6.

Western, Bruce. 1997. *Between Class and Market: Postwar Unionization in the Capitalist Democracies*. Princeton, NJ: Princeton University Press.

Western, Bruce, and Kieran Healy. 1999. "Explaining the OECD Wage Slowdown: Recession or Labour Decline?" *European Sociological Review* 15: 233–249.

Wilensky, Harold L. 2002. *Rich Democracies*. Berkeley, CA: University of California Press.

——. 1997. "Social Science and the Public Agenda: Reflections on the Relation of Knowledge to Policy in the United States and Abroad." *Journal of Health Politics, Policy, and Law* 22: 1241–1265.

——. 1975. *The Welfare State and Equality*. Berkeley, CA: University of California Press.

Williams, Donald R. 1991 "Structural Change and the Aggregate Poverty Rate." *Demography* 28: 323–332.

Wilson, George. 1996. "Toward a Revised Framework for Examining Beliefs about the Causes of Poverty." *Sociological Quarterly* 37: 413–428.

Wilson, William Julius. 1999. *The Bridge over the Racial Divide*. Berkeley: University of California Press.

——. 1996. *When Work Disappears*. New York: Alfred A. Knopf.

——.1993. *The Ghetto Underclass: Social Science Perspectives*. Newbury Park, CA: Sage Press.

——.1991. "Studying Inner-City Social Dislocations: The Challenge of Public Agenda Research." *American Sociological Review* 56: 1–14.

——.1987. *The Truly Disadvantaged*. Chicago: University of Chicago Press.

Woldendorp, Jaap, Hans Keman, and Ian Budge. 2000. *Party Government in 48 Democracies*. Boston: Kluwer.

Wolfe, Barbara. 1994. "Reform of Health Care for the Nonelderly Poor." Pp. 253–288 in *Confronting Poverty*, edited by S. H. Danziger, G. D. Sandefur, and D. H. Weinberg. New York: Russell Sage Foundation.

Wright, Erik Olin. 2004. "Introduction." *Politics and Society* 32: 3–6.

——.2000. "Working Class Power, Capitalist-Class Interests, and Class Compromise." *American Journal of Sociology* 105: 957–1002.

Wright, Erik Olin, Andrew Levine, and Elliot Sober. 1992. *Reconstructing Marxism: Essays on Explanation and the Theory of History*. New York: Verso.

Wright, Robert E. 1995. "Women and Poverty in Industrialized Countries." *Journal of Income Distribution* 5: 31–46.

Wrong, Dennis H. 1988. *Power*. Chicago: University of Chicago Press.

Wu, Lawrence L., and Barbara Wolfe. 2001. *Out of Wedlock: Causes and Consequences of Nonmarital Fertility*. New York: Russell Sage Foundation.

Ziliak, James P., David N. Figlio, Elizabeth E. Davis, and Laura S. Connolly. 2000. "Accounting for the Decline in AFDC Caseloads: Welfare Reform or the Economy?" *Journal of Human Resources* 35: 570–586.

Zuberi, Dan. 2006. *Differences That Matter: Social Policy and the Working Poor in the United States and Canada*. Ithaca, NY: Cornell University Press.

Zylan, Yvonne, and Sarah A. Soule. 2000. "Ending Welfare as We Know It (Again): Welfare State Retrenchment, 1989–1995." *Social Forces* 79: 623–652.

Index